Differentiating Science Instruction and Assessment

FOR LEARNERS WITH

Special Needs, K-8

Differentiating Science Instruction and Assessment
FOR LEARNERS WITH
Special Needs, K–8

Kevin D. Finson
Christine K. Ormsbee
Mary M. Jensen

CORWIN
A SAGE Company

CORWIN
A SAGE Company

FOR INFORMATION:

Corwin

A SAGE Company

2455 Teller Road

Thousand Oaks, California 91320

(800) 233-9936

Fax: (800) 417-2466

www.corwin.com

SAGE Ltd.

1 Oliver's Yard

55 City Road

London EC1Y 1SP

United Kingdom

SAGE India Pvt. Ltd.

B 1/I 1 Mohan Cooperative

Industrial Area

Mathura Road, New Delhi 110 044

India

SAGE Asia-Pacific Pte. Ltd.

33 Pekin Street #02-01

Far East Square

Singapore 048763

Acquisitions Editor: Jessica Allan

Associate Editor: Allison Scott

Editorial Assistant: Lisa Whitney

Production Editor: Cassandra Margaret Seibel

Copy Editor: Gretchen Treadwell

Typesetter: C&M Digitals (P) Ltd.

Proofreader: Victoria Reed-Castro

Indexer: Shapiro Indexing Services

Cover Designer: Rose Storey

Permissions Editor: Karen Ehrmann

Copyright © 2011 by Corwin

Printed in the United States of America.

Library of Congress Cataloging-in-Publication Data

Finson, Kevin D.

Differentiating science instruction and assessment for learners with special needs, K-8/Kevin D. Finson, Christine K. Ormsbee, Mary M. Jensen.

p. cm.

Includes bibliographical references and index.

ISBN 978-1-4129-9399-9 (pbk.)

1. Science—Study and teaching (Elementary) 2. Science—Study and teaching (Middle school) 3. Learning disabled children—Education (Elementary) 4. Learning disabled children—Education (Middle school) 5. Individualized instruction. 6. Inclusive education. I. Ormsbee, Christine K. II. Jensen, Mary M. III. Title.

LB1585.F543 2011 372.3'5—dc22   2010048974

This book is printed on acid-free paper.

11 12 13 14 15 10 9 8 7 6 5 4 3 2 1

Contents

Acknowledgments

In the spring of 1994, the basic idea encompassed in this book was conceived, eventually resulting in grant support from the Illinois State Board of Education's (ISBE) Office of Scientific Literacy. With that support, a collaborative group was formed consisting of university faculty in science education and special education, and of K–8 science and special education teachers from eight school districts. It was through the combination of all these elements that this book had its beginnings. A special thank you is extended to each of the following individuals (teachers, principals, and colleagues) whose contributions and help made the project a success:

Cris Altgilbers	Newton Fink	Donald Powers
Carol Anderson	Kara Harper	Sheila Rafferty
Julie Aten	Maureen Hazell	Scott Rigg
Louise Bassett	Carol Holland	Ida Rosenau
John Beaver	Dana Jenkins	Steven Russell
Karen Bhear	Jane Kliffmiller	Barbara Shrode
Joan Biswell	Gail Lester	Barb Spitzer
Patty Bloom	Edna Lotz	Diana St. John
Karen Burtch	Perry Lotz	Sarah Talley
Liz Burton	Peggy Ma	Judy Trotter
Wayne Caparoon	Sharon Maroney	Sue Underwood
Sherrie Cullen	Jack McKinnon	Barb Wagner
Marie Dunstan	Mary McMahon	Carrie Walkington
Linda Engel	Carolyn Phillips	Sherri Zimmerman
Jason Finch	Gwen Pollock	

PUBLISHER'S ACKNOWLEDGMENTS

Corwin gratefully acknowledges the contributions of the following reviewers:

Charre Todd
Science Instructional Facilitator, Science Teacher
Crossett Middle School
Crossett, Arkansas

Sheila Smith
Science Specialist/Consultant
Jackson Public Schools
Ridgeland, Mississippi

Robert E. Yager
Professor Emeritus of Science Education
University of Iowa
Iowa City, Iowa

Kelli S. Kercher
Special Education Team Leader
Murray School District
Murray, Utah

Douglas Llewellyn
Director of Science
Faculty of Educational Leadership
St. John Fisher College
Rochester, New York

Sharon Schulze
Director of The Science House
College of Physical and Mathematical Sciences
North Carolina State University
Raleigh, North Carolina

About the Authors

Kevin D. Finson (PhD, Kansas State University) is a Professor of Science Education at Bradley University in Peoria, Illinois, where he teaches elementary and secondary science education courses. His teaching has included middle- and high-school level life, physical, and earth sciences; college-level earth science content courses; a foundations course in strategies and techniques; and graduate courses in instructional theory and program evaluation.

He has served as a member of the board of directors for the international Association for Science Teacher Education (ASTE), and chaired its Professional Development Committee and Inclusive Science Education Forum. He has also contributed to the standards for the Early Adolescent Science Committee of the National Board of Professional Teaching Standards. He has edited the international *Journal of Elementary Science Education,* served on editorial boards of several national science education journals, and served on the publications committees of two national professional organizations. During this time, he has maintained a consistent record of his own publication in national refereed and practitioner journals.

With two primary areas of research interest, the first focuses on making science more accessible to students who have special learning needs. In particular, Dr. Finson explores how teachers can make adjustments and modifications to written materials, procedures, and simple equipment so students who have specific learning disabilities can successfully engage in doing science. The second area of interest focuses on students' perceptions of scientists, which has included development of a framework to guide science educators in dealing with students' conceptions of scientists.

Christine K. Ormsbee joined the Oklahoma State University College of Education June 2006 as Professor and Head of the School of Teaching and Curriculum Leadership. She holds a PhD in special education from the University of Kansas, a master's degree in special education from Emporia State University, and a bachelor's degree in psychology and special education from Emporia State University. As a faculty member in special education, she teaches an undergraduate introductory special education course and graduate special education methods and research courses.

With over two decades in the profession, she has established a consistent record of scholarly publications and presentations, which address her interests in providing strategies and supports for teachers who work with children with learning and/or behavioral concerns. Specifically, her research has focused on collaborative processes including peer coaching, co-teaching, and preassessment.

Very active in teacher education, Dr. Ormsbee is serving her second term as a commissioner on the Oklahoma Commission for Teacher Preparation, is a member of the Oklahoma P-20 Education Council, and serves on the advisory board for the Oklahoma Board of Education's State Improvement Grant. She served as an associate editor of the journal *Intervention in School and Clinic* until 2009 and now serves as a field reviewer for this journal and other special education–related journals.

Mary M. Jensen has been a Professor of Special Education at Western Illinois University (WIU) in Macomb, Illinois, since 1990. She teaches college students to be outstanding special education teachers for students with mild to moderate disabilities. The special education courses she teaches relate to behavior management methods and characteristics and teaching methods for students with mild to moderate disabilities. Her past experience teaching special education includes working with students in the elementary grades in public school, and with high school students in residential treatment.

Dr. Jensen has been honored to receive the Outstanding Teacher Award at WIU in 1993 and 2006. In 2008, she won the Teaching With Technology Award and the WIU Provost's Award for Teaching With Technology. In 2009 and 2010, she was a recipient of the WIU Honoring Our Professors of Excellence (HOPE) Award.

Dr. Jensen makes presentations for professional development at schools, conferences, and for other organizations on a variety of special education topics for teachers and parents. Topics include proactive and positive behavior management methods, differentiated instruction methods, ADHD, social skills, and bully behavior. The programs focus on practical teaching, management skills, and content that will help students with mild to moderate disabilities increase academic achievement and improve social skills and behavior.

Introduction

THE PURPOSE OF THIS BOOK

In today's K–8 general education classrooms, teachers are aware of students who have been mainstreamed into their classes. Most are also aware that there are resource and special education teachers available to help them with these students and their Individualized Education Plans (IEPs). Unfortunately, most teachers are also aware that the amount of resource help they can actually get is limited due to the demands placed on resource teachers from the rest of the faculty and staff. So, much rests on the shoulders of general education teachers with respect to developing and delivering instruction that meets the needs of their students who have special needs. The purpose of this book is to provide some suggestions, guidelines, and examples of things teachers can do to make science activities and assessments more accessible to their students with special needs. Indeed, as the authors found in the years of pilot testing these guidelines, even gifted students have said the changes made things clearer for them. Teachers have also found these ideas to be of help in addressing issues of universal design and Response to Intervention (RTI).

This book is for general K–8 elementary teachers who teach science, and for their special education colleagues who wish to work with them to improve instruction in the classroom. With this in mind, the ideas in a book such as this cannot, nor should they, replace IEPs or innovations like RTI. However, teachers can have more ownership in the ways they prepare for helping their students learn science, and be more effective doing it. There is considerable value in general education teachers learning more specifics about the needs and characteristics of their students having special needs, and there is concurrently considerable value in special education teachers learning more about science and science instruction. Working together, both can be a dynamic pair having positive impact on the students in their charge. All that being said, it is important teachers clearly understand that even though the bulk of this book focuses on attending to the materials (written and otherwise) used in science teaching, the ultimate focus is to make science instruction more student centered and to use revised materials as one of the tools to enable effective inquiry learning to take place.

RATIONALE FOR THIS BOOK

The basic premise behind the design of this book is that in today's schools, most students with special needs are taught in inclusion classrooms. One of the challenges related to inclusion is preparing educators to teach science education with activities, laboratories, and assessments that are appropriately designed for students with exceptional education needs. As designed, most standard science activities and assessments fail to accommodate for the difficulties encountered by students with learning disabilities, behavioral disorders, and other special characteristics. In many states, such issues have come to the forefront as school improvement plans have been designed and implemented, requiring all schools to assess all students' learning at specified grade levels. The need to do so has been further underscored by the effects of the No Child Left Behind Act (NCLB) passed by Congress. It is no surprise to educators that students who are not appropriately and actively engaged in learning science will likely fare poorly on science assessments. The National Research Council (NRC) has addressed the importance of high-quality science activities and assessments in its *National Science Education Standards* (1996). This document describes assessment as necessary for providing teachers the information required to plan and conduct teaching in appropriate ways. Assessment data guide teachers by providing knowledge about student progress and understanding. Further, assessment tasks must not be afterthoughts, but must be

1

explicitly designed into the teaching process. The effective science teacher uses care in the selection and design of both classroom activities and assessments, and uses assessment tasks that are at the same time positive learning experiences for students.

LIMITATIONS OF THIS BOOK

As noted earlier, this book is intended for Grades K–8 general and special education classroom teachers, and contains outlines of strategies, or guidelines, useful in "retooling" traditional science activities and assessments so that they are more appropriate for students with special needs who are mainstreamed into general education classrooms. At the same time, the activities and assessments must be appropriate for the "typically achieving" student. Considering the variety of disabilities extant in the student population and space constraints, only two disabilities have been addressed in these retooling guidelines: learning disabilities and behavioral disorders. For similar reasons, the guidelines described in this book were developed specifically for science activities and assessments for Grades K–8. Although many of the guidelines have some applicability to other grade levels, and perhaps to other student disabilities, the reader should be aware of the original target audience for the guidelines. The ideas included in them have been teacher developed and teacher tested in actual classroom settings.

This book does not attempt to address or describe the myriad examples of settings and circumstances possibly encountered in inclusion classrooms, nor does it attempt to outline general classroom and behavior management strategies. The materials contained in this book focus exclusively on how to revise science activities and assessments and then use them.

BASIC REMINDERS

The process of developing these guidelines rested on several premises, discussed briefly as follows. They provide the context in which this book should be read and used.

1. Guidelines must be developed and used by K–8 general and special education teachers working as co-teachers in inclusion classrooms. Each teacher must have equal opportunities for input, each must respect and value the other's contributions, and each must be willing to help the other learn about their special knowledge (i.e., general classroom teachers need to learn more about specifics of special education, and special education teachers need to learn about specifics peculiar to science teaching). Hence, teachers can enhance success with their revising endeavors by working collaboratively as teams, having equal responsibilities, and sharing in the outcomes (sometimes including the actual teaching).

2. Retooled science activities and assessments must remain suitable for general education students. An aim here is for the teacher not to create activities useful only to one segment of the student population. This would simply shift the problem as it presently exists from one side of the coin to the other. Such efforts are untenable, particularly considering the time and effort teachers would invest in the process or in revising science activities and assessments.

3. When making modifications to activities and assessments, teachers should *not* lower their expectations of what students can do or learn from the activity. Expectations should remain high. The revised activities and assessments should contain changes that make them more readily usable for students possessing learning disabilities and behavioral disorders.

4. Revised activities and assessments for students with special needs should not be viewed as being lower-grade level activities and assessments. Because many students with learning disabilities and behavioral disorders are quite intelligent, providing them "easier" or lower-grade level activities and assessments is not an appropriate strategy. Such students need to be actively engaged in challenging and interesting learning activities and assessment tasks.

Finally, as with most useful tools, the guidelines in this book may need to be adjusted, added to, deleted from, and so on as time passes. This is necessary if such a tool is to remain vibrant and in touch with the reality in today's schools and classrooms.

SUMMARY OF CHAPTER CONTENT

Although some K–8 science teachers may be prepared to deal with any special education situation that confronts them in their classrooms, many are not. Hence, it becomes important for teachers to have some knowledge of what resources are available to help them when the need arises. One such resource can be found in colleagues down the hall: the special education teachers. Chapter 1 takes a look at the importance, in fact—necessity—of science teachers collaborating with special education teachers to provide appropriate instruction for students having special needs. The chapter then moves into looking at what some of those special needs are, and provides a short description of the most common ones that are found in mainstreamed classrooms.

In Chapter 2, the theme from Chapter 1 continues with considerations science teachers should make when planning science instruction. Characteristics of learners with special needs are noted, along with some suggestions teachers may follow in dealing with these characteristics. Such characteristics include writing difficulties, reading difficulties, language processing difficulties, attention deficits, perceptual and spatial orientation deficits, impulsivity problems, and memory deficiencies. In addition, some motivational strategies are explored that can help teachers get their students moving in the desired direction with respect to learning in science. Finally, most science teachers recognize that science (indeed, the English language) is replete with words that mean different things in different contexts, even though the words are spelled and pronounced the same. What are some problem words that might affect students? Chapter 2 provides a list to help teachers get started in their thinking on this issue.

Colleagues who have reviewed this book have noted that its heart begins in Chapter 3. In this chapter, specific suggestions guide teachers in preparing for differentiated science instruction, beginning with identifying specific competencies to be targeted, moving to vocabulary and prerequisite skills, and then looking at things that can be done to improve written and printed materials and verbal directions.

Building on the suggestions in Chapter 3, some actual examples of science activities and how they can be revised using the guidelines appear in Chapter 4. Specific examples ranging from primary to middle school are provided, as are examples from biological, earth, and physical sciences. The annotated activity examples include specific notes about what revisions can be made, along with some rationales for making those changes.

Similar to Chapter 4, Chapter 5 assists the teacher with how to revise science assessments. Included in the chapter is a middle-grade traditional assessment and an example of how such an assessment can be revised using the guidelines from Chapter 3. Also in this chapter are some performance-based assessment samples, spanning primary through middle-school levels. As in Chapter 4, there are annotated examples that include specific notations regarding what revisions have been made and some rationales for them.

Chapter 6 provides a brief examination of assessment rubrics, including a discussion of types of rubrics and general suggestions for starting to make them. After these rubric basics are covered, teachers are provided a sample performance-based assessment, its rubric, and two student work samples for the assessment. Teachers are guided in using the rubric to score the work samples, and then the scores are discussed with respect to what is assessment and what is evaluation. The chapter concludes with some consideration of what a teacher can do to differentiate science instruction in an appropriate way based upon the results of the assessment for one of the students.

Finally, the Resource section helps place the differentiation of science instruction in the context of the national science education standards promulgated through the NRC (*National Science Education Standards,* 1996), the American Association for the Advancement of Science (*Benchmarks for Scientific Literacy,* 1993), the National Science Teachers Association's documents on scientific literacy, scope-sequence-coordination, and pathways to scientifically literate and inquiry-based instruction. The chapter concludes with mention of state science learning standards. Overall, the themes that emerge from these various standards documents are that science instruction should be inquiry based, and it should be for all students—including those with special education needs.

SOME HELPFUL RESOURCES

Institute of Education Sciences, U.S. Department of Education. (2007). *Fast facts*. Retrieved from http://nces.ed.gov/fastfacts/display.asp?id=59. The National Center for Education Statistics (NCES) is the primary federal entity for collecting and analyzing data related to education.

National Research Council. (1996). *National science education standards*. Washington, DC: National Academy of Sciences. This is the primary science education standards source used by the science education community.

U.S. Department of Education. (n.d.). *Building the legacy: IDEA 2004*. Retrieved from http://idea.ed.gov. This site was created to provide a "one-stop shop" for resources related to IDEA and its implementing regulations.

1

Collaborating to Teach Students With Mild to Moderate Disabilities in the Inclusion Classroom

VIGNETTE WITH MARIE

Marie has just started her first teaching job at Anyplace Elementary School, and has been assigned to teach third grade. She begins preparing for the year by ensuring her classroom is well stocked with materials and supplies to engage her students in some quality hands-on/minds-on science like she learned in college. When she receives her class roster and student information, she is surprised to see the number of students who have special learning needs. Although she had some college courses and limited clinical experiences that dealt with this, the assignment now seems almost overwhelming. Marie loves science, but feels she needs some help because her science background simply won't be enough to meet the needs of all these students. The IEPs are of some help, but she's not sure exactly what she can do to meet all the specified requirements detailed in them. Fortunately, Marie has befriended a colleague, Tanya, who is one of the special education teachers. The two decide that some collaboration will be helpful, and the results should be beneficial for Marie's students. Marie's immediate questions are, "Exactly what does collaboration entail?" and "How can I make it work?"

STUDENTS WITH MILD TO MODERATE DISABILITIES AND INCLUSION

There are more than six million students with special needs being educating in preK–12 schools in the United States. That means about one out of every ten students in classrooms across the country can be labeled *exceptional* (Kirk, Gallagher, Coleman, & Anastasiow, 2009). These students may have any number of special needs including but not limited to learning disabilities, emotional or behavioral disorders, attention deficit disorder, cognitive disabilities, and autism. This group of special education categories is often referred to as mild to moderate disabilities.

Students with mild to moderate disabilities are a heterogeneous group of individuals all with unique learning and behavioral differences. However, as many teachers, parents, and other professionals come to discover, most of these students are more like their typically developing peers than they are different. Many simply need some adaptation or modification to the curricula, teaching materials, or special management strategies in order to perform up to their highest potential achievement levels.

The Individuals with Disabilities Education Act of 2004 mandates that students with special needs be educated in the *least restrictive environment* (LRE). The LRE is defined as the educational setting which best meets a student's individual learning needs while being educated with students without disabilities to the greatest extent possible (Rosenberg, Westling, & McLeskey, 2008). Inclusion is a process for providing education to students with mild to moderate disabilities in the general education classroom along with whatever necessary academic or behavioral *supports* they need to be successful. Supports may be in the form of curricular adaptations or modifications, a paraprofessional, special equipment, or assistive technology.

Students may have inclusion classes scheduled for any part of the day up to and including the full school day. Prior to placement in inclusion classes, students with mild to moderate disabilities should be prepared and capable to successfully handle the academic and behavioral expectations of the inclusion classroom when provided with their necessary supports.

The Institute for Education Sciences (IES), under the U.S. Department of Education, indicated in a national survey from the fall of 2007 that 95 percent of students with special needs are educated in inclusion classrooms for some part of the school day (IES, 2007b). Another report from the IES stated that during the 2004–05 school year, 50 percent of students with special needs spent 80 percent or more of their school day in inclusion classrooms (IES, 2007a). Most general educators, then, will have students with special needs in their classrooms. With this, the process of collaboration between general and special educators has been suggested as an effective means of educating all students in inclusion classrooms (Friend, 2005; Friend & Cook, 2007).

TEACHER COLLABORATION

When working with students who have mild to moderate disabilities in inclusion classrooms for science education, special education teachers and science teachers may work together, or *collaborate*, to teach students with and without disabilities. Friend and Cook (2007) provided the following definition for collaboration:

> Interpersonal *collaboration* is a style for direct interaction between at least two co-equal parties voluntarily engaged in shared decision making as they work toward a common goal. (p. 7)

Collaboration in inclusion classrooms is an equitable process where teachers value the importance of sharing educational responsibilities for students with and without educational disabilities. Friend (2005) related that effective collaboration is dependent on a foundation of trust, respect, and shared responsibility for all students' educational achievement. Teachers' approaches to collaboration continually evolve as they learn more about working together. The educators involved in collaborative teaching must perceive each other as equal professionals and understand that they can learn from each other. They cooperate to plan the entire teaching process including preparing class lessons, sharing materials and resources, co-teaching the lessons while managing the inclusion classroom, and making decisions about assessment of common goals for teaching and for student learning.

All of these components emphasize the ongoing developmental cycle of collaborative teacher relationships. As with any type of successful partnership, educators must understand that establishing effective collaborative relationships is an activity that requires commitment and a strong belief in the importance of the process. For example, collaboration usually begins with two professionals who are coworkers but have little knowledge of each other's philosophies, teaching methods and skills, and goals. In order to establish positive collaborative relationships, both parties must work together to plan their collaborative activities and take specific action to maintain the collaborative process in an inclusion classroom. While effective collaborative relationships take a great deal of time and personal commitment to establish, an important result of those efforts is the increased academic success and progress of students with mild to moderate disabilities in inclusion classrooms.

TEACHING PHILOSOPHY

Research has shown that teachers who carefully plan and consistently implement their own *professional conceptual framework* have a positive influence on student achievement in the classroom (Rosenberg et al., 2008). Professional conceptual framework is described as the teacher's plan for the curriculum and total classroom management. This boils down to *what to teach* and *how to teach it*. Meticulous planning of curriculum along with individual lesson plans, activities, and lesson materials; and proactive classroom management are all important components of a teacher's professional conceptual framework.

Another concept related to teaching philosophy is called *personal teaching efficacy*. This perception is a key component in overall teacher effectiveness and successful student learning outcomes. Personal teaching efficacy is defined as the teacher's faith in his or her own ability to have a positive impact on the learning and behavior of all students.

In order to be able to teach compatibly in the inclusion classroom, teachers in collaborative partnerships need to share their ideas related to their teaching philosophies. Being a teacher is not an easy job. When times get tough and difficulties arise, collaborative teachers who have discussed their ideas related to professional conceptual framework and personal teaching efficacy may have an easier time solving problems and maintaining a compatible partnership.

COLLABORATION AND COMPATIBILITY

General compatibility is another factor that can affect the collaborative partnership. An assessment instrument called the *Co-Teacher Relationship Scale* (CRS) (Friend & Cook, 2007) presented a number of factors that emphasize the importance of communication and cooperation when co-teaching in an inclusion classroom. The purpose of the CRS was to measure the degree to which co-teachers believed they were the same or different in their beliefs and philosophies about professional conceptual framework and personal teaching efficacy. The co-teachers who believed that their philosophies, values, and beliefs about teaching were more like their co-teacher than different achieved higher scores on overall program quality measures. The following concepts from the CRS were considered to be important points of agreement between co-teachers for successful collaboration:

- Philosophy related to curriculum, assessment, and teaching style (professional conceptual framework)
- Beliefs about the developmental learning process
- Adaptations and modifications of teaching materials to improve student achievement
- Parent involvement and collaboration
- Proactive behavior management methods
- Effective communication

Effective communication skills are critical for co-teachers who share teaching and behavior management responsibilities. Verbal communication is the primary mode of interaction and information sharing during collaboration. Co-teachers need to use open, honest, and direct communication methods that convey information clearly to share their knowledge about the course content, classroom management, and behavior management methods. Teachers who build an effective partnership learn to trust and respect each other's professional skills and abilities and this allows both teachers to expand and improve their own personal teaching skills.

CO-TEACHING

Collaboration is based on sharing ideas and strategies in a professional manner with a focus on meeting the diverse and unique needs of all students. The teachers must be able to productively communicate and work together.

Co-teaching, a common form of collaboration for general and special education teachers, involves two or more teachers who share a classroom and teaching responsibilities for a heterogeneous group of students. Co-teaching requires cooperation in planning, presenting the lessons, assessing student learning, and problem solving. Many teachers are asked to co-teach in inclusion classrooms, but are not provided with any guidelines or specific direction on how to go about the process. Following are suggestions for teachers interested in getting started with co-teaching.

Suggestions for Co-Teachers

1. Obtain administrative support for the co-teaching venture. Administrative backing is vitally important because the teachers may need additional planning time for preparing lessons, modifying and adapting lesson materials, evaluating lesson outcomes, and learning about each other's teaching style and philosophies.

2. Brainstorm co-teaching lesson ideas and pick one. Begin with simple lessons to allow co-teachers to build their comfort levels before tackling more involved lessons.

3. Carefully plan how to share teaching, paperwork, and behavior management responsibilities for each co-teacher. Be sure all materials are modified, adapted, and prepared for optimal learning for all the students in the inclusion classroom.

4. Collaboratively teach the lesson. Demonstrate the equal status and shared teaching responsibility of co-teachers to the students.

5. Evaluate the lesson upon completion, providing feedback and reflection in a constructive manner. Note what worked and what needs to be revised.

6. Plan the next co-teaching lesson, making necessary changes and improvements.

7. View co-teaching as a strategy that can continually evolve over time. Focus on improving content that teaches knowledge and skills, adaptations and modification of lesson materials, and behavior management knowledge and skills.

8. Remember to provide enthusiasm, positive reinforcement, and support to one another throughout the entire experience.

Using the co-teaching method, both teachers actively plan and teach the lesson. Students benefit from the combination of the talents and expertise of two teachers. With experience and reflection, co-teachers will find the methods that work best for them based on the curriculum to be taught and the needs of the students.

ACADEMIC AND BEHAVIORAL CHARACTERISTICS OF STUDENTS WITH MILD TO MODERATE DISABILITIES

Co-teachers in inclusion classrooms will need to communicate and plan for necessary curriculum and behavior management adaptations and modifications to provide the supports that will help students with mild to moderate disabilities achieve success in inclusion classrooms. Some students demonstrate a variety of academic and behavioral characteristics that interfere with learning and achieving in traditional science classrooms.

It is important for all teachers to remember that these students do want to learn and succeed at school. Their academic and behavioral problems are not intentional. Providing accommodations and making adaptations and modifications to lesson materials will assist these students to achieve at higher levels and show more appropriate behavior in the inclusion classroom. Illustrating these improvements, the collaborative pairs of science and special education teachers who participated in the original revising project upon which this book is based noted an interesting observation. They indicated that the adaptations and modifications made to science class materials and assessments not only benefited the students with mild to moderate disabilities, but also made the learning process more effective and efficient for all the students in the science inclusion classrooms.

COGNITIVE AND SOCIAL CHARACTERISTICS

Expressive and Receptive Language

Many students with mild to moderate disabilities experience difficulties with *expressive* and *receptive language*. Expressive language relates to an individual's ability to speak coherently and receptive language relates to comprehending spoken language. For a lot of these students, processing verbal communications from the teacher is significantly slower than that of their peers (Jordan, 2006). If the teacher asks a question, the student may need extra time to process the question before he can begin to process the response or answer. Because of the *time lag in processing* the *question* and the time lag in processing an *answer* to a question, by the time the student finally figures out a possible response, the teacher and the rest of the class have already moved on to the next question, which this student has missed entirely.

A teacher's understanding of the cognitive processing differences for students with mild to moderate disabilities has practical implications for a language-intensive topic like science. The cognitive and social characteristics typical of these students often make it difficult for them to adequately complete traditional paper and pencil tasks and assessments. Science has customarily been taught using lectures, verbal descriptions, and explanations supplemented by demonstrations and lab activities. Adapting and modifying curriculum materials and assessments can provide the necessary support for the students to demonstrate science class competencies.

If a student has poor receptive language skills and is unable to effectively understand and remember the verbal information spoken by the teacher, she will not be able to show adequate learning progress or achievement. Hands-on classroom activities, and tasks based on a student's preferred learning style (verbal, auditory, or kinesthetic), will help her to more accurately demonstrate individual learning outcomes. Authentic assessments that focus on performance-based activities, which reflect class instructional tasks, help students demonstrate their knowledge and progress.

Attention Problems

Many students with mild to moderate disabilities also have problems with *selective attention* and *sustained attention* (Rosenberg et al., 2008). Selective attention refers to the student's ability to filter out unimportant noise and other distractions in the classroom and to focus directly and specifically on the teacher. Sustained attention is the skill of being able to maintain attention through completion of a given task or class period. The students may miss all or portions of directions and instructions due to these attention problems.

Jordan (2006) provided an interesting real-life example to explain the problem of sustained attention. He hypothesizes that these students *are* motivated to learn. At the start of the lesson, they "plug their plugs in" when the teacher calls for attention and begins the lesson. Then, because of their neurological processing problems, their "plugs" fall out like a vacuum cleaner's motor dies when the vacuum is pulled a little bit further than the length of the cord allows. If the prongs of the plug are pulled even just a little bit out of the electric socket to break the connection, the vacuum cleaner loses power. The same thing happens with students who have these processing problems. Through no fault of their own, the tenuous connection between the teacher presenting the concepts of the lesson and their brain comprehending the material is broken.

An additional processing difficulty relates to how the students actually comprehend verbal presentations and directions. Because of the difficulty they have with listening for details, they may not catch all the fine points of the directions or may miss whole words or parts. It is suspected that they often miss as much as two of every three words spoken by the teacher (Jordan, 2006). These processing problems may be observed in students who have attention and memory problems. Consequently, these students may not understand or remember what they hear.

Memory Skills

Many students with mild to moderate disabilities have poor memory skills. In particular, their short-term memory does not function as effectively as it should. As a result, they have difficulty remembering information they learned. This memory problem is called *encoding*. The information is not stored efficiently in their neurological memory banks. Because of this, when they need to go back and pick a concept or idea out of their memory bank, they can't do it. It's almost like the information in their memory banks is scrambled, rather than neatly and logically organized. Due to the encoding problems, students may not be able to respond to simple comprehension questions following extensive instruction.

To help students cope with memory deficits, teachers need to frequently review important points of the lesson, elaborate on pertinent details, model methods and strategies, and frequently check for understanding. In addition, teachers should offer memory strategies within the lesson structure to help all students remember important concepts.

Performance Inconsistency

Students with mild to moderate disabilities seem to have good days and bad days at school. Some days they just seem to be able to remember facts and information better than they can on other days. Unfortunately, many are punished for their bad days. The students are accused of being lazy, apathetic, unmotivated, and uncaring. Ironically, they are also often punished for their good days as teachers comment that they can, after all, achieve when they "really try." Mel Levine, a pediatrician who specializes in research and treatment for children who have learning and behavioral disorders stated:

> It will be a great day when we recognize performance inconsistency as part of the learning disabilities profile, rather than as evidence for the prosecution. (Levine, 2003)

Levine further describes the good-day, bad-day phenomenon as a disruption in the flow of mental energy (see also Gunther, Bieber, & Lavoie, 1997). Levine reports that an individual has no control over this. It is very discouraging for students who do their homework, study for tests, but then, cannot produce knowledge or information on demand when they need it. Performance inconsistency happens to students with mild to moderate disabilities over and over in their daily lives. It is frustrating for them as well as their teachers.

Social Characteristics

Students with mild to moderate disabilities present a unique social profile that sets them apart from their typically achieving and developing peers. As a direct result of their disabilities, these students may show poor peer relationships, emotional instability, impulsivity, and low self-concept and poor self-esteem. The daily life problems experienced by students with mild to moderate disabilities can be so frustrating that many students develop and then demonstrate behavioral and emotional disorders that are triggered by various situations at home, at school, or in the community. Their behavior often interferes with expected academic achievement at school. The average sixth grader with mild to moderate disabilities may already be two years behind academically (Rhode, Jenson, & Reavis, 1992).

All of these social characteristics have the potential to negatively affect the student's motivation and progress in school. Teachers often misinterpret the behavior problems as evidence suggesting that the students are being willfully noncompliant, defiant, or that they just don't care (Jensen, 2005). This is not necessarily the case. These students may not be able to express their thoughts and feelings effectively. Teaching structured social skills classes such as *Skillstreaming* (Goldstein & McGinnis, 1997) can be of great practical benefit to students who have social skill deficits.

Jensen (2005) provided a set of proactive suggestions for positively focused behavior management. These strategies are structured for teachers to help students learn what to do to be successful:

1. Be proactive in setting up the classroom management. Set realistically high standards for behavioral and academic expectations to help more students learn to be successful.

2. Establish rules and expectations for appropriate classroom behavior. Teach, post, and review the classroom expectations to help students remember. They have to understand precisely what is expected to be able to follow through.

Figure 1.1 Student Behavior Checklist

Student Name: _____ Date: _____ Time: _____

Please check yes or no to indicate the student's current behavior.

The student:

1. Is in assigned seat ❑ Yes ❑ No
2. Has all required materials ❑ Yes ❑ No
3. Is quiet and ready to listen ❑ Yes ❑ No
4. Works consistently on the assigned task ❑ Yes ❑ No
5. Works independently on the assigned task ❑ Yes ❑ No
6. Follows directions consistently during class ❑ Yes ❑ No
7. Uses appropriate language ❑ Yes ❑ No
8. Works cooperatively with peers ❑ Yes ❑ No
9. Shows appropriate behavior and attitude with teacher ❑ Yes ❑ No
10. Has homework completed on time ❑ Yes ❑ No

Other specific behaviors for this student:

11. _____

12. _____

13. _____

14. _____

15. _____

Use a minimum of ten behaviors to compute the percentage of behavioral compliance using the following formula:

Total marked Yes (_____) divided by (Yes + No _____) × 100
= Percent of Compliant Behaviors _____ %

Comments:

_____

_____

_____

(continue on back or another page as needed)

Source: Adapted from Rhode, Jenson, & Reavis, 1992.

3. Use functional behavioral assessment to identify priority problem behaviors for each student and teach new target behaviors to help them learn appropriate skills and to be more successful. Teach and give positive reinforcement for new appropriate target behaviors rather than simply punishing old problem behaviors.

4. Consistently use positive reinforcement to teach students new target behaviors. The main idea is to pay more attention to appropriate behaviors. Rule of thumb: The behaviors the teacher pays the most attention to in the classroom tends to increase. Focus, then, on the positive.

5. Use verbal praise and activities, and extend privileges that are academically and socially beneficial for positive reinforcement.

6. Collect data consistently to monitor student behavior. Graph results. Troubleshoot and revise when necessary.

7. Teach students self-management skills so that they can assess, monitor, and reward their own behavior. Self-management helps students to internalize and generalize their new target behaviors. This will help the students to become more successfully independent and less reliant on the teacher.

Student Behavior Checklist

One of the primary benefits of retooling science activities for students with mild to moderate disabilities is the increase in academic achievement and appropriate social behavior that occurs when the students are actively engaged in learning science concepts with materials adapted to meet their individual learning needs. As students become more motivated and engaged in learning, they naturally experience increased academic achievement and success in inclusion classrooms.

Sometimes it is difficult for teachers to objectively determine changes in students' behavior. For data collection, a simple student behavior checklist (adapted from Rhode et al., 1992) may be helpful. Results of the checklist can provide teachers with an ongoing picture of a student's academic and social behavior progress.

The checklist (Figure 1.1) can be used daily or weekly to collect samples of a student's behavior. The teacher may use the checklist in the beginning of the observation period for several days to establish a baseline or representative sample of the student's activities. Then, weekly or biweekly observations allow the teacher to compare baseline information to current behavior to determine if the student is functioning effectively in the classroom. Because this is a simple checklist of typical classroom behaviors, the teacher only needs a few minutes to complete it during the class while the student is there. The teacher could also make a weekly graph of this data for comparisons.

CONCLUSION

One of the significant themes of this chapter is the importance for teachers to work together to address the needs of their students. Another purpose of this chapter is to provide a primer, of sorts, about the characteristics of a number of learning needs teachers will find in students in today's classrooms. The idea of teamwork, whether through some form of collaboration, through co-teaching, or some other mechanism, is critical if successful science instruction and learning are to be achieved in mainstreamed classrooms. Many teachers prepared for teaching science are not experts in special education, and many special education specialists are not experts in teaching science. A major focus of this book, then, is how teachers can make science more accessible to their students who have special needs, and a key to achieving that is for everyone involved to work, plan, and deliver together as a team, doing what is best for each child.

2

Addressing Specific Learning Difficulties

INTRODUCTION

Logically, before one begins to fix something, it is best to know as much as possible about what it is that needs to be fixed. Preparing for differentiated science instruction is no different. In the case of preparing for differentiated science activities, assessments, and so forth, the teacher seeks to revise (more so than "fix"). Exactly what those revisions entail depends upon the intended target audience. In the science classroom, that audience is the student. If activity and assessment revisions are to hold promise of success, teachers require a clear understanding of students' needs and learning characteristics. In this chapter, those specific learning difficulties are briefly examined in order to provide teachers some context in which they can then proceed to make necessary and appropriate revisions in their instructional science materials and procedures.

VIGNETTE WITH MS. BURRELL

Ms. Burrell was taken aback by Joel's behavior. Whenever the class was at their lab stations, it seemed Joel would intentionally break a piece of glassware or be across the room poking at another student. If not that, then he'd be disorganizing the materials at his workstation so his lab partners would have trouble getting through the activity. Letting this behavior continue was no way to run a sixth-grade science class. So, Ms. Burrell decided to create some special rules for Joel to follow. First, during lab times, he would have to stay in a designated space at his work area unless he needed to go retrieve or return materials from the supply table. Second, he would only be allowed to manipulate one thing at a time and must leave other materials in their place on the worktable until it was their turn to be used. Third, Joel would be given only nonbreakable items to use—no more glassware, if at all possible. As Ms. Burrell reviewed her "Joel rules," she realized that these rules could also be helpful to other students. In fact, she had several other students who had some behavior and learning issues (although not as extreme as Joel's). And, it would be better to have rules that applied to everyone rather than singling out one student—more equitable application, that way.

Ms. Burrell thus began implementing the new rules, and found the lab area was sometimes (but not always) much calmer and the students were more productive (but not always)—not to mention safer. Moreover, Joel's behavior during labs showed improvements as well. In the following section of this chapter, you will find some guidelines that specifically address what Ms. Burrell desired to do—as well as other guidelines to improve operations in her classroom.

PREPARING TO MAKE INSTRUCTIONAL CHANGES

In order for Ms. Burrell to devise a plan of action to deal with Joel's behavior, she first needs to understand something about the characteristics of behavior disorders. Chapter 1 presented information about various learning needs, including behavior disorders, that would be helpful for Ms. Burrell. Whenever teachers make changes in activities or assessments, it affects learning outcomes for all their students, especially for those who have learning differences. Although it is impossible to predict what type of changes will be effective for all students, teachers should attempt to be as fair as possible in making those alterations. Some teachers use a trial-and-error method to determine task adaptations that will result in all students achieving academic success in the classroom. Ms. Burrell may find it helpful to consult her special education colleague about Joel's situation, as well as his IEP or 504 plan, to identify the strategies that have the best chance for success.

Teachers like Ms. Burrell are likely correct in their thinking that the changes in classroom rules might be beneficial to all their students, although they should be mindful that not all such changes impact every student in the same way. Some students will still need their own special rules to follow. Further, unless teachers understand the particular difficulties their students face with writing, reading, comprehending, and so on, teachers' rules may lack the effectiveness they desire. Teachers need to address the difficulties themselves rather than their symptoms (such as negative classroom behaviors).

Teachers will also find it necessary to change some of the personal protocols and procedures in their own teaching. For example, they may reorganize their course schedules so that they give tests on Tuesdays, Wednesdays, or Thursdays, rather than on Mondays or Fridays. Mondays are particularly problematic for students who take medication. Oftentimes, the medicine is not given on the weekend for various reasons. It may take several hours for medications to take effect on Monday mornings when students resume their medications. Teachers may also need to be more judicious in selecting work partners for their students. Work partners may be available adults (e.g., paraprofessionals, parent volunteers) or other students who are interested in being assistants. Teachers should not hesitate to seek assistance in meeting the varied needs of their students, including those with special needs.

Chapter 1 examined major categories of special learning needs, and many teachers will recognize how some of their students exhibit specific difficulties that seem to cut across these categories. For example, they may find students with attention deficit disorder (ADD) and learning disabilities (LD) both have some difficulty with writing while students with autism spectrum disorder (ASD) may struggle with comprehending textbooks and gaining information from class lectures. The remainder of this chapter looks at considerations teachers should make, as they plan their science instruction, regarding specific difficulties their students may have. Some suggestions can apply to more than one difficulty students experience in their science learning.

CONSIDERATIONS FOR STUDENTS POSSESSING WRITING DIFFICULTIES

Many students with learning challenges experience difficulties with writing, both the physical and the cognitive processes. As students progress through the science curriculum, writing demands increase. By the time they are in middle school, science students are expected to be able to write answers to questions, listen to a teacher's presentations and take notes, complete lengthy exams using multiple answer formats, and prepare written reports. Difficulties in writing may include being able to produce clear, legible answers or products as well as preparing well thought out and constructed responses to academic tasks. Some students with learning difficulties also have poor fine motor skills, particularly in the early elementary years, and may have very slow, laborious writing that impedes their completion of tasks in the same time frame as their peers.

Teachers can provide assistance to these students in various ways. With the technology available in schools today, one solution is to allow students to use computers or word processors to do their written assignments. By allowing the use of a computer, the student may be a much faster typist than writer, and this strategy emphasizes clarity as well. In addition to addressing the physical demands, a computer can also assist in improving potential mechanical and composition concerns by employing the spell- and grammar-check tools. This can be a motivating method of writing for two reasons. First, computers facilitate the writing process for students; it is not so much physical effort, and it can assist students in organizing their ideas (Access Center, 2004). Second, the completed writing project will be more readable, polished, and better in quality (Lipson & Wixson, 2003).

Another digital option for teachers is to allow students to audio-record their answers. With this response mode, students will record their answers to questions or complete tasks orally using a tape recorder for later transcription or computer software that uses word recognition technology. Teachers may find student answers are much more complete compared to those they get when students physically labor with writing. If the technology is unavailable, the student can dictate to an adult (such as a teaching assistant or volunteer).

One of the biggest challenges for students with learning difficulties is taking notes during teacher presentations. Note taking is an important skill for students and teachers should help students with this for many reasons, including because it helps students understand and remember instructional information, it keeps students engaged in the learning process, and it improves students' performance on tests. Thus, it is important for students with special needs to learn how to take notes effectively. To facilitate note taking for students with special learning needs, teachers can provide outlines of their lecture notes to students or audio-record their lectures so those who need it can listen to the presentation again.

Additionally, unless prescribed by IEPs, 504 plans, or state standardized test protocols, teachers can use performance-based assessments rather than paper-pencil tasks or tests for students to demonstrate skill mastery. Teachers may find that some of their students are more relaxed and can demonstrate their learning more effectively through a more authentic task than through an abstract writing task or formal test. For example, if teachers want to assess whether students know the parts of an atom, they can ask them to draw and label the atom in lieu of one or two multiple-choice items on a test.

CONSIDERATIONS FOR STUDENTS POSSESSING READING DIFFICULTIES

Reading is a very complex task, and for students with learning challenges often represents difficulties. Reading is not a single process, but instead is comprised of the simultaneous implementation of several operations that address decoding (which includes phonemic awareness and phonics), and comprehension (vocabulary knowledge and fluency). Good readers apply all of these skills to written text to gain meaning and acquire information. Neuroscience (Medina, 2008) has shown us that the human brain doesn't read whole words or individual letters, but rather interprets graphic portions—such as the vertical portion of the letter *R*, the individual horizontal portions, the slanted portion, and so on. When seeing the letter, the brain must put the images of the portions of the letter together in order to recognize it as the letter. Once decoded, the student then continues to apply phonics' rules, and ultimately derives meaning (comprehension) from the print. Hence, reading is a very labor-intensive process.

Science reading materials can usually be placed into one of two kinds of text: narrative or technical. Technical reading is characterized by much information, definitions, terms, and so forth. Narrative reading is characterized as more storytelling, much like what one finds in trade books. Each requires different types of reading skills that need to be taught, and technical reading is particularly difficult for many students.

To help students use written science material effectively, teachers should consider potential barriers for those students who deal with printed materials less effectively because of special learning needs. Many of the difficulties that students with special learning needs encounter relate to the mechanics of reading, including the size and print quality of the text or learning materials. When providing reading material for students, teachers should type the materials, with a font that is as clean as possible with few or no tails (serifs) such as Geneva or Helvetica. Fonts of 12 to 14 point are easier for students to work with than are smaller font sizes. In addition, double-spacing print helps students track the text better. In addition, teachers should avoid glossy paper selected for printing or copying learning materials. Flat-finish papers reduce visual glare and are easier on the eye. (Many textbook pages are printed on glossy paper because it helps with colored text and figures.) Some colored papers work well for copying, particularly if they are softer tones.

Teachers report wide variability in student reading level, and this is also true of students with special learning needs who are placed in general science classrooms. That is, some of these students will not be reading on grade level and will have trouble gaining information from the adopted text or supplemental reading and instructional materials. Planning for this ongoing problem will be very beneficial to teachers if they determine the readability of the written materials that they plan to use with their students, including their own personally developed ones. The easiest way to do this is to determine the readability through a manual or computer process. There are several readability formulas that can be easily implemented. In general, readability formulas determine the level of text by weighing the impact of the complexity of sentences and phrases and the difficulty of vocabulary. There is software available for free or to purchase for checking readability of print materials. In addition, most word processing software has an integrated readability tool so the teacher simply types in a 100-word section, selects the readability function, and the software performs the calculation. With this information, teachers can make better choices regarding the print materials they choose to use with their classes, and particularly, for those students with special learning needs.

In Microsoft Word 2007, the Flesch Reading Ease and the Flesch-Kincaid Grade Level, built into the program, determine the readability of written text through the following steps:

1. Type a 100- to 200-word passage from the text into Microsoft Word.
2. Click on the Microsoft Office Button and then click Word Options. Next, click Proofing.
3. Ensure there is a check in the box for "Check grammar with spelling." Then check "Show readability statistics."

When Microsoft Word finishes checking spelling and grammar, it displays information about the reading level of the document.

In addition to identifying a text's readability, teachers may also want to determine if their students will be able to use the adopted classroom text effectively. They can do this by conducting a *cloze procedure*, where words are deleted from a selected passage. Students insert words, filling in the deletions, to make the text meaningful.

To prepare materials for cloze exercises, teachers may use the following procedure:

1. Select a self-contained passage from the textbook of an appropriate length for the grade level of the students being assessed (100 words for elementary students, and 200 words for secondary students).
2. Leave the first and last sentences and all punctuation intact.
3. Carefully select the words for omission using a word-count formula, such as every fifth word or other criteria (every eighth word for elementary students, and every fifth word for secondary students).
4. Leave lines for the students to fill in the missing words.
5. Score the completions, assigning 1 point for each correct answer. (Synonyms are okay as well.)
6. Determine the percentage of correct word replacement with this scale:

61% correct	Independent level
41%–60% correct	Instructional level
Below 40%	Frustration level

If teachers find themselves using materials that are written at a level higher than their students' reading abilities, they may need to consider some general supports to implement as part of their overall teaching approach. For those students whose reading abilities are significantly below what is needed to learn efficiently from the text, teachers may devise some alternative strategies. Alternative approaches may include:

- Providing the text on a recording
- Having someone read the text aloud to the student
- Providing the text with the relevant or key ideas highlighted, as shown in the following example:

Example of Highlighted Key Ideas

The cell is the structural and functional unit of all known living organisms. It is the smallest unit of an organism that is classified as living, and is often called the building block of life.[1] Some organisms, such as most bacteria, are unicellular (consist of a single cell). Other organisms, such as humans, are multicellular. (Cell, n.d.)

- Providing a different text written at a lower level
- Providing the content of the text through another format, such as an instructional video
- Providing a reading guide to help the student identify important text information

These general strategies, when provided to students with special learning needs or students who have reading problems but are not assisted through disability services, can help them more successfully interact with written science materials.

Specific Strategies for Addressing Reading Comprehension Difficulties

In addition to the general reading adaptations and adjustments that teachers make for their students with special learning needs, they may also need to implement adaptations or interventions to address more specific and unique reading difficulties to improve comprehension.

One common problem that students with inadequate reading skills present is poor fluency, which negatively affects comprehension. Teachers can help these students by using an index card technique, whereby a 3 × 5 index card helps students track the reading text while reading alone or with others. The student places the card on the page so the long edge of the card is parallel to the lines of text. The student then moves the card down the page as he reads, revealing only one additional line at a time as he progresses through the text. The card improves the student's overall fluency by discouraging word-for-word reading, helps the student stay on the appropriate line of text, and can support an appropriate reading pace. It may be helpful to mark the edge of the card with a bright color to help keep the student's attention.

Another index card technique uses a window card to limit distractions while reading. A window card is simply an index card that has a small window cut out of it so the opening is as long as a line of text and is limited in its height. This simple device permits the student to see only one or a few lines of text at once. It helps keep the reading place, limits distractions on the page, and improves student concentration and comprehension.

Teachers can also help their students by making and giving them reading guides for organizing the assigned reading material. The reading guide accompanies the student through the assigned reading, asks the student to identify relevant information, and supports acquisition of content using a skimming and scanning procedure. To accomplish this, reading guides should be organized sequentially based on the text and include clues (page numbers, paragraphs, and sentences) for finding the answers. Reading guides can use a variety of formats including short-answer, fill-in-the-blank, or multiple-choice responses. These response formats allow the teacher to adjust the writing demands based on student needs.

Figure 2.1 provides an example of items on a reading guide using different response formats. In parentheses, the student is provided clues to where in the text the to find the answers. *P* stands for page,

Figure 2.1   Reading Guide Example

Chapter 2: Matter, Atoms, & More

1. There are _____ naturally occurring kinds of atoms. (P 4, pg 2, s 3)

2. Atoms are made up of what **three particles?** (P 4, pg 3, s 2)

3. Protons carry a − + charge. (P 4, pg 4, s 1)

4. How many electrons and protons does an atom have? (P 4, pg 6, s 3)
   a. The same number of electrons as protons
   b. More electrons than protons
   c. More protons than electrons

---

pg for paragraph, and *s* for sentence. Thus, to find the answer to the first question on the reading guide, the student needs to refer to page 4, paragraph 2, and sentence 3.

Written directions are often overlooked as a potential reading problem for students. Some students with special learning needs struggle to implement the directions they have read. When providing written directions, teachers should use bold print or a highlighter to emphasize important, new, or unfamiliar words. Following a term in bold, teachers can facilitate student comprehension by using parentheses to describe the term in language more understandable to their students.

While a student reads, either aloud or silently, teachers should engage their students in comprehension checks. Asking students questions to check their understanding of the reading content can monitor comprehension. It is important for teachers to ensure that their students are retaining important points along the way, rather than waiting until the end of the reading to check for comprehension. Additional strategies for supporting reading include:

- Providing prereading organizers and end-of-text summaries
- Asking students to create their own questions about assigned readings
- Providing vocabulary lists with simple definitions

By following these strategies, teachers can be more assured they are correctly interpreting their students' comprehension of materials.

CONSIDERATIONS FOR STUDENTS POSSESSING LANGUAGE PROCESSING DIFFICULTIES

A difficulty that parallels reading issues involves auditory aspects of student learning. Specifically, teachers need to consider two auditory difficulties with respect to their students' language processing: auditory comprehension and auditory memory. Auditory comprehension problems interfere with students' ability to effectively process what they hear in learning environments. Students who have auditory comprehension problems will process verbal information much slower than average. These students need to be provided with extra time because they must process the question asked as well as their answers. An example of such processing follows:

Verbal question: "What are the names of the nine planets in the solar system?" The student must process three specific pieces of information: (1) what = a thing, (2) are = currently existing, and (3) nine planets = quantity clue.

Because of the slower than average processing speed, some students will still be processing the first question while the class is answering and possibly moving on to the second and third questions or other parts of the discussion. To help the slower group, teachers can use a strategy that is effective for all learners, but particularly important for students with processing issues, which is *wait time*. Thus, a teacher helps improve everyone's thinking process by preceding verbal questions with, "I would like everyone to take a minute and think about this question." At that point, the teacher can ask the question, repeat the direction for students to think about it a minute, wait ten or more seconds, and then call on a student for an answer. This questioning procedure will give all the students adequate processing time. Teachers may also repeat certain pertinent portions of the question that give clues to the answer. It is important during the wait time that the teacher stops talking so that students can focus on the question without other auditory distractions.

Some students will experience difficulty following verbal directions. This can be addressed by providing verbal directions on a recording so a student can replay and listen whenever necessary. Also, teachers should be concise in providing verbal directions. Students may get bogged down in the irrelevancies of the language. For supporting homework completion, a recording can again be particularly helpful. The teacher may also consider videotaping or creating a podcast that can be accessed on a class website to provide a visual model for a student. While this may seem like a lot of work for one student, students without identified disabilities have been found to also use these tools to their benefit.

Teachers may also want to provide a visual model or example for the entire class by projecting it using a documents camera, projector, or smart board technology. A teacher does not need to possess the latest in technology to provide large-scale models. Whatever approach used, teachers should be sure the images are large enough for easily and clearly viewing their details throughout the classroom.

Of course, using multiple modalities to provide an enriched environment is always preferred. Teachers can pair verbal directives with modeling and visuals. If the directive to students is to put their names in the right-hand corner of the paper, the teacher should have an example on the board or projected to show students what is expected.

In addition to auditory processing issues, some students may have difficulty with auditory memory. That is, students with auditory memory problems will have difficulty remembering what they hear. Given that most classrooms rely heavily on oral communication, this can create a significant barrier to learning. Some specific strategies teachers may use to assist their students with remembering (and perhaps with auditory comprehension as well) include:

- Putting visual reminders of the instructions on the board for students to follow
- Providing an individual card for each student that contains reminders to refer to when following directions
- Providing students with a checklist of directions so that each can be checked off as it is finished
- Using mnemonics to help remember processes (e.g., FOIL for first, outside, inside, and last for completing polynomial math problems) or details (e.g., PENS for parts of the atom: proton, electrons, neutrons, and shell)

Whatever strategies teachers select and use, they should use them consistently with an eye toward modifying the usage as appropriate as their students' needs change.

CONSIDERATIONS FOR STUDENTS POSSESSING ATTENTION DEFICITS

Students who have attention deficits need many prompts and cues to stay on task. Teachers should consider several factors to help these students function more effectively in the science classroom, including seating decisions and ways to sustain attention. First, teachers should carefully consider where students are seated. For example, they may want to assign a student with attention concerns away from distractions such as display cases with specimens or animal habitats frequently found in science classrooms, and in a place where the teacher can easily be on hand to provide attention supports.

However, it may not be advisable to seat these students in the front row if this results in the student continually turning around to see what is happening behind her. Sometimes, the sides of the classroom are the best places because this allows students to use their peripheral vision to track activity while also staying engaged in their desk work. Additionally, these spots are out of the main traffic areas, and they only have one other student on one side, thus, reducing possible prospective human distractions.

Once teachers place students in appropriate locations, they should plan for sustained attention by keeping the students actively involved with the learning process and by giving them many opportunities to respond. Asking students planned questions during lessons helps teachers accomplish this, giving students special bits of information to be responsible for during the lesson, or having them participate in demonstrations. When teachers give directions, they can ask students to repeat the directions back to check for understanding. Teachers should also not overload their students with too many directions at once—students may function better when given one or two steps at a time, rather than an entire set of directions. Listing the directions on the board or providing students with a written list at their desk can also be effective.

CONSIDERATIONS FOR STUDENTS POSSESSING PERCEPTUAL AND SPATIAL ORIENTATION DEFICITS

Some students may have perceptual and spatial orientation deficits that affect how they perceive and process visual information. That is, some students will have difficulty focusing on the important information in written sources because of the way their brain interprets visual stimuli. This can be prevented if the teacher formats handouts, worksheets, and other learning materials mindfully considering the management of the content, the use of space to emphasize topics or skills, and the use of color and graphics to enhance concept development.

One of the biggest concerns with paper resources is overcrowding information. Everyone wants to be efficient with their limited resources and teachers frequently use very small print, single-spaced on a handout or slide. Many students with perceptual and spatial orientation issues will see a jumbled mess when they look at this material. Slides or transparencies should have no more than eight to ten lines of information. Handouts need white space separating lines, paragraphs, or sections, and around graphics. Teachers should limit distracting bits of clip art and restrict artwork to those items that can help illustrate or inform.

The materials also need to be organized to support memory links, by formatting worksheets or sheets of directions so that connected tasks are grouped together. This can give students a concrete idea of where a separate problem or task begins and ends. To help further, teachers can number the boxes so students will know which one to do first, second, third, and so on. As an example, the Silent Smell science activity in Chapter 4 shows how the use of graphics, lines, and white space helps students distinguish the steps and key vocabulary.

CONSIDERATIONS FOR STUDENTS POSSESSING IMPULSIVITY PROBLEMS

Just about every teacher seems to be able to recall at least one student who was impulsive. In the science classroom, this can be problematic when such students jump into some action before fully receiving the teacher's directions or understanding what the task is that needs to be completed. For teachers like Ms. Burrell who have impulsive students, there are some strategies to help these students maintain self-control. When using questioning sessions, they can precede questions with suggestions for students to stop and think before responding. They can also remind students to raise their hand and wait to be called on for a response. During those times when teachers want their students engaged in a task, there are four specific strategies that can be used:

1. Before allowing students to begin, tell them how long the task should take to finish it successfully.

2. During the work, periodically tell students at what point they should be on the task. Having the student fold the paper in half, or place a line at the midpoint of the task, to indicate where they should be at the halfway point in time is also a helpful visual reminder to help students monitor their pace. Simultaneously, those who are moving too quickly through the task and leaving parts undone will be reminded to slow down and be more attentive and thorough. This strategy also can help those students who get bogged down in minutiae and aren't moving along rapidly enough.

3. Use a visual reminder such as a clock face on the board to tell students when they should be halfway.

4. Use verbal reminders to tell students there are a specific number of minutes left to complete the task.

Teachers may also want to plan ahead to prevent behavioral concerns related to impulsive student acts. One of the best ways to prevent impulsive student behaviors is to make expectations explicit for students. In practical terms, this means that class rules are discussed, posted, and reviewed regularly to ensure that the students know well the behavioral expectations of that teacher.

In addition, for science classrooms, rules for the lab should also be addressed before each lesson using lab materials. For some students, the laboratory environment is perceived as a less formal, uncontrolled, or basically unstructured setting. As a result, students may have a harder time focusing on the task, not be mindful of safety concerns, and miss a great opportunity to engage in an authentic learning experience without the barriers of the typical classroom. If teachers carefully structure the laboratory lesson and class time to prevent off task behavior, students with attentional concerns will benefit to the fullest extent possible. For example, in the Bouncing Ball experiment shared in Chapter 4, where students drop balls of varied mass from different heights and measure the bounce heights, the possibility of balls flying across the room is high. To prevent this, teachers may want to create space parameters for each group by using masking tape to demark work areas on the floor and create a defined work space. A rule for that day could be for balls that stray from the designated space to be confiscated from the group. This preventive strategy is likely to reduce or even eliminate an inappropriate and potentially dangerous behavior that could easily ripple across the class. Because science lab work changes with each experiment, lab rules may need to be a mixture of common and situation-specific rules. A list of possible science lab rules for students is as follows:

1. Follow lab safety rules at all times.
2. Follow all experiment steps carefully.
3. Follow the teacher's directions exactly.

In the Testing for Sugars activity (Chapter 4), safety reminders and rules are added to the task between steps to remind students to be safe. For example, during the first steps when students are preparing a hot water bath, there are two safety warnings listed between Steps 3 and 4, reminding students to take care when boiling the water. In addition, safety warnings appear throughout the task, reminding students to wear their safety goggles and lab apron.

Some students with special learning needs have difficulty sitting through an exam. Teachers can prevent some of the difficulty associated with testing by making adaptations to specifically address this issue. A lengthy test of multiple-choice questions can be very overwhelming for many students. The practical result of this anxiety may be an inability to respond effectively. That is, the students will become too anxious to recall the test information that they studied. Sometimes simply splitting the test into smaller sections helps a student see the test as a manageable event. To accomplish this, the teacher prints out a special test formatted in three or four sections and simply tells the student to use one-fourth of the time to complete that section. The student returns that part to the teacher when it is complete, and then gets the next section. This reorganization facilitates a more effective pacing for the student to work through the exam, provides the teacher with several opportunities to reinforce the student as he completes each section, and helps the student manage his anxiety related to testing.

It is always easier to prevent inappropriate behavior than correct it, so when there are students in a classroom with potential for impulsive or distracting behaviors, "an ounce of prevention is worth a pound of cure."

CONSIDERATIONS FOR STUDENTS POSSESSING MEMORY DEFICIENCIES

At times, certain students exhibit difficulties with retaining information or making use of their memory. Teachers like Ms. Burrell can help students use study enhancements to improve their overall learning and success in the science classroom. Teachers should be more concerned with their students' knowledge of and ability to apply a process than simply achieving the end product. Study enhancement sheets or cards help remind students of basic facts so the process can be followed and completed in a meaningful way. Study enhancements can also address basic factual information.

Most students with special learning needs require a clear and organized delivery of content. An effective strategy for improving memory of content and processes is to group similar or connected information. With this, teachers organize science details in short lists, graphic organizers that show meaningful connections between items, and pictorial representations that serve as reminders of the concept. These memory supports help increase the recall of critical information for students who often have the ability to comprehend the material but do not possess strong memory systems. In Chapter 4, the Radioactive Dating and Half-Life activity has a brief, easy-to-read introduction designed to give the student the big picture using simple vocabulary.

Teachers can improve student learning outcomes by employing simple strategies to help improve memory. Mnemonics are a simple strategy that can be very helpful in improving students' recall of science content. Memory devices, such as a rhyme or acrostic sentence, have often been individually developed by more sophisticated learners to help them remember information. "My very educated

Figure 2.2 Spider Map Visual Organizer

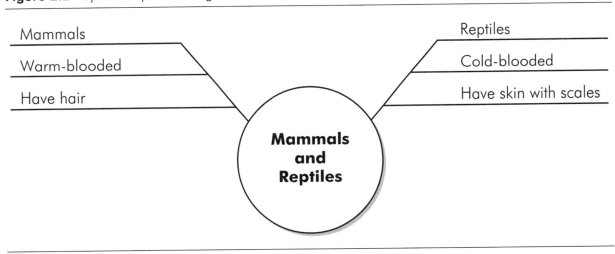

mother just served us nine pizzas" is an example of an acrostic for the planets: Mercury, Venus, Earth, Mars, Jupiter, Saturn, Uranus, Neptune, and Pluto. Teachers can design these and present them to the class or work with the students to develop these on their own so that they resonate more powerfully based on individual understandings and interests. Regardless of how they are created, many students can improve their recall of relevant science information using this strategy.

Another very effective strategy for supporting memory is the use of graphic aids. Graphic aids may be in various forms including pictures, bulleted lists, Venn diagrams, illustrations, or other visual representations. These visual models help organize information into pictorial representation that improve information retention. Figure 2.2 provides an example with a spider map comparing mammals and reptiles.

There are many examples of graphic organizers in teachers' materials and on the Internet. In addition, both teachers and students are quite good at developing their own pictorial representations. In all of the revised science activity samples found in Chapter 4, included for use are graphics, drawings, illustrations, and clip art to help describe the task or concept and support the student's memory.

In test situations, teachers may want to consider if the student can effectively and efficiently complete a paper-pencil test without output adaptations; this includes changing the overall look of the exam, the way it is completed, and the item format. When preparing an exam, as mentioned previously, teachers should be careful not to put too many items on one page, making the test harder to read and track. In addition, again, a simple, readable-sized font will improve comprehension. Clustering the same types of questions about similar concepts also helps improve a student's performance on a test. For instance, if the exam has multiple-choice items, the teacher can group items about cells together. This helps students who have less efficient memory processes by helping them focus their memories on similar concepts as they take the test rather than having to search for varied concepts with each succeeding item.

Moreover, limiting the types of items of the test will have an immediate positive impact on students with special learning needs who struggle with tests that contain multiple types of questions like true-false, matching, multiple choice, and essay. All of these formats place different cognitive demands on students and require them to recall information in different ways, and can result in overload for them. A test that has just one or two types of questions organized together makes the exam more accessible to students with special learning needs. Once the test format is determined, it will help for teachers to keep that format for each test scheduled thereafter. Chapter 5 provides examples of assessments using these same format suggestions. The Rubber Band Stretch assessment looks very much like a science activity with illustrations and clear directions designed to support the student's approach to completing it successfully.

MOTIVATIONAL STRATEGIES

Motivational strategies can be effective for all students. Specific teacher behaviors can help motivate students to achieve up to their highest potential. For students with special learning needs who have experienced more difficulties associated with school and learning than their peers, motivation can be an issue. Teachers may consider implementing a particular strategy to improve a student's approach to science learning. One approach found to be effective with children with special learning needs, but is also beneficial for all students, is the use of *antecedent strategies*. An antecedent strategy is one that a teacher would activate prior to beginning an assigned task. The purpose of the strategy is to provide motivation or an incentive for increased student achievement. Rhode, Jenson, and Reavis (1992) described four main antecedent strategies all teachers can use to benefit students in all grade levels. They are (1) encouragement, (2) structuring incentives, (3) hype, and (4) relating academic accomplishments to outcomes.

Encouragement

To use the antecedent strategy of encouragement, teachers make verbal statements designed to influence a student to achieve. In effect, they make statements that indicate faith in the student's ability to succeed at the task. For example, the teacher might say, "I know you will be able to do a really good job on your science today," or "You did such nice neat work on your science vocabulary; I'll bet you can do even better this week."

Structuring Incentives

Teachers use structuring incentives by first setting up reward situations related to behavior prior to the start of a specific task. The idea is to challenge students to demonstrate positive learning behaviors—such as arriving on time, being prepared, and showing continuous appropriate behavior—and then to reinforce the students for the positive behavior. Essentially, when planning and structuring incentives, teachers establish specific reinforcements to be given for specific behaviors or performances. A teacher might state, "Students who are in their seats when the bell rings will be allowed to choose a peer partner to work with during science class."

Some educators make use of *token reward systems* as structured incentives, meaning students receive tokens for completing identified tasks or exhibiting certain behaviors (Chapman, 2003; Cotton, n.d.). The tokens can be exchanged at a later time for a reward. For example, students who stay in their work areas throughout a science activity may be given a chip or marker that they can later trade with the teacher for a reward. Rewards can vary from tangible items like fancy pencils, small toys, trinkets, to extra time or activities such as a game at the reading center.

Hype

Teachers most effectively use hype if they develop and demonstrate something of a "game show host personality." They show enthusiasm and excitement about classroom events and daily lessons. Enthusiasm is contagious, so their students begin to mirror the same attitude. Teachers' hype may be exhibited when with statements such as, "Remember, the first cooperative learning group to complete their project with a minimum of 95 percent of the points on the rubric will earn time to go to the planetarium. It is the neatest place! All the kids like to spend time in there! I know you will really like it!" or "The big lottery drawing is in only two more days! Try to earn as many lottery tickets as you can by getting good grades and following the classroom rules. There are some really neat prizes up there that I know you would all love to win. And also remember, we have the mystery bonus prizes! Earn those lottery tickets!" Nonreward or nontoken hype might be exemplified by statements such as, "Tomorrow, Mr. Jones the chemist will be here to show us some demonstrations. This is so exciting to have him coming! I know you'll really like it, too!"

Relating Academic Accomplishments to Outcomes

With this antecedent strategy, teachers set up rewards for students who achieve at a certain level or higher on specified assignments. The rewards are set up prior to the task, with the students all knowing the incentive to be awarded. For example, "Everyone who passes the pretest today can skip the science lesson and go to Mrs. Johnson's first-grade room to be a tutor for 25 minutes," or "Today we are having a review lesson in science. Anyone who scores 95 percent or better on the comprehension exercises will be allowed to have a free homework pass for tomorrow night." This strategy highlights the importance of helping students with special learning needs connect their efforts and successes to positive outcomes.

PROBLEM WORDS

Watching Language

Students with special learning needs often experience tremendous difficulties with written and oral language. They lack adequate vocabulary, don't have effective self-monitoring skills to determine if they understand concepts, and fail to ask for assistance when needed. This becomes most problematic when dealing with directions to instructional tasks. Students may not understand the terms used in the directions and will not be able to complete the task without assistance.

To avoid this problem, teachers can use simple language, model all tasks for students, provide explanations to all directions, and if possible, provide a pictorial model to help students understand what they are to do. In the proceeding section, a compilation list of words that may cause problems for students with special learning needs is provided. The list also offers alternatives to those words. However, two points of caution are in order: (1) Every student is different, and it is incumbent upon teachers to learn the particular needs of their students. (2) Additionally, there are simply some science terms that students must learn, and for which clean alternatives are not readily available.

In the normal course of classroom discussion and on many papers handed out to students, teachers might use words that prove to be confusing to students with special learning needs. In general, many of these meanings can be clarified with brief phrases or definitions that relate them to other words better understood by the class. For other words, it is best to find different words to substitute for them. An example of the former is *measure*. If a teacher tells students to measure something, what is it that the teacher wants them to do? How much, how far, which dimension (l, w, h), and so on? Simply adding a few words clarifies the teacher's intent for this instruction. An example of the latter, substituting a new word or phrase, is *differentiate*; perhaps *explain the difference between* is a better choice. There are also words that have different meanings depending upon the context in which they are used. This occurs frequently in science instruction. For example, depending upon the context, *conductor* could mean material that allows electric charge to pass through it, material that allows heat energy to pass through it, a person who manages a train, or a person who directs an orchestra. Examples of problem words along with some alternatives teachers can use are provided in the next section.

Problem Word Alternatives

In this section, the problem word appears first, followed by the possible alternative. Of course, the suggested alternatives are not all inclusive, and teachers may know other alternatives that are more useful for their classroom situations. Further, the list is not a complete list of problem words. It is only a beginning; teachers should begin to develop their own lists of problem words based on their own experiences with their students. In general, directions should avoid using the word *not*, because many students with special education needs have difficulties processing reverse positives. Congruent terms may also be unfamiliar to students, even though the terms may mean the same thing. For example, if the term *characteristics* is used in instruction, *properties* or *attributes* should not be substituted for that term in activities or assessments. Overall, teachers should aim for more informal language whenever possible (while being sure students understand terms necessary for successful completion of state tests, etc.).

Problem Word	Example or Alternative
Benefit	Get some good from
Compare	Show similarities between things
Complete	Finish
Conclude	Decide or bring to an end
Consider	Think

Contrast	Show differences between things
Criticize	Give the positive and negative points of a subject
Define	Give the meaning of a term
Delineate	Give details
Describe	Tell in detail about something
Determine	Find out
Diagram	Make a drawing and label it
Differentiate	Tell the difference between
Discuss	Give details and the positive and negative points
Enumerate	List points and number them
Essay	Define what you want; "in three to five sentences . . ."
Evaluate	Give the positive and negative points of a subject as well as your opinion
Identify	Name
Illustrate	Explain by giving examples
Interpret	Explain the meaning of something
Justify	Give reasons for something
List	Give a series of points and number them
Outline	Give the main points and important supporting points
Prove	Show to be true by giving facts or reasons
Relate	Show connections among things
Select	Choose
Similar	Alike, almost the same
State	Give the main points
Study	Learn, look at closely, think about
Summarize	Give the big picture of the main ideas
Trace	Describe the order of events

CONCLUSION

While teachers probably adapt instruction both as planned and ad hoc decisions, it is important that high expectations for student performance drive those decisions. By using adaptations carefully, teachers ensure that students with special learning needs are engaged in high-quality learning tasks to increase the likelihood that they will meet age-appropriate learning outcomes necessary to make regular progress in their education. That is, teachers must remember that these students need to acquire the same skills as their nondisabled peers, so adaptations should not be used that impede the academic progress.

3

Suggestions for Revising Science Activities and Assessments

INTRODUCTION

The purpose for this chapter is to provide some specific suggestions teachers can apply when revising science activities and assessments. To put it in context, it begins with a brief examination of how differentiated science lessons allow students to practice inquiry-based science. It is important to keep this in mind to avoid science instruction that is too teacher centered or too "cookbookish." Next, ideas are presented regarding the lesson planning phase, followed by preactivity or preassessment considerations. Then, the chapter provides some suggestions for written and print materials, and concludes with suggestions for verbal directions. These suggestions are basically a starting point for teachers. Not all suggestions will work for everyone or in every context, and teachers may develop some of their own as they determine what works best with their particular students.

VIGNETTE WITH MR. JAMES

Francis threw down the activity book on the tabletop, shoved his chair away from the table, turned, and stomped away with his arms folded and a frown on his face. Obviously, Mr. James thought, Francis was angry. Knowing Francis, Mr. James could foresee a tantrum coming that would disrupt the entire class. And once third graders got stirred up, it would be a while until they could be settled down and refocused on their work. Mr. James walked over to Francis, who by now had taken a position at the back wall of the classroom with his back toward the other students. Mr. James began calmly, asking Francis if he needed help with something. Francis slightly turned his face, and Mr. James could see the tears running down his cheeks. The look in his eyes was not one of anger, but of something else. "I can't do it, Mr. James," Francis said. "I don't understand what it wants me to do!" The tears kept rolling. "You don't understand what?" Mr. James asked. "I can't tell what the sentences want me to do!" sobbed Francis. Mr. James realized Francis was really controlling himself very well considering the circumstances, but Francis was frustrated to the point of giving up. Mr. James calmed Francis as best he could, and at least got him to return to his worktable to sit quietly.

Later in the day, Mr. James was sharing this experience with a colleague, Mrs. Keller, who had Francis in class the year before. As it turned out, Francis had difficulty reading. In fact, Francis was dyslexic. He could look at a page of text, and half the letters seemed to him nothing more than a jumble of figures on the page. It would be quite a task for Francis to read a complete sentence, let alone really understand what it was saying. Mrs. Keller shared that she found providing Francis some pictures or diagrams really helped him understand what the reading material was about. Mr. James decided that he could try that, and began to determine what kinds of diagrams he could add to the worksheets, and where to place them, to help Francis with his class work. In the end, Mr. James retooled the first of many science activity handouts, resulting in activities with multiple diagrams and simplified sentence structure for his students, and also ensured that Francis could do the inquiry successfully.

When considering how to proceed in revising science activities and assessments, Mr. James will be most successful if he keeps in mind the various steps and guidelines to follow in creating something that will help students like Francis. Attention should be paid to preactivity preparation, to the written and printed materials that will be used, and to the verbal directions that will need to be given to students. The majority of suggestions in this chapter are not difficult to incorporate into handouts and worksheets for activities or for assessments, and should be useful to teachers.

HOW DIFFERENTIATED LESSONS ALLOW STUDENTS TO PRACTICE INQUIRY-BASED SCIENCE

If there is a single issue embedded throughout the *National Science Education Standards* (*NSES*) (National Research Council [NRC], 1996), the American Association for the Advancement of Science (AAAS, 1993) *Benchmarks,* and most state-level learning standards, it is that inquiry, investigations, and problem solving are critical elements of any science program. Another common theme among the various standards is they apply to all students, not just those regarded as "general" education students (i.e., students not receiving special education services). The *NSES* Standard A (see NRC, 1996, pp. 30–33, 121, 143, 173) is explicit that the ability to do inquiry and achieve understanding about scientific inquiry should be developed by students in each grade range (K–4, 5–8, and 9–12). Beginning in their early years, students should be engaged with investigating and actively constructing ideas and explanations. In the middle grades, students should begin to recognize relationships between explanations and evidence, and progress from partial inquiry toward more full inquiry. In the upper grades, students should develop sophistication in their inquiry abilities and understandings.

In a real sense, differentiated science lessons can be considered as guided inquiry. With such an approach, teachers use organizing questions and steps to guide students. Guided inquiry is not restricted to the student finding something entirely new to the world, but is a matter of the student internally rearranging data to form new concepts. Something a student discovers independently is remembered while concepts a student is only told about can be quickly forgotten. The student must be actively involved in the learning. By differentiating inquiry lessons, teachers can help students be more actively involved and successful in this endeavor. Further, teachers can use either inductive or deductive approaches with positive results.

Inductive inquiry is illustrated by an instructional strategy called the *learning cycle,* consisting of three phases: exploration, concept invention, and application. In the exploration phase, students are given some guidance (hints, questions, etc.), but are not given answers or labels. In the concept invention phase, teachers serve as guides to channel thinking, and encourage students to construct appropriate labels for the relationships they have just discovered. Students, then, are asked to explain concepts in their own terms. In the application phase, students apply their knowledge of a concept or skill to other situations, thus reinforcing the newly acquired knowledge. The role of differentiated science instruction would be most prevalent in the exploration and concept invention phases. In using the revising suggestions in this chapter, teachers carefully plan instruction so students can more easily recognize the relevant stimuli that constitute the concepts and principles being taught.

Another way differentiated science lessons can be inquiry oriented is through more deductive approaches. Teachers using this approach commonly provide certain rules or information first, and then expose students to some exploration. For example, in the expository phase, a teacher may provide definitions of acids and bases, and in the exploration phase students use that information to determine which solutions are acids and which are bases. The role of the differentiated lesson is to help students focus on a limited set of stimuli or phenomena rather than on the whole realm of stimuli or phenomena. This process of "focusing down" proceeds through several steps until the phenomena is of a size or scope that can be handled easily by students. For example, if the subject is the formation of rocks, rather than trying to focus on all types of rocks and how they are formed, the process first narrows down the scope to examine a single type of rock. Then, each of the various processes involved in the formation of that rock type might be examined. Finally, specific examples of rocks formed by each of the processes might be studied. Care needs to be taken to ensure that students are guided in this, but not provided with "cookbook" activities or activities that basically involve verification rather than inquiry about the topic.

From the viewpoint of the national and many state standards, there are seven readily identifiable advantages for using scientific inquiry in differentiated lessons in the classroom:

1. Scientific inquiry helps students develop the process skills of doing science. In the suggestions for revising science activities found later in this chapter, as well as in the sample revised activities in Chapter 4, the skills students are asked to perform and practice are more clearly identified and articulated, providing them more focus and less guessing about what skills they need to apply when doing an activity.

2. Inquiry helps children learn how to learn independently. As students learn how to identify or ask a question, investigate it, and then draw reasonable conclusions from it, they are prepared to learn more on their own. Using the revised procedures and steps in differentiated lessons can help clarify the questions students are being asked as well as help them learn to formulate their own questions to investigate.

3. Inquiry shifts the motivation of the student from that of seeking external rewards (extrinsic motivation) to internal satisfaction (intrinsic motivation). The inquiring student develops a desire to find out, to come to understand "why." Students will seek to inquire if the target they are to pursue is made clearer, and if the steps to follow are sequenced in a manner that makes the activity more accessible for them. Their frustration reduces, and their engagement increases.

4. Inquiry equips the learner with practical problem-solving procedures. Differentiated lessons make science more accessible to students, so they learn about science, and how to do science, through doing more science. As learning improves, students more adequately apply problem-solving and investigative procedures, whether it be for activities presented in science class or something encountered beyond the classroom.

5. Inquiry often results in fewer behavior problems in classroom settings, and, in fact, can at times prevent some. When students actively engage in learning, they are not engaged in problem behavior. Inquiry provides teachers with the opportunity to design relevant, interesting, hands-on, and student-controlled learning activities. Differentiated lessons help students better understand what they need to do, consequently increasing their engagement in the activities

6. Inquiry focuses on *how* students process data more so than *what* the process produces at the end. This is the old "process versus product" paradigm. As one moves through the inquiry process, learning occurs. At the end of the process, a product—sometimes several products—emerges. From an inquiry-practicing teacher's perspective, the learning derived from how to approach solving a problem or in investigating something may be more valuable and useful than the actual end product. Differentiated lessons help students approach problem solving and investigations in ways that make more sense to them.

7. Inquiry places emphasis on the student. Teacher-centered organization of classroom or field experiences subsides, while the learner is required to be an active participant in seeking knowledge. Not only does this help students develop the ability to learn how to learn, but it also contributes to building their self-confidence that they can learn on their own. With differentiated lessons, if designed properly, teachers reduce direct instruction and increase student engagement.

Applying the suggestions in this chapter will help teachers design and deliver inquiry instruction that is more appropriate for their students; teachers will also learn to better understand the inquiry skills and understandings emphasized in the standards. This chapter's suggestions are not a replacement for inquiry, but should help teachers facilitate it. It is beyond the scope of this book to discuss all the different types of inquiry and ways it can be done, so the purpose of this chapter is to help teachers find ways to make inquiry science more accessible to their students, regardless of the form the inquiry takes.

PLANNING BEFORE BEGINNING

As Mr. James prepares to teach his science class, and recognizes students who have special needs mainstreamed into it, he needs to consider some management and instructional issues. These include: (1) identifying the specific competencies targeted in the lesson, (2) identifying key concepts to emphasize, (3) identifying pertinent vocabulary for the lesson, (4) determining prerequisite skills needed for the lesson, (5) considering the most effective instructional approaches, and (6) determining the assessment procedures to determine mastery.

1. **Identifying the specific competencies targeted in the lesson.** Before teachers can plan effective lessons, they should delineate the intended academic and social outcomes that are desired targets of the instruction. When working with students who have special needs, it is even more important to identify the targeted behaviors and skills to ensure that instruction is specific and direct.

2. **Identifying key concepts to emphasize.** When preparing the instructional activities, teachers must first identify important concepts, and then be prepared to tell students what the themes or ideas are that require understanding and mastery. This specificity will help students who have special needs to focus on the critical ideas and not be distracted by supportive details.

3. **Identifying pertinent vocabulary for the lesson.** Most lessons have, as a major component, terminology that is specific to the subject; science is no exception. In order to increase students' comprehension of key ideas, teachers should identify five or six key terms necessary for their students, and teach these prior to the lesson or as part of the lesson. Students who have special needs may need access to the terminology at least a day before the lesson to master the terms and their meanings.

4. **Determining prerequisite skills for the lesson.** Every lesson or activity requires specific skills to complete. Before planning a lesson, teachers should first consider the skills that students need to master the new content. Not only should teachers identify the prerequisite skills, but they should also decide whether the students possess those skills. If they do, then the lesson likely will be successful in adding new skills to the students' repertoires. If the students do not have the prerequisite skills, teachers need to plan to teach those skills before implementing the lesson.

5. **Considering the most effective instructional approaches.** Teachers should always try to use the most effective instructional approach. A common misconception is that efficient teaching is also effective teaching. For example, lectures are quite efficient; a large amount of information can be covered in a short period of time. However, while lectures are efficient, they are not necessarily effective unless the students have strong listening and note-taking skills. In addition to finding the most effective approach, it is also important for teachers to vary instruction so students do not become bored with redundant teaching approaches.

6. **Determining the assessment procedures to measure mastery.** As teachers plan their instruction, they must consider how they will determine student achievement. Assessment activities can take many forms other than paper-pencil tests. Teachers can use observation, student work products, performance tasks, and so forth to accomplish this. Whatever form of assessment they choose, it is important to consider mainstreamed students who have special needs in terms of reading and communication skills and make sure that the particular assessment activities are not ones that only depend upon students performing academically well with writing, reading, and other specific subject areas.

PREACTIVITY AND PREASSESSMENT PREPARATIONS

As teachers move forward with their materials preparations for science instruction, they can also prepare their students for what is to come. The following steps will facilitate a smoother transition into the planned lesson or assessment.

1. Two to three days prior to a laboratory activity or assessment, announce to students that they will be doing a lab or assessment (whichever applies). Then, announce this again each day up to the day of the lab activity or assessment. If the activity or assessment is not to be conducted at the beginning of the day, it might be announced in the morning that it will be done later that day. For assessments, consider providing "mini-cues" such as, "Remember, you need to know the three steps A, B, and C for tomorrow." These procedures will help students with special education needs mentally prepare for the change in routine that will occur.

2. Be sure to connect activities and assessments with students' previous experiences. This is true for experiences in classroom instruction as well as couching activities and assessment items in terms of what students experience in their world beyond the classroom.

3. Begin instruction with things that are simple and familiar to students—a strategy that has been shown effective time and again—and as they progress, gradually introduce those things that are more complex and less familiar. As an example, if assessing the student's understanding of the life cycle of animals, begin first with that of a frog or mealworm, and later progress on to more complex, less familiar organisms.

4. Consider how students may benefit from learning mnemonic strategies for remembering. An example for remembering the order of planets in our solar system is "My very educated mother just served us nine pizzas." Perhaps provide and teach memory associations as well.

5. The day before an assessment, give students a "dry run" through some of the steps they will follow. For example, if the assessment will include items for which a balance is to be used, then students could work with a balance in a dry run. Students do not necessarily need to use the balance for exactly the same item as that which will be on the assessment.

6. Immediately prior to handing out an assessment, complete a quick review of key points students will need to remember.

7. To help actions in the classroom run more smoothly, first establish rules and relay these to students prior to starting a lab activity or assessment. Rules should be straightforward and uncomplicated. Here are four examples:
   a. Mark certain sized areas and tell students they must keep their materials within those marked spaces.
   b. Tell students that, except for the materials being tested, all other materials must stay in their containers. For example, if students are to test several balls for their bounciness, require that all balls stay in the container except for the one that is being tested at that moment.
   c. Emphasize that activity directions must be followed with no deviation. Referring back to the bouncing ball testing, allow students to only drop balls from the heights given in the activity.
   d. Remind students that during a performance-based assessment, there is to be only one student at any station at one time (unless the assessment is designed for partners working together on some or all of it).

8. Color-code, rather than label, items. For example, provide a blue ball rather than Ball A or Ball 1. If this is not feasible, then clearly label the items (e.g., place a label directly on the blue ball that identifies it as Ball A).

9. When possible, select equipment that is less potentially damaging than others, such as Nerf balls or ping-pong balls rather than hard rubber balls.

10. When planning to use devices such as meter sticks, consider placing colored marks at the decimeter marks (10 cm, 20 cm, 30 cm, etc.) to help students more easily locate the measures on the device. If possible, color-code entire sections of meter sticks so that one-decimeter section is red, another yellow, and so forth. This enables students to quickly "eyeball" measurements, especially if what they are measuring occurs relatively quickly, such as the height to which a rubber ball bounces. If a wall or floor target is used, color-code the different zones on the target.

11. Try to eliminate distractions in the classroom, such as flickering lights or buzzing fixtures. This is particularly important when students are doing assessments.

12. Review laboratory safety procedures and rules with students before each activity or performance assessment, and provide safety information both verbally and in writing. Be sure students clearly understand those procedures, and consider asking students to explain those procedures back in their own words to determine their comprehension.

13. Consider providing students with practice exercises that parallel those on an upcoming assessment. This does not mean the practice exercises should be identical to what will be on the assessment. As an example, if the assessment will require students to measure 45 milliliters of water using a graduated cylinder, then allow them advance practice filling a graduated cylinder to differing volumes.

14. When giving assessments, consider making provisions for students to continue their work on assessments beyond the time provided in the class period. Students may complete the remainder of the assessment in another room, at a later time, and so forth, with extended time limits established. Some teachers have found that giving students with learning disabilities (LD) or behavior disorders (BD) a placebo test to do while other students complete the real test is one solution. In such cases, students with LD or BD then complete the real test later with the resource teacher, for example. This helps avoid stigmatizing students during the regular class period when assessment is given.

15. Devise and implement some noise-control measures, especially during assessment. This helps keep noise levels from getting out of hand and provides "signals" for students to quiet in order to hear directions, announcements, and so on.

16. Consider using cooperative groups, when possible, during activities and performance-based assessments. Give each group member a specific job, allowing each student to be actively engaged in that job. For example, one student may be the manager, one the experimenter, one the recorder, and the fourth the observer. Allow for these roles to rotate among the group members over time. The student with special learning needs may not be first assigned a leadership role (experimenter), but ensure that student has the opportunity to serve in that role later. To further facilitate group work, the teacher might consider the following:

   a. Provide role modeling. Have the group's best reader do the reading, and have the student with special learning needs do much of the action (e.g., dropping balls, measuring bounce heights, etc.). Similarly, avoid assigning the student with special learning needs to first record data and answers to questions. As skill development occurs over time, gradually allow students with special learning needs to fulfill these roles. This should prove helpful in the long term as attempts are made to shift students from group to individual work (e.g., homework or individual performance-based assessments).
   b. Try to place high-ability students in cooperative groups with low-ability students.
   c. Change lab partners occasionally, if possible, to provide students experiences working with different people.

17. For activities and performance assessments, if the activity or assessment activity is novel to the student, consider modeling the procedures for students before they begin. Show students how to do the steps of the procedures. This may include setting up a laboratory apparatus correctly as a model for students to follow. In this case, the apparatus would be set up so the students can see it constructed, piece by piece. Consider, also, having students sketch or draw the apparatus before starting the assessment activity.

18. Try to use equipment that is as simple as possible. For example, rather than using a bottle and an eyedropper for dispensing a solution, use a dropper bottle that has the dropper built in.

19. If possible, reduce the number of trials students must make during a set of procedures. Try, for example, to reduce the trials to two or three rather than five or six. In some instances, reduce the number of trials to one or two. While some science educators will debate this point, a key, regardless, is to have students conduct as many trials as necessary to derive a set of usable data that conveys the basic concept or idea to them. It may be unnecessary to have students repeat ten or twelve trials of an event when three to five would suffice.

20. Give partial credit whenever possible, and consider modifying grading requirements, according to the abilities of individual students and according to their IEPs or 504 plans.

REVISING WRITTEN AND PRINTED MATERIALS

Selecting and Changing Written Materials

When science teachers attempt to accommodate students with LD, their first concern should be the types of instructional materials they use. In particular, determining a good fit of textbooks and other materials requires teachers to analyze instructional materials for (1) the reading level, (2) the visual accessibility, (3) the use of visual cues, (4) the organization of materials, and (5) the substitution of more appropriate items. Suggestions follow for determining the use and effectiveness of science materials for students with special needs.

Selecting and Adapting Textbooks

Since many science activities are located in textbooks, or student manuals that accompany textbooks, teachers may find it necessary to consider criteria for selecting and adapting such materials. As a beginning point, teachers should determine the readability level of the textbook. They might use a readability formula to determine the reading level and difficulty of any textbooks or materials they are using. Two examples are the cloze procedure and the Fry Test for Reading Levels. However, depending upon the science terms present in the passages analyzed, a teacher may find a variation of one grade level up or down in the results obtained—so some caution is warranted.

Once teachers have established the readability level of the text or other written material they plan to use, they next need to determine the degree of *considerateness* of the textbook. Text considerateness is the accessibility and usability of a book. Teachers should evaluate the text by reviewing all of the features of the book. For example, looking at text features, does the book pose prereading questions to help the student prepare to read the content? Are headings and subheadings used to organize the chapters? Does the author use bolded vocabulary, pictures, and diagrams to help the student identify key ideas? Finally, is the textbook written in a way that is motivational for students?

Finally, teachers should prepare students to use the textbook. At the beginning of the school term, they should review the textbook with students to teach them how to use the text. This may mean spending several days acquainting students with the text through activities such as a scavenger hunt that requires students to find information using all of the features of the book.

Substituting the Text

Sometimes, the text (textbook, handout, etc.) is far too difficult for students with special needs. In fact, many students with special needs have reading levels up to three years below their grade placement. In these cases, it is difficult, if not impossible, for those students to acquire information effectively from the textbook. When this occurs, science teachers may need to consider substitutions for the class science text. How much teachers can do in these instances may be limited by an individual student's IEP or 504 plan, so teachers should be sure to check that document before proceeding. Provided teachers can substitute the text, they can consider the following suggestions for providing information in science books or other text material:

1. Audio-record the science text. A fairly simple answer for students experiencing difficulty with a textbook is for teachers to provide a recorded version. If the student has an identified learning disability, recorded books can be requested through Readings for the Blind. If the student is not in special education

or is not registered with Readings for the Blind, then teachers can arrange for the text to be recorded at the school by a teacher's aide, a student, or a volunteer. Some publishers may also provide their books in audio formats. In either case, it is prudent to check with the publisher to avoid infringing on copyrights.

2. Read the text aloud to students. One way to address the reading difficulties of all students is to provide time for the textbook to be read during instruction—in large groups, small groups, or pairs. By having students read the text aloud, teachers can ensure that all students are reading the assigned material and even conduct follow-up comprehension activities. While this takes a great deal of time, the benefits to students who have difficulty reading assigned materials are potentially large.

3. Pair students to master text content. Teachers might assign students to work in pairs to complete activities that demonstrate comprehension of the text materials. Students with special needs tend to work well in small groups or pairings. One hint when pairing students is that partnerships will be more successful when the students are more alike in their academic skills (i.e., pair a student with a low reading ability with one who is slightly higher, but not dramatically superior in academics). This reduces the dissonance in skills and eliminates the potential for one partner relying too much on another. However, when assigning small groups, make sure the groups are heterogeneous in skills, gender, and culture. Avoid having high, medium, and low groups.

4. Construct abridged versions of text content. Teachers may wish to rewrite the text and eliminate difficult terminology, reduce sentence length, and remove extraneous material. When rewriting a text, the focus should be on presenting the key ideas in a clear manner and providing very specific examples for each concept.

5. Provide an overview of an assignment before reading. An excellent teaching technique for improving comprehension is to provide an overview of the concepts that will be encountered in the assigned reading. A prereading activity can be used to present vocabulary, connect previously learned information to new material, present prediction questions, and organize the students' approach to the reading.

6. Structure opportunities for students to activate prior knowledge before they start reading the assignment. Student comprehension increases when the information encountered is familiar and relates to previous experiences. Thus, teachers can increase comprehension by helping their students make important connections between new and old concepts. This can be done quite easily by taking a few minutes to preview the reading assignment and review pertinent information that was previously taught.

7. If the text does not have one, teachers can develop a reading guide to direct learning from it. (Some textbooks include such guides, alleviating the need for teachers to do this.) This makes content reading more structured for students. A reading guide may be a list of questions students are to answer as they are reading, or may be a set of competencies the student should be able to meet after reading the assigned material. The guide should be set up sequentially so students can use it as a road map through the materials. If the reading guide consists of questions, those may need to be reworded. Some students have difficulty understanding the vocabulary used in review questions found at the end of chapters. Teachers can increase student responses by rewriting the questions using more understandable or less complex vocabulary. The idea is not to reduce the number of questions that the student is to answer, but rather, to use vocabulary that the student understands. Additionally, teachers may find it helpful to students if they provide them clues for finding answers to text questions. For students who have difficulty manipulating texts, a simple way to help them find answers to text questions is to give them the page number where the answer can be found. This gives students a running start, but still requires them to read and find the appropriate answer.

8. Highlight key ideas in texts. For students who have difficulty distinguishing important concepts in reading materials, teachers can help by highlighting those terms or language that represent pertinent information. Teachers may select two or three texts for each class, highlight those texts, and use them each semester or year with those students who need the extra guidance. If teachers plan to highlight textbooks, they may need to first obtain approval from their administration before marking in any books purchased by their school or district.

9. Divide reading into smaller portions and distribute them over time. Many students with special needs have reading fluency and rate problems that cause them difficulty in completing reading assignments in limited time frames. Therefore, teachers might consider distributing a reading assignment over

a week's time rather than assigning a lengthy chapter to be read in one night. This will help the student in terms of the volume that must be read, as well as increase understanding because the student will encounter fewer ideas to absorb.

10.   Use direct experiences, videos, and computer programs. The more active science instruction is, the more students with special needs are able to relate the content to their own experiences and, thereby, increase their acquisition of information. Videos, experiments, and simulations, all of which are relatively active tasks, engage students in learning far more than does a lecture.

Guidelines for Revising Written Materials

Once teachers have addressed matters concerning reading text, they should turn attention to the handouts, tests, and other self-made materials they (or colleagues) have written for use with students. When undertaking this task, teachers need to be mindful that the purpose is to make the written materials more accessible to students through their learning modalities rather than "watering it down" to a lower grade-level status. Further, teachers should know that revising written materials using the guidelines provided here takes some time. Teachers may judiciously select a few key materials for starters, and then continue with other materials as time allows. Eventually, they may revise all of the written materials, but it likely won't occur in a single year. Finally, teachers should note that not all the suggestions will necessarily work in their situation—and they may need to devise others that are not included in this compendium. (Some of the guidelines teachers may need to follow have already been shared in previous parts of this chapter or book, so not all will be repeated here.) Some concrete examples of the application of the guidelines are shown in Chapter 4 (revising activities) and Chapter 5 (revising assessments).

1.   Avoid using hyphenated words, particularly when they appear at the right margin of the page. Words that begin at the right end of one line and continue at the left margin of the next line down sometimes prove difficult for students to follow.

2.   Provide a box or line to the left of each direction or step so students can check them off as they complete one.

3.   Use photocopies that are clean and not grainy or grayed.

4.   If budgets are problematic, consider making class sets of directions, such as one per group, rather than giving each individual student a set. Some teachers may wish to laminate the directions and keep them for reuse as permanent copies. Even so, they may find it necessary to provide students having LD or BD their own sheets on which they can write.

5.   Substitute graph papers as necessary and appropriate, and use graph papers with large grid spaces, if possible. Teachers may find it useful to use graph grids larger than what fits on a normal size sheet of paper. For example, large bulletin board–size grids or grids marked out on the floor may be useful for some activities. In addition, teachers may find it helpful to students if they prepare graph grids ahead of time with their axes prelabeled and marked. (This, of course, may not apply if one of the objectives is for students to learn how to do this themselves as part of data representation.) Also, use colors on graphs when possible, and along with having students use different colors for graphed data, have them use different colors for different lines of the grid itself. The zero line might be black, the next line might be green, the next red, and so forth. If teachers want to use colored graph paper, they can make it by photocopying a dark grid master onto colored sheets of paper, purchase it at office supply stores, or even get it through free online sources that allow them to select color, grid sizes, and other specifications. (Two such online sources are http://incompetech.com/graphpaper/lite/ and http://freebies.about .com/od/freeprintables/p/graphpaper.htm.)

6.   Consider using different colored papers for different worksheets or handouts. For example, use yellow for one worksheet, light blue for another, light green for yet another, and so on. In any case, avoid using fluorescent paper for printed materials.

7.   Include rationales at the front end for doing the activities that explain to students why they are doing the activity. This may relate the activity to things that are done in the world outside the classroom, regardless of whether or not the student personally is likely to do them. This tells the student that there is value in the activity's learning and it is not simply busywork.

8.   At the beginning of the activity, include vocabulary words that may be new to students. Students can work on these as a warm-up activity either individually or in their work groups, or the teacher may

go over them in class prior to the activity. Put these words on the handouts so students see them as well as hear them.

9. Highlight verbs in directions given to students. This can be done by putting the word in boldface, underlining it, italicizing it, making its font different colors, changing its font size, and so forth.

10. If a procedure contains more than one step, use space to separate each step and number each one. Keep steps that apply to a single task together, and consider outlining the group using a box, graphic, or AutoShape figure.

11. Illustrate steps in the activity with pictures or diagrams. Either include these pictures or diagrams in the text of the activity or provide them on large posters or overhead screens for students to see. Many students with LD and BD are visual learners. Visual cues (illustrations, drawings, demonstrations, etc.) are likely beneficial for them (as well as for other students). Also, don't undersize the illustrations, and try to make and provide pictures or illustrations of actual individual steps in the activity unless one can serve for a cluster of steps. Make these large enough to show critical details students need to comprehend the task and procedures better. It may be desirable to have students make their own drawings of things, such as laboratory apparatus.

12. Use clip art or digitally copied illustrations of equipment and materials when needed. Teachers may find such an illustration of a graduated cylinder is better than a stylized one they could draw. If the clip art or copied illustration is not public domain, be sure to follow copyright provisions.

13. Simplify directions, adjusting to a more step-by-step format. Simplification can include reducing the complexity of sentence syntax, length of sentences, and so forth. Longer sentence directions can be broken into two or more shorter sentences that, together, convey the same information.

14. Simplify or reduce the number of questions. For simplifying directions, consider the length of sentences used in questions, the syntax, and other features that can affect comprehension.

15. When students are asked to write down information, data, answers to questions, and other responses, provide about twice the writing space on the page than normally given.

16. If the activity includes paper patterns that must be both cut and folded, highlight the lines along which to cut in order to distinguish them from the "fold" lines. Conventionally, solid lines represent cut lines and dashed lines represent fold lines.

17. Provide students a behavior sheet that goes along with the activity. The behavior sheet should list and describe expected behavior while doing the activity.

18. If students are to do numeric operations, prepare and provide worksheets or flowcharts on which they can enter the numbers and then do the necessary operations. For example, if two numbers are to be added and then multiplied by a third, and later divided by a given value, the worksheet may look like Figure 3.1.

Figure 3.1 Formula Flowchart

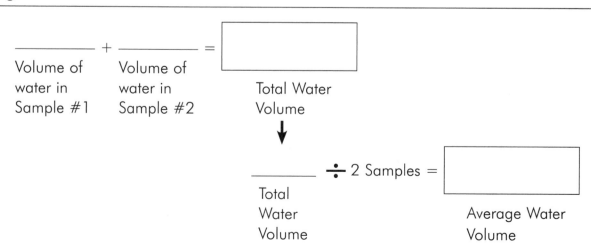

19.   When formulae are to be used, do not rely only on symbols and letters. Provide versions that are word formulae using terms with first letters that correlate with the variables' symbols, such as

$$d = distance, h = height$$

Also, sequence the example so it progresses from the word formula to the symbol formula as shown in the Figure 3.2.

Figure 3.2   Illustration of a Formula

$$speed = distance\ divided\ by\ time$$

$$speed = \frac{distance}{time}$$

$$s = \frac{d}{t}$$

The remainder of the guidelines for revising written materials primarily deals with assessments—both performance-based and more traditional, objective types. Teachers should keep in mind that most of the guidelines already shared are also applicable to assessments.

20.   Prepare students to give responses in the desired format. If responses are to be in complete sentences, prepare students accordingly. This helps obtain student responses that more closely meet teacher expectations.

  a.   When designing the assessment, consider including on it models of expectations or what is meant by a "complete" response. Provide a language model (have a complete sentence as an example) if that is important. In another example, if using a mark-in "bubble" sheet for student answers and desiring students to darken bubbles in a certain way, provide a model to guide the students, as shown in Figure 3.3.

Figure 3.3   Sample Response Guide

Be sure to completely darken the circle for your answer. If your answer is C, then be sure to darken in the circle marked C. Darken it completely, and stay inside the lines.

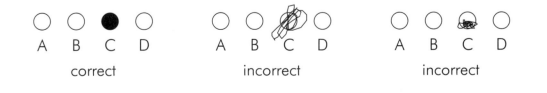

21. When having students identify parts of a diagram, such as one showing the parts of a flower, try to have the parts labeled A, B, C, and so on, and have foil A be for label A, foil B be for label B, and so forth. Format the foils as follows:

A) A   B) B   C) C   D) D

Avoid designating foils with letters that do not match the labels. For example, avoid the following format:

A) D   B) C   C) A   D) B

Finally, for tests, rather than arranging the foils horizontally, stack them vertically.

22. Whenever possible, photocopy the actual item for use on assessments. For example, if the desire is to show a thermometer, try to use a photocopy rather than a stylized drawing of one. However, if a photocopy is used, be sure it is very clear and crisp. Otherwise, a clear line drawing is better.

23. When vocabulary words are included as part of the assessment, try to identify vocabulary words that are similar and separate them into different groupings of the vocabulary words. If the word list is lengthy, consider breaking it down into a series of smaller word groups. For example, if there are fifteen vocabulary words, try breaking the list down and provide students with three lists of five words each. Further, consider placing similar words in different groups. If, for example, words are *balance* and *scale*, place *balance* in one word grouping and *scale* in another.

24. Include rationales for doing the various sections of the assessment. Explain to students what they are expected to do in each section. For example, "This section will measure your understanding of the water cycle." Add section headings throughout the assessment so students can readily and easily identify what the test sections are.

25. If using performance stations located around the room, consider providing identifying signs that are colored (yellow for one, blue for a different one, etc.). To augment this color-coding, consider using place mats at each station with the same colors as the station-identification labels (yellow place mats for the station with the yellow identification label, etc.).

26. For each object shown on the assessment, provide a sample of the actual object for students to see if needed.

27. When using multiple pieces of equipment that are similar, try to use identical items. For example, if the assessment item involves the use of three 100 milliliter graduated cylinders, try to have all three cylinders exactly the same (100 mL graduated cylinders come in different diameters, etc., and using nonmatching cylinders together may confound some students).

28. Provide student-response sheets or worksheets with templates onto which students can find spaces for taping test materials such as pH papers when doing pH testing or for placing picture cards in a life cycle assessment, or other activities where templates can assist (see Figure 3.4).
   a. Consider posting a large model of what to do to remind students of procedures.
   b. Do not overload the example. In other words, avoid providing drawings with arrows attempting to show how to move or place the cards onto the template. Students should have used these activities prior to assessment, making this unnecessary.
   c. Avoid transferring numbers or letters if possible. For example, in the life cycle template shown in Figure 3.5, avoid asking students to write in the card numbers on the circular template sections labeled A, B, C, and D (and vice versa).

29. Remove unnecessary steps from procedures in a performance-based assessment item. For example, if students are working with batteries, bulbs, wires, or other similar materials, strip the ends of the wires ahead of time so students do not have to do it during the assessment. Unless a specific item is to be assessed, such steps have little to do with assessing what the student has learned and are extraneous and time-consuming.

Figure 3.4 Template for Taping pH Papers to Paper

Testing the pH of Solution X

Procedure 1
Add a drop of distilled water to the red litmus paper. Then tape the red litmus paper to the proper place on the chart.

Procedure 2
Next, add a drop of distilled water to the blue litmus paper. Then tape the blue litmus paper to the proper place on the chart.

Procedure 3
Next, add a drop of distilled water to the pH range paper. Then tape the pH range paper to the proper place on the chart.

Procedure 4
Repeat Procedures 1, 2, and 3, except this time use drops of Solution X rather than distilled water.

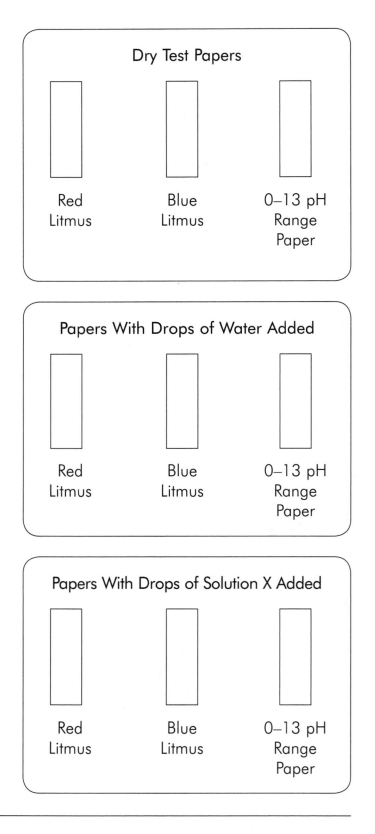

Figure 3.5 Life Cycles Numbering Template

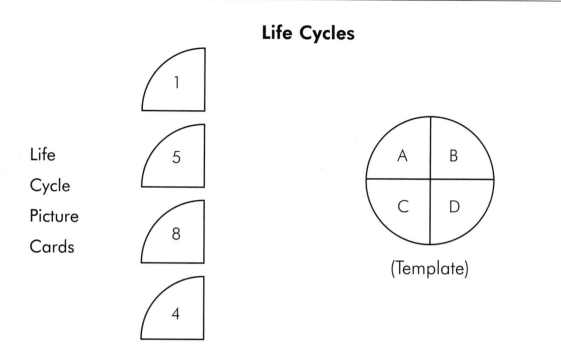

Life Cycles

(Template)

Question 4.

Place the life cycle picture cards on the circle diagram to the right. Place the first stage of the life cycle in the pie-shaped area marked A. Then place the next stage of the life cycle in the area marked B. Then go to C, and finish with D.

---

30. Consider breaking larger assessments into two or more smaller assessments, or at least into smaller sections less overwhelming to students. Students should complete one section (or smaller assessment) prior to going on to the next one. Teachers may even consider providing students with a brief review of the information to be assessed in upcoming, smaller assessments or assessment sections.

31. For objective-type assessments, remember that fill-in-the-blank and true-false questions are particularly difficult for students with LD or BD. Objective-type assessments best suited for students having LD or BD are those comprised of multiple-choice and matching items.

    a. Consider the following precautions with multiple-choice items:

- Limit the possible number of responses to four.
- Have students circle a correct answer rather than transcribe the answer's letter/or number to a blank next to the question. This helps students with LD or BD reduce transcription errors.
- Avoid question stems containing "not" formats. For example, "Which of the following is not a part of the digestive system?" Special education students often have difficulty distinguishing double negatives or in processing inverse statements.
- Avoid including in the possible answer (foils) responses such as "all of the above," "none of the above," and so on.

    b. Consider the following with respect to matching items:

- Group matching items by topic, so that all things in a single matching item relate to the same topic.
- Limit the possible number of items to be matched to five for any single question or series.
- Keep the number of items to be matched equal to the number of items that can be matched. For example, if students are to match items in Column A with those in Column B, be sure there is the same number of items in each column. Avoid having one or more additional items in Column B.
- Consider using pictures in lieu of words in matching items.

c. Try to separate multiple choice and matching items so the same kind of items are not clustered one after another. For example, provide some multiple choice items, then have a matching item, then include some more multiple choice items. Avoid grouping all items of one type together without a break in question type.

32. For essay questions, consider providing students a short outline at the top of the answer space for them to follow (see Figure 3.6). This may simply be the format to follow, with students providing the information for the blanks. Consider limiting students to answers of a certain length (e.g., one paragraph). Students with LD or BD characteristics often have difficulty deciding just how much (or how little) is necessary to write.

Figure 3.6 Outline Guide

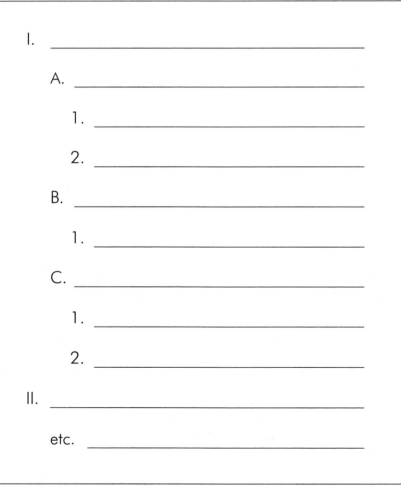

Guidelines for Verbal Directions

When giving verbal directions—whether in a regular classroom, a special education classroom or a classroom containing both types of students—many of the same considerations apply. First, make sure the students are paying attention. To ensure their attention, remove as many distractions as possible. Unless absolutely necessary, do not have materials that students will use located where they can manipulate them while directions are being given. Second, give as specific verbal directions as possible. If there are new vocabulary words used in the directions, review those words with the students before starting the directions, being sure students understand the words correctly.

As directions are being given, also be sure to review with students any laboratory safety procedures that might apply. Remind students they are to do only what they are told, and not to try new configurations of the equipment or mixtures of chemicals other than what is given in written or verbal directions. Also explain the rationale of the activity to the students. This will assist the students in relating the present activity to their previous work.

As the directions are being given, it is helpful for students to have a visual set of directions to which they can refer as verbal directions are given. Visual directions may be in the form of an overhead transparency, a poster, or a printed desk copy of the directions. Pairing written directions with verbal directions allows students to focus on the words as well as the sounds of the directions. Using illustrations while delivering the directions verbally is as much of a key consideration as it is when preparing written directions. As with written directions, verbal directions should be grouped with their respective tasks as closely as possible. If the activity consists of many separate tasks requiring different directions for each, give the directions for the first task and have the students complete the task before giving directions to subsequent tasks. This grouping of directions will hopefully avoid page turning, and other distracting movements of the handouts as verbal directions are given.

In some situations, it is advisable to audio-record directions. By having the directions on a recording, the students can replay the verbal directions, focusing on each part of the directions. If the technology exists, video recording of the teacher giving the directions might be appropriate. This then allows the student to not just listen to the directions again, as a recording allows, but to actually see the delivery of the instructions.

Understanding verbal directions requires students to employ their audio mental capabilities. With many students, this can be difficult because of the many audio distractions present inside and outside of the classroom that are within their hearing range. Therefore, forms of visual directions should support verbal directions as often as possible. Verbal directions need to be stated clearly and simply, but as specifically as possible for students—both those with special needs and those without special needs—if the students are to understand the directions.

Application Exercise

After reading through these suggestions and guidelines for revising science activities and assessments, try to apply them. Select a laboratory-type activity or a test (perhaps a short one would be best to start with), and make some revisions based on the suggestions in this chapter; then, as you continue with the book, compare the product with the revised activities or assessments provided in the proceeding chapters.

CONCLUSION

The science education standards at both the national and most state levels emphasize that science is something all students should do. This includes students with special learning needs. The standards also stress that effective science is inquiry based. Hence, the teacher is called upon to provide quality inquiry-based science instruction to all students. Aside from IEPs and 504 plans, many teachers find the need for some guidelines that will help them in accomplishing this task. In this chapter, a number of those guidelines were provided with respect to preparation and planning, prelesson activity, during-lesson activity, and assessment. Teachers should be mindful that not all the suggestions provided in this chapter will necessarily work for them, nor that this compilation of suggestions is all-inclusive. Indeed, teachers may find their own guidelines to help them reach the end goal: making science accessible to all students.

4

Revising Science Activities

The purpose of this chapter is to illustrate how the revision suggestions in Chapter 3 can actually be applied to science activities. This chapter includes activities spanning the lower-elementary grades through upper-elementary/middle-school grades, and also representing each major science subdiscipline: biological, earth, and physical science. For each one, the original activity is provided to help contextualize a beginning point. While some of the activities are older classic ones, and others are newer, both types are prevalent in some form in many classrooms today. Following each original activity is a revised version that uses the suggestions from Chapter 3. To provide some rationale for the revisions, an annotated copy is then shown that highlights significant aspects of the changes made.

Previous chapters started with a vignette of a situation a teacher faced with his or her students and the science instruction at hand. Since a single vignette does not suffice for this chapter, three are shared. The solutions to each of these teachers' problems can be found in the revised science activities (following later in the chapter), again based on the revision suggestions from Chapter 3.

VIGNETTE WITH MRS. STROTHERS

Mrs. Strothers teaches a sixth-grade class departmentalized for mathematics and science. Several years ago, the school district adopted a science textbook series that covers life, earth, and physical sciences. For each of these content areas, the curriculum includes a set of kits that are designed for use in a hands-on approach. For sixth grade, the kits focus on physical science.

Each year Mrs. Strothers has used the textbook and kits, she has found that some of her students struggle with understanding what it is they are supposed to do with the materials. This year, she has one particular student, Sarah, who is very bright and pleasant, but has difficulty staying focused on her work. Earlier that year, Sarah was diagnosed with attention deficit hyperactivity disorder (ADHD), and Mrs. Strothers has noted that Sarah begins her work eagerly enough, but soon is inattentive to the science activity and uses her science time to mess with other things, such as art materials. In her conversations with Sarah, Mrs. Strothers has found that Sarah likes science, but has trouble staying with it and completing the activities. Mrs. Strothers thus decided that Sarah needed something to help her stay on track, and thought a simple way to begin would be for Sarah to check things off on a list (or steps in an activity) as she completed them. This would provide a guide for Sarah so she could clearly see what she had completed and what she still had left to do. To augment this, Mrs. Strothers decided she would also make more of an effort to give verbal time cues to the class as they worked through their materials.

VIGNETTE WITH MRS. LOWELL

Walking by the teacher's workroom, Mrs. Lowell caught a whiff of cinnamon rolls. Mmm! Fond memories came to mind about when she was a child at home and her mother would make cinnamon rolls. She could remember the smell of the rising dough, remember the feel of the dough as she kneaded it with her mom, and reveled in the sumptuous depths of the warm sweetness when the rolls came fresh out of the oven.

Mrs. Lowell then returned to the present, aware that she was going to have a room full of precocious second graders anxious for a day of learning. In the back of her mind, she also thought of a recent in-service program she had attended about how students with special needs often learned better when multisensory experiences were available to them. She was just beginning a unit on wildlife, and realized most of the material was textbook reading or videotapes. What could she do, she thought, to engage more of the students' senses with respect to learning about wildlife? She knew she had some poor readers in class, and she also knew some students had short attention spans. An activity would be useful, but it would need to be one about wildlife, and hopefully more than a cut-and-paste activity. Since the wildlife unit began with a story about wolves and how they lived, and many of the children had dogs, this would be a good way to make connections with wolves. Like dogs, wolves would need a good sense of smell to survive in the wild. Could she find an activity that involved smell? She had a number of activities that could employ tactile senses, but not much with smell. Later that day, she stumbled across a *Ranger Rick* magazine that focused on wolves, and it contained an activity illustrating how mother wolves could tell which pups were theirs—and it involved smell. With a little effort, Mrs. Lowell could make this activity work for her students, regardless of their reading ability, and it should keep all of them attentive.

VIGNETTE WITH MR. WAXELL

Mr. Waxell decided it was time for his fourth-grade class to do some investigation about "mystery powders." As part of his teaching leading up to this point, Mr. Waxell had taught students how to perform certain tests, such as using iodine to test for the presence of starch, or using Benedict's solution to test for sugars. For the mystery powders investigation, Mr. Waxell wants to give five white powders to his students and have them not only make observations about the powders, but to also do some tests with the powders to try and determine what they were.

In his class, Mr. Waxell has a student named Azjen, who would probably have difficulty with the mystery powders investigation. Azjen's broad reading score placed him in the 25th percentile and his written language was at the 20th percentile. Azjen's overall achievement showed him functioning at the 53rd percentile, and his language abilities were in the average range. However, Azjen has difficulty with complex sentence structure. He is able to repeat sentences up to eleven words in length, but is frustrated with longer sentences or with sentences having complex structure. He struggles with reading comprehension after silent reading. Oral vocabulary is one of his strengths, but his clerical speed and accuracy are weaknesses.

For students like Azjen, the mystery powders investigation handout can be lengthy. Consequently, Mr. Waxell found the need to revise the handout. In his revision, the sentence structure was simplified and sentences were shortened. A few diagrams were added to help illustrate what the text of the handout was saying. In addition, Mr. Waxell designed the handout so it could be broken down into different sections, making it possible to have students do one section per class period. His plan was to have students work in groups on their investigation.

INTRODUCTION

To illustrate how science activities can be revised, this section of the book includes three versions of six science activities. In most cases, the original activities came from sources that have undergone several revisions or iterations, and what are presented as "original" may not be identical to that found in the very first source. For example, the Bouncing Ball activity, which originated with *Science: A Process Approach* (American Association for the Advancement of Science, 1961), or *SAPA*, has undergone a number of teacher revisions since its original publication. Hence, the "original" example provided here may not be identical to that found in the *SAPA* materials. However, the example given is one that has been used with students.

For each of the science activities, each is presented first in this aforementioned original form, followed by its retooled version, and that is followed by its retooled version with annotations. In these third versions, the retooled version has been reduced in size so that comments or annotations concerning specifics of the revising could be added around the margins. A comparison of the revised versions with the suggested guidelines from Chapter 3 helps illustrate how those guidelines are directly applied to improving each of the activities.

Science activities selected for inclusion in this chapter are at both the upper- and lower-elementary levels, and in each of the three major science subdisciplines (biological, earth, and physical science), as detailed in Table 4.1, in which the names of the activities are provided. The activities are presented in the following sequence: lower-elementary biology, lower-elementary earth science, lower-elementary physical science, upper-elementary biology, upper-elementary earth science, and upper-elementary physical science (note that upper elementary includes middle-school grades, up to and including Grade 9). The one exception is the Mystery Powders activity, which has been placed in the upper-elementary section to avoid repeating it in both places.

Table 4.1 Selected Activities for Revision

	Biological Science	**Earth Science**	**Physical Science**
Lower-Elementary Level	Silent Smell Tracking	Granite Mosaic	Mystery Powders* and the Bouncing Ball
Upper-Elementary Level and Middle School	Testing for Sugars	Radioactive Dating and Half-Life	Mystery Powders*

* Mystery Powders can be used at either level, depending upon the amount of work the teacher desires for students to engage. For example, if the teacher simply expects students to do some basic observations of the powders, then the activity lends itself to the lower-elementary levels. If the teacher wishes students to make use of diagnostic tests (e.g., iodine testing, heating, etc.), then the activity is more suitable for upper-elementary students.

STANDARDS ADDRESSED IN THESE ACTIVITIES

Alongside the modified activities, the appropriate *National Science Education Standards* (*NSES*) are added as a guide. Initiated by the National Research Council (NRC, 1996) and published by the National Academies Press, they are a central component guiding high-quality science instruction. Tables 4.2 and 4.3 summarize the standards addressed in the activities. (The page numbers noted are the pages in the *NSES* rather than pages in this book.) Since teachers can engage their students in differing levels of inquiry with any of these activities, only the main inquiry standards are noted rather than the specific "abilities to do" or "understandings about" scientific inquiry.

The *NSES* Unifying Concepts and Process Standards applicable to these activities include:

Grades K–4: Systems, Order, and Organization (p. 116) and Form and Function (p. 119)

Grades 5–8: Changes, Constancy, and Measurement (p. 117)

Grades 9–12: Systems, Order, and Organization (p. 116); Change, Constancy, and Measurement (p. 117); and Evolution and Equilibrium (p. 119)

Table 4.2 Lower-Elementary Level (Grades K–4)

Activity Title	NSES **Content Standards** (NRC, 1996)	NSES **Inquiry Standards**
Silent Smell Tracking	Standard C (p. 129): Characteristics of Organisms; Organisms and Environments	Standard A (p. 122)
Granite Mosaic	Standard D (p. 134): Properties of Earth Materials	Standard A (p. 122)
The Bouncing Ball	Standard B (p. 127): Position and Motion of Objects	Standard A (p. 123)
Mystery Powders	Standard B (p. 127): Properties of Objects and Materials	Standard A (p. 123)

Table 4.3 Upper-Elementary Level and Middle School (Grades 5–8 and Grade 9)

Activity Title	NSES **Content Standards** (NRC, 1996)	NSES **Inquiry Standards**
Testing for Sugars	Standard C (p. 156): Structure and Function in Living Systems	Standard A (p. 145)
Radioactive Dating and Half-Life	Grades 5–8 Standard D (p. 160): Earth History Grades 9–12 Standard B (p. 178): Structure and Properties of Matter Grades 9–12 Standard D (p. 189): Origin and Evolution of the Earth System	Standard A (pp. 145 & 148)
Mystery Powders	Grades 5–8 Standard A (p. 154): Properties and Changes of Properties in Matter Grades 9–12 Standard B (p. 178): Structure and Properties of Matter	Grades 5–8 Standard A (pp. 145 & 148) Grades 9–12 Standard A (pp. 175–176)

AN EYE TOWARD UNIVERSAL DESIGN

In each case of a revised version of an activity, a concept known as *universal design* is employed, which is a must in today's classrooms. One of the tenets of universal design is that instructional materials and content, as well as the design of a course, should be beneficial to all students with all learning styles. This means that each student should be able to cognitively access course materials and effectively function with them.

The goal is to remove barriers to access, and thus facilitate students' learning processes. A barrier to access may be something as simple as having too many words in small print on a single page. In the Introduction to this book, the major intent of the text was described so as to help teachers find a way to make science more accessible to their students. This is addressed through the retooling guidelines shared in previous chapters, and through the examples of revised science activities listed in Tables 4.1, 4.2, and 4.3. Common revision themes should emerge as each revised activity is perused—anywhere from the font used to separating steps to including diagrams, and so forth. Overall, there is a consistent pattern with applying the revision guidelines throughout each of the revised activities.

Teachers' experiences with students who have used activities designed with these revising guidelines reveal that what is being asked and expected of students now makes more sense to the students. Even gifted students have agreed with this, according to their comments, such as, "Why didn't we do this before?" Hence, such efforts at employing a universal design approach with the revision of science activities and assessments demonstrate success.

There are a number of good sources for finding more information on universal design. A few are noted as follows:

Universal Design Education Online: www.udeducation.org/

Adaptive Environments: www.adaptenv.org/Do-It

Universal Design of Instruction: www.washington.edu/doit/Brochures/Academics/instruction.html

An important consideration when going through this chapter is that one obvious result of the revision is the increase in the number of pages required for an activity—often more than doubling the original's number of pages. While doubling the page requirements may put an unwelcome load upon both the teacher and the school budget, caution and experience recommends against printing both front and back to save paper, since this may not be appropriate for some students with special needs. However, classroom teachers have suggested providing one copy (perhaps laminated) per cooperative group of students. Single copies (nonlaminated) of the activity can be provided to students as needed on an individual basis. This strategy reduces the total volume of paper consumed, as well as the time to print the activity for class use.

SILENT SMELL TRACKING

Introduction

Wolves, like many animals, rely on their senses for learning. Almost from the time they are born, wolf pups use their sense of smell to tell them where they are and to help them find their mother for each meal. To wolves, like other animals, the sense of smell is often more sensitive than it is in humans. For example, although we might be able to detect smells in the air like perfumes or smoke, wolves can sense odors much earlier and in more diluted quantities than we can. Animals often mark their territories by leaving scents that other animals can smell. Further, animals can identify their relatives by their individual smells. The scents come from glands located in various places on the wolves' bodies: the base of the tail, the skin, their feet, and so on. Wolves often spread their scent by rubbing parts of their bodies against trees.

In this simulation, you will be lost wolf pups. You will try to find your mother, or your den, as well as other members of your wolf pack by using your sense of smell.

Objective

After completing this activity, the student should be able to

1. determine how the sense of smell can be used to learn about an object.

Materials

6 cotton balls per group

6 35-mm film canisters with lids per group

1 box

6 food extracts (e.g., lemon, vanilla, etc.)

6 color dots per group (same colors per group, different colors for different groups)

Procedures

A. For each group of five students, open six 35-mm film canisters. If you wish, mark the bottoms of each canister with a color dot. (If you do this, be sure to not tell students so they will not simply match color dots later in the activity.) One canister will be the "mother" or "den" scent while the others are for the wolf pups.

B. Take six cotton balls and soak each with the same food extract (e.g., vanilla).

C. Place one cotton ball in each film canister, and then fasten the lids on each canister.

D. Repeat Procedures A, B, and C for different groups, using a different food extract for each group.

E. Place one film canister of each scent (food extract) randomly around the room.

F. Mix up all the remaining film canisters. Place them in a box.

G. Have students reach into the box and withdraw one film canister each.

H. Tell students they are to remove the top of the film canister and smell what is inside. Then, instruct students to do the following two things *without speaking to one another:*
   1. Find all the other members of their pack.
   2. Find their den.

I. Advise students to remove the lids of their film canisters to smell each other (each others' scents) as well as the canisters representing the dens and mothers. However, advise students to keep the lids on their canisters when they are not smelling the scents.

J. As an option, extend this activity by having students smell their individual scents for long periods of time (such as two minutes) and then try to locate identical scents. (The olfactory sensors in the nose will become fatigued, and for a while, will fail to respond to scents of the same kind.)

Source

Barber, J., Barrett, K., Beals, K., Bergman, L., & Diamond, M.C. (1996). *Learning about learning.* Berkeley, CA: Great Explorations in Math and Science, Lawrence Hall of Science, University of California.

SILENT SMELL TRACKING

Teacher Introduction

This first page is for the teacher only. The essence of the activity is that animals, such as wolves, have scent glands and they use their particular scents to identify each other as well as their territories. Students will use scents to locate their wolf mothers and dens during this activity.

Standards Addressed

NSES Content Standard C (NRC, 1996, p. 129); *NSES* Inquiry Standard A (p. 122)

Materials

1 box

6 cotton balls per group

6 food extracts for smells (e.g., lemon, vanilla, peppermint, etc.)

6 35-mm film canisters with lids per group

6 color dots per group (same colors per group, different colors for different groups)

Teacher Preactivity Preparation

1. For each group of five students, open six 35-mm film canisters. If you wish, mark the bottoms of each canister with a color dot. (If you do this, be sure to not tell students so they will not simply match color dots later in the activity.) One canister will be the "mother" or "den" scent while the others are for the wolf pups.
2. Take six cotton balls and soak each with the same food extract (e.g., vanilla).
3. Place one cotton ball in each film canister, and then fasten the lids on each canister.
4. Repeat Procedures 1, 2, and 3 for different groups, using a different food extract for each group.
5. Place one film canister of each scent (food extract) randomly around the room.
6. Mix up all the remaining film canisters. Place them in a box.

Note for Procedural Step 4

The olfactory sensors in the nose will become fatigued and will fail, for a while, to respond to scents of the same kind.

SILENT SMELL TRACKING

Rationale

Wolves, like many animals, rely on their senses for learning. Almost from the time they are born, wolf pups use their sense of smell to tell them where they are and to help them find their mother for each meal. For wolves, like other animals, the sense of smell is often more sensitive than it is in humans. For example, although we might be able to detect smells in the air like perfumes or smoke, wolves can sense odors much earlier and in more diluted quantities than we can. Animals often mark their territories by leaving scents that other animals can smell. Further, animals can identify their relatives by their individual smells. The scents come from glands located in various places on the wolves' bodies: the base of the tail, the skin, their feet, and so on. Wolves often spread their scent by rubbing parts of their bodies against trees.

In this simulation, you will be lost wolf pups. You will try to find your mother, or your den, as well as other members of your wolf pack by using your sense of smell.

Vocabulary

canister   scent   home den

Objective

After completing this activity, the student should be able to

1. **determine** how the sense of smell can be used to learn about an object, and

2. **explain** how animals can use scent to identify their families.

Materials

1 35-mm film canister per student   1 home den canister per group

Silent Smell Tracking   Page 3

Procedures

- -

Step A

____ 1. When it is your turn, **reach** into the teacher's box of canisters and **take out** one film canister.

____ 2. **Wait** until everyone has picked a film canister.

____ 3. **Remove** the cap of your film canister.

____ 4. **Move the canister** close to your nose and **smell** what is inside the canister.

____ 5. Try to **identify** the scent you smell.

Question for Step A

a. What do you think the scent is (name it)?

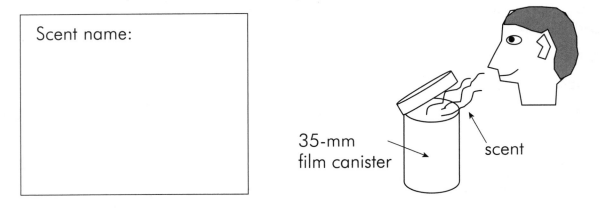

Scent name:

35-mm
film canister

scent

- -

Step B

____ 1. **Find** your family wolf pups.

____ 2. **Do this WITHOUT SPEAKING** to one another.

____ 3. **Go to other students and smell** their film canisters. When you **find a matching scent** for the smell in your canister, **stay** with that person.

> **NOTE:** Keep the lid on your film canister unless you are smelling it or having someone else smell it.

____ 4. When you **find** someone with the same scent as you have, **continue to search** for other members of the family. **Continue until** you have found all family members (there should be five total in a family).

Silent Smell Tracking   **Page 4**

Procedures Continued

Questions for Step B

a. How easy or difficult was it for you to find someone else who had the same scent as you had?

b. How long did it take you to find all the wolf pups for your family?

- -

Step C

___ 1. **Look** around the room. You will **see** some film canisters located in different parts of the room.

___ 2. Once you have all your family members identified, **find** your home, or your den.

___ 3. **Go** to each of the film canisters located around the room to **find** the one that has a scent that matches the one in your film canister.

> **NOTE:** Keep the lid on your film canister unless you are smelling it or having someone else smell it.

___ 4. When you have found your home den, **stay** there until all students have found their dens.

Questions for Step C

a. Describe how you and your family located your home den.

b. Did your family have any difficulties finding your home den? Explain.

Silent Smell Tracking

Procedures Continued

- -

Step D: Optional Only (You do not have to do this)

___ 1. **Get** a new film canister with a different scent.

___ 2. **Smell** your individual scent (in your film canister) for a long period of time (such as two minutes) and then **try to locate** identical scents.

___ 3. See if you are successful **finding** members of your family or your home den.

Questions for Step D

a. How well were you able to smell your scent after smelling it for a long period of time?

b. Based on your answer to a, do you think being around your scent a long time would help you or hinder you in finding your home den? Explain your answer.

c. Do you think real wolves would have similar problems? Explain why you think so or why you don't think so.

Source

Barber, J., Barrett, K., Beals, K., Bergman, L., & Diamond, M. C. (1996). *Learning about learning.* Berkeley, CA: Great Explorations in Math and Science, Lawrence Hall of Science, University of California.

Lower-Elementary Biological Science Activity
Revised Activity: Silent Smell Tracking

SILENT SMELL TRACKING

Teacher Introduction

This first page is for the teacher only. The essence of the activity is that animals, such as wolves, have scent glands and they use their particular scents to identify each other as well as their territories. Students will use scents to locate their wolf mothers and dens during this activity.

Standards Addressed

NSES Content Standard C (NRC, 1996, p. 129); *NSES* Inquiry Standard A (p. 122) ◄—

> The specific content and inquiry standards from the *National Science Education Standards* (NRC, 1996) are identified to help guide the teacher.

Materials

1 box
6 cotton balls per group
6 food extracts for smells (e.g., lemon, vanilla, peppermint, etc.)
6 35-mm film canisters with lids per group
6 color dots per group (same colors per group, different colors for different groups)

Teacher Preactivity Preparation

1. For each group of five students, open six 35-mm film canisters. If you wish, mark the bottoms of each canister with a color dot. (If you do this, be sure to not tell students so they will not simply match color dots later in the activity.) One canister will be the "mother" or "den" scent while the others are for the wolf pups.
2. Take six cotton balls and soak each with the same food extract (e.g., vanilla).
3. Place one cotton ball in each film canister, and then fasten the lids on each canister.
4. Repeat Procedures 1, 2, and 3 for different groups, using a different food extract for each group.
5. Place one film canister of each scent (food extract) randomly around the room.
6. Mix up all the remaining film canisters. Place them in a box.

Note for Procedural Step 4

The olfactory sensors in the nose will become fatigued and will fail, for a while, to respond to scents of the same kind.

> This particular activity includes a teacher's page. This page provides information about necessary preactivity preparations, as well as an informational note about the last procedure in the activity.

- Although not readily apparent here, the font has been changed. The font selected is one with few serifs (curlicues) on the tails of letters. In addition, the font size increased to 14 point.

SILENT SMELL TRACKING

Rationale

Wolves, like many animals, rely on their senses for learning. Almost from the time they are born, wolf pups use their sense of smell to tell them where they are and to help them find their mother for each meal. For wolves, like other animals, the sense of smell is often more sensitive than it is in humans. For example, although we might be able to detect smells in the air like perfumes or smoke, wolves can sense odors much earlier and in more diluted quantities than we can. Animals often mark their territories by leaving scents that other animals can smell. Further, animals can identify their relatives by their individual smells. The scents come from glands located in various places on the wolves' bodies: the base of the tail, the skin, their feet, and so on. Wolves often spread their scent by rubbing parts of their bodies against trees.

In this simulation, you will be lost wolf pups. You will try to find your mother, or your den, as well as other members of your wolf pack by using your sense of smell.

The Introduction header changed to Rationale so it is consistent with other model activities.

Vocabulary

canister   scent   home den

Vocabulary words are identified and added to help students.

Objective

After completing this activity, the student should be able to

1. **determine** how the sense of smell can be used to learn about an object, and

2. **explain** how animals can use scent to identify their families.

The objectives are spread out more for easier reading, and key verbs are highlighted (put into boldface) to help guide students in knowing what actions they need to take.

Materials

1 35-mm film canister per student   1 home den canister per group

The list of materials was reduced and now shows only those that students will need. The more complete list of materials is located on the previous (teacher) page.

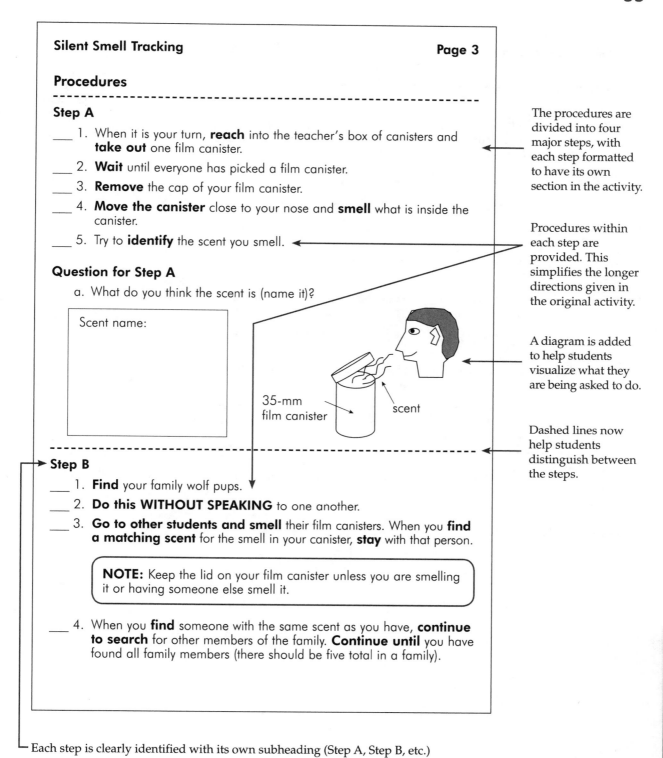

Silent Smell Tracking   **Page 3**

Procedures

Step A

___ 1. When it is your turn, **reach** into the teacher's box of canisters and **take out** one film canister.

___ 2. **Wait** until everyone has picked a film canister.

___ 3. **Remove** the cap of your film canister.

___ 4. **Move the canister** close to your nose and **smell** what is inside the canister.

___ 5. Try to **identify** the scent you smell.

Question for Step A

    a. What do you think the scent is (name it)?

> Scent name:

35-mm film canister   scent

Step B

___ 1. **Find** your family wolf pups.

___ 2. **Do this WITHOUT SPEAKING** to one another.

___ 3. **Go to other students and smell** their film canisters. When you **find a matching scent** for the smell in your canister, **stay** with that person.

> **NOTE:** Keep the lid on your film canister unless you are smelling it or having someone else smell it.

___ 4. When you **find** someone with the same scent as you have, **continue to search** for other members of the family. **Continue until** you have found all family members (there should be five total in a family).

The procedures are divided into four major steps, with each step formatted to have its own section in the activity.

Procedures within each step are provided. This simplifies the longer directions given in the original activity.

A diagram is added to help students visualize what they are being asked to do.

Dashed lines now help students distinguish between the steps.

Each step is clearly identified with its own subheading (Step A, Step B, etc.)

- The entire content of a section or step is kept on the same page, so part of a step isn't on one page and the rest of it on the next page.

Lower-Elementary Biological Science Activity
Annotated Revised Activity: Silent Smell Tracking

Silent Smell Tracking   **Page 4**

Procedures Continued ◄─────────────────────────────

The Procedures Continued heading is added to help students understand the activity extends onto this page.

Questions for Step B

a. How easy or difficult was it for you to find someone else who had the same scent as you had?

b. How long did it take you to find all the wolf pups for your family?

- -

Step C

▼ ___ 1. **Look** around the room. You will **see** some film canisters located in different parts of the room.

___ 2. Once you have all your family members identified, **find** your home, or your den.

___ 3. **Go** to each of the film canisters located around the room to **find** the one that has a scent that matches the one in your film canister.

> **NOTE:** Keep the lid on your film canister unless you are smelling it or having someone else smell it. ◄─

A note is added to provide a helpful pointer for students so that the scent material doesn't fade too quickly through the duration of the activity.

___ 4. When you have found your home den, **stay** there until all students have found their dens.

Questions for Step C

a. Describe how you and your family located your home den. ◄─────

b. Did your family have any difficulties finding your home den? Explain.

Each procedure within a step has a blank line to its left. Students can place checks in the blanks to help keep track of what they have completed.

Questions for each section are added, and the questions that pertain to a particular step or section are included within that step. In addition, space is provided for students to write their answers. This reduces the chances of transcription or translation errors that occur when separate sheets of paper are used.

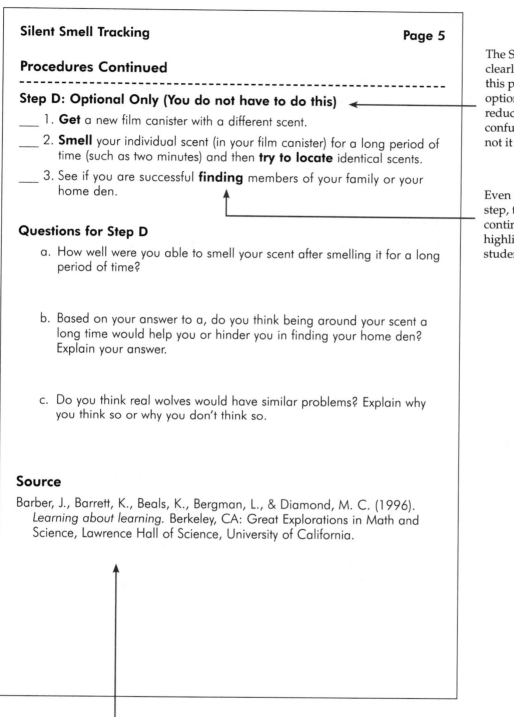

Silent Smell Tracking   **Page 5**

Procedures Continued

Step D: Optional Only (You do not have to do this) ←

___ 1. **Get** a new film canister with a different scent.

___ 2. **Smell** your individual scent (in your film canister) for a long period of time (such as two minutes) and then **try to locate** identical scents.

___ 3. See if you are successful **finding** members of your family or your home den.

Questions for Step D

a. How well were you able to smell your scent after smelling it for a long period of time?

b. Based on your answer to a, do you think being around your scent a long time would help you or hinder you in finding your home den? Explain your answer.

c. Do you think real wolves would have similar problems? Explain why you think so or why you don't think so.

Source

Barber, J., Barrett, K., Beals, K., Bergman, L., & Diamond, M. C. (1996). *Learning about learning.* Berkeley, CA: Great Explorations in Math and Science, Lawrence Hall of Science, University of California.

The Step D subheading clearly indicates that this procedure is optional. This helps reduce potential confusion whether or not it must be done.

Even in the optional step, the key verbs continue to be highlighted to help students.

The original source that the activity is based upon is provided at the end of the last page of the activity.

• Throughout the revised activity, additional white space is provided to prevent a cluttered appearance and to help students read the content and directions.

A GRANITE MOSAIC

Introduction

Rocks are usually classified by identifying the minerals that are in them. The amount of any particular mineral can vary compared to the amount of other minerals in a type of rock. For example, granites are made of combinations of the minerals quartz, feldspar, and mica. Some granites tend to contain more mica than others, some contain more quartz than others, and so forth.

In this activity, you will explore how a single type of rock can have different amounts (proportions) of minerals.

Objectives

Upon completion of this activity, the student should be able to

1. describe how a single type of rock can contain varying proportions of minerals yet still be that rock type, and
2. create a model of granite showing its mineral contents.

Materials

1 magnifying lens

3 sheets of construction paper (1 yellow, 1 black, 1 pink)

1 Magnifying Lens Worksheet

2–3 samples of granite

1 pair of scissors

1 bottle of glue (or glue stick)

Procedures

A. Take your scissors and the yellow construction paper. Cut the paper into small rectangles. These will represent the mineral quartz.

B. Next, cut the black paper into small triangles. These will represent the mineral biotite (mica) and/or hornblende.

C. Finally, cut the pink paper into small squares or circles. These will represent the mineral feldspar.

D. Glue the paper pieces in the magnifying lens area of the worksheet. (Be sure to glue one paper piece in the "key" portion of the worksheet!) You may use any combination of paper pieces and any arrangement you wish, just as long as all three types of paper (minerals) are glued onto your worksheet.

E. When finished, you will have created a model of the rock granite. Compare your granite to that of other students.

F. Use the magnifying lens to examine the samples of granite. See if you can identify the three minerals in your samples. Then compare the granite samples with the paper model you just made.

Questions

1. In what way(s) was your granite the same as that created by other students?
2. In what way(s) was your granite different from that created by other students?
3. Describe how your paper "granite" was similar to and different from the real samples of granite you examined in Procedure F.
4. Were all the samples of granite you examined the same? Explain. (If yes, in what way were they the same? If not, how were they different?)
5. Why do you think one granite can form so it contains different amounts of minerals compared to another granite?

Source

National Wildlife Federation (1988). Mineral mosaics. *Geology: The active earth, Ranger Rick's nature scope.* Washington, DC: Author.

A Granite Mosaic

Page 2

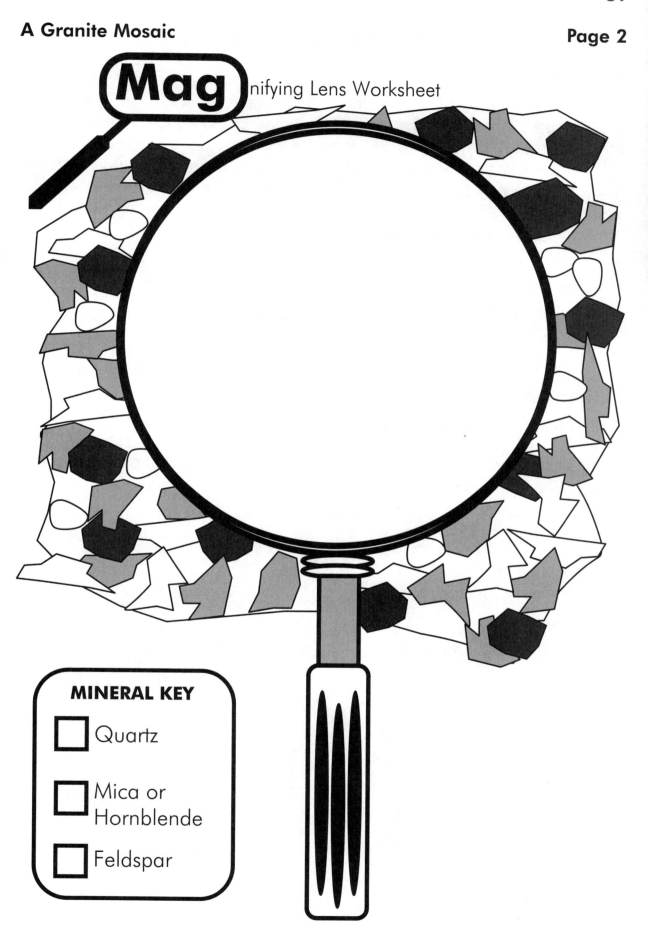

Magnifying Lens Worksheet

MINERAL KEY

☐ Quartz

☐ Mica or Hornblende

☐ Feldspar

A GRANITE MOSAIC

Rationale

Rocks are usually classified by identifying the minerals that are in them. The amount of any particular mineral can vary compared to the amount of other minerals in a type of rock. For example, granites are made of combinations of the minerals quartz, feldspar, and mica. Some granites tend to contain more mica than others, some contain more quartz than others, and so forth. In this activity, you will explore how a single type of rock can have different amounts (or different proportions) of minerals.

Vocabulary

quartz	feldspar	biotite mica
hornblende	proportion	granite

Objectives

Upon completion of this activity, the student should be able to

1. **describe** how a single type of rock can contain varying proportions of minerals yet still be that rock type, and

2. **create** a model of granite showing its mineral contents.

Materials

1 magnifying lens

1 pair of scissors

1 Magnifying Lens Worksheet

2–3 samples of granite

1 bottle of glue (or glue stick)

3 sheets of construction paper (1 yellow, 1 black, 1 pink)

A Granite Mosaic   **Page 2**

Procedures

- -

Step A

___ 1. **Get** the yellow construction paper and the scissors.

___ 2. **Cut** the yellow paper into small rectangles.

___ 3. **Put** the yellow rectangles in a pile to the side.

> **NOTE:** These yellow rectangles will represent the mineral quartz.
>
>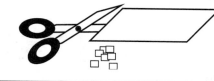

- -

Step B

___ 1. **Get** the black construction paper and the scissors.

___ 2. **Cut** the black paper into small triangles.

___ 3. **Put** the black triangles in a pile next to the yellow rectangles.

> **NOTE:** These black triangles will represent the mineral biotite mica (or the mineral hornblende).
>
>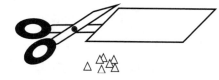

- -

Step C

___ 1. **Get** the pink construction paper and the scissors.

___ 2. **Cut** the pink paper into small squares or circles.

___ 3. **Put** the pink squares or circles in a pile next to the yellow rectangles.

> **NOTE:** These pink squares or circles will represent the mineral feldspar.
>
>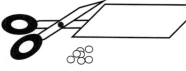

- -

A Granite Mosaic

Procedures Continued

- -

Step D

___ 1. **Place** the worksheet titled "Magnifying Lens Worksheet" on the table in front of you.

___ 2. Be sure to **glue** one piece of each kind of construction paper in the "key" portion of the worksheet on page 5.

___ 3. **Glue** the cut pieces of construction paper into the middle section of the worksheet on page 5.

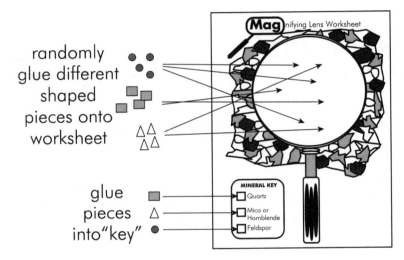

___ 4. Randomly **select** pieces and glue them in the magnifying lens area of the worksheet on page 5.

___ 5. Be sure to **mix** different pieces of paper together on the worksheet.

___ 6. **Use** any combination of paper pieces and any arrangement you wish, just as long as you **glue** all three types of paper (minerals) onto your worksheet.

- -

Step E

When finished, you will have created a model of the rock granite.

___ 1. **Compare** your granite to that of other students.

- -

Step F

___ 1. **Use** the magnifying lens to examine the real samples of granite. See if you can **identify** the three minerals in your real samples. Then **compare** the real granite samples with the paper model you just made.

- -

A Granite Mosaic   **Page 4**

Questions

1. In what way(s) was your granite the same as that created by other students?

2. In what way(s) was your granite different from that created by other students?

3. Describe how your paper "granite" was similar to and different from the real samples of granite you examined in Procedure Step F.

4. Were all the samples of granite you examined the same?

   a. If yes, explain in what way were they the same.

   b. If not, how were they different?

5. Why do you think one granite can form so it contains different amounts of minerals compared to another granite?

Standards Addressed

NSES Content Standard D (NRC, p. 134); *NSES* Inquiry Standard A (p. 122)

Source

National Wildlife Federation (1988). Mineral mosaics. *Geology: The active earth, Ranger Rick's nature scope.* Washington, DC: Author.

A Granite Mosaic   **Page 5**

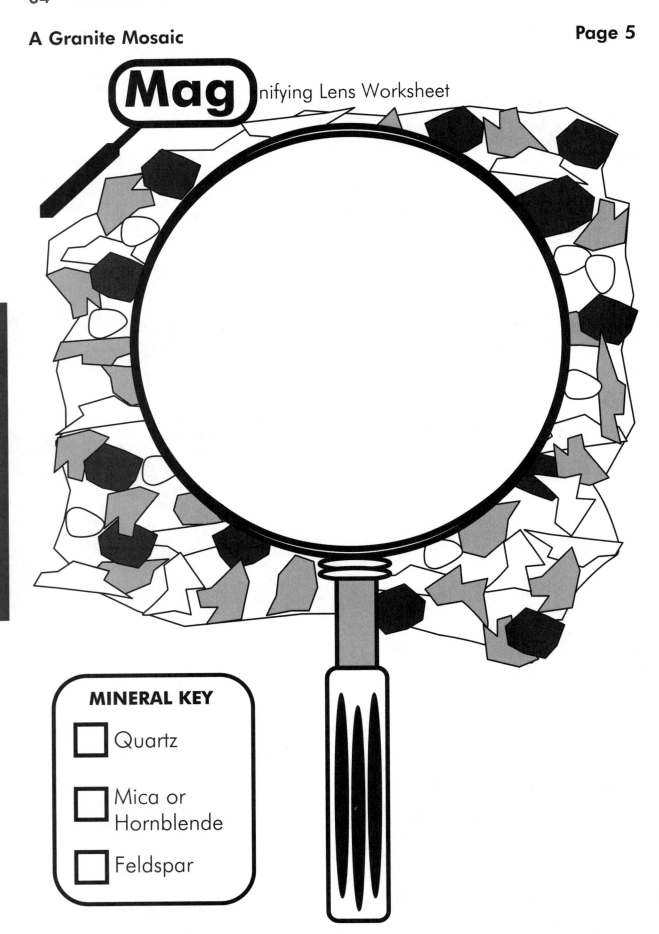

Magnifying Lens Worksheet

MINERAL KEY

☐ Quartz

☐ Mica or Hornblende

☐ Feldspar

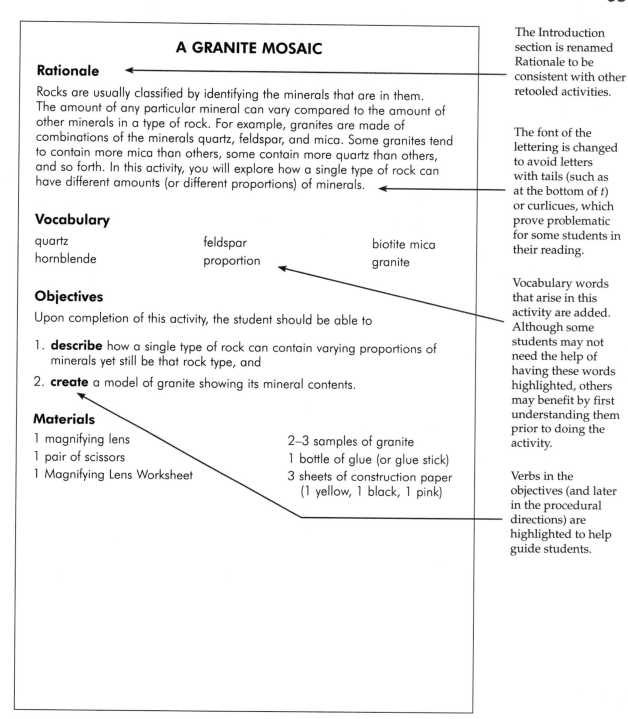

A GRANITE MOSAIC

Rationale

Rocks are usually classified by identifying the minerals that are in them. The amount of any particular mineral can vary compared to the amount of other minerals in a type of rock. For example, granites are made of combinations of the minerals quartz, feldspar, and mica. Some granites tend to contain more mica than others, some contain more quartz than others, and so forth. In this activity, you will explore how a single type of rock can have different amounts (or different proportions) of minerals.

Vocabulary

quartz	feldspar	biotite mica
hornblende	proportion	granite

Objectives

Upon completion of this activity, the student should be able to

1. **describe** how a single type of rock can contain varying proportions of minerals yet still be that rock type, and
2. **create** a model of granite showing its mineral contents.

Materials

1 magnifying lens	2–3 samples of granite
1 pair of scissors	1 bottle of glue (or glue stick)
1 Magnifying Lens Worksheet	3 sheets of construction paper (1 yellow, 1 black, 1 pink)

The Introduction section is renamed Rationale to be consistent with other retooled activities.

The font of the lettering is changed to avoid letters with tails (such as at the bottom of *t*) or curlicues, which prove problematic for some students in their reading.

Vocabulary words that arise in this activity are added. Although some students may not need the help of having these words highlighted, others may benefit by first understanding them prior to doing the activity.

Verbs in the objectives (and later in the procedural directions) are highlighted to help guide students.

- Although the sample shown here is reduced in size, the print size used on the page is 14-point font.

- Efforts were made to provide more white space to avoid a cluttered appearance (such as the spaces between the items in the materials list). Margins on all sides have not been reduced.

- The activity is photocopied in clear copies (not mottled or grayed).

Lower-Elementary Earth Science Activity
Annotated Revised Activity: A Granite Mosaic

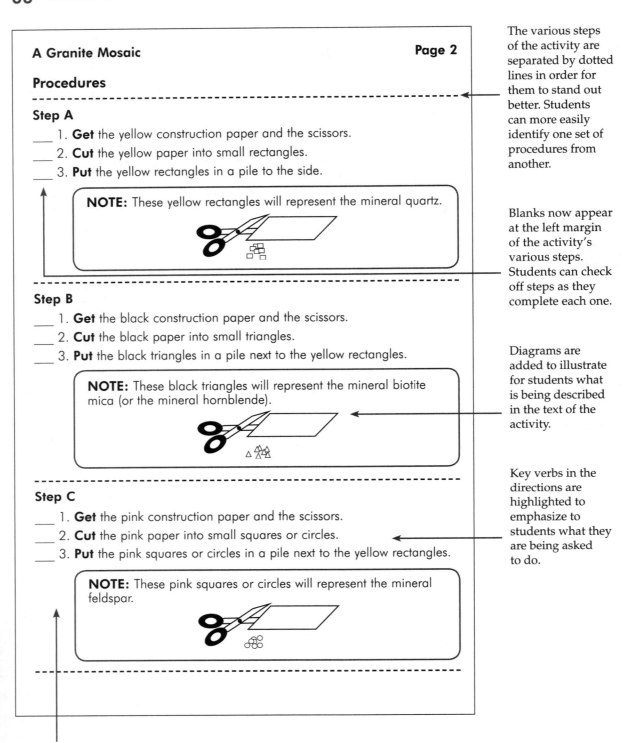

A Granite Mosaic   **Page 2**

Procedures

- -

Step A

____ 1. **Get** the yellow construction paper and the scissors.

____ 2. **Cut** the yellow paper into small rectangles.

____ 3. **Put** the yellow rectangles in a pile to the side.

> **NOTE:** These yellow rectangles will represent the mineral quartz.

- -

Step B

____ 1. **Get** the black construction paper and the scissors.

____ 2. **Cut** the black paper into small triangles.

____ 3. **Put** the black triangles in a pile next to the yellow rectangles.

> **NOTE:** These black triangles will represent the mineral biotite mica (or the mineral hornblende).

- -

Step C

____ 1. **Get** the pink construction paper and the scissors.

____ 2. **Cut** the pink paper into small squares or circles.

____ 3. **Put** the pink squares or circles in a pile next to the yellow rectangles.

> **NOTE:** These pink squares or circles will represent the mineral feldspar.

- -

The various steps of the activity are separated by dotted lines in order for them to stand out better. Students can more easily identify one set of procedures from another.

Blanks now appear at the left margin of the activity's various steps. Students can check off steps as they complete each one.

Diagrams are added to illustrate for students what is being described in the text of the activity.

Key verbs in the directions are highlighted to emphasize to students what they are being asked to do.

Directions in each step are separated by more white space. This helps avoid a cluttered appearance and is easier for students to read.

Lower-Elementary Earth Science Activity
Annotated Revised Activity: A Granite Mosaic

A Granite Mosaic   **Page 3**

Procedures Continued ◄

- -

Step D ◄

___ 1. **Place** the worksheet titled "Magnifying Lens Worksheet" on the table ◄ in front of you.

___ 2. Be sure to **glue** one piece of each kind of construction paper in the "key" portion of the worksheet on page 5.

___ 3. **Glue** the cut pieces of construction paper into the middle section of the worksheet on page 5.

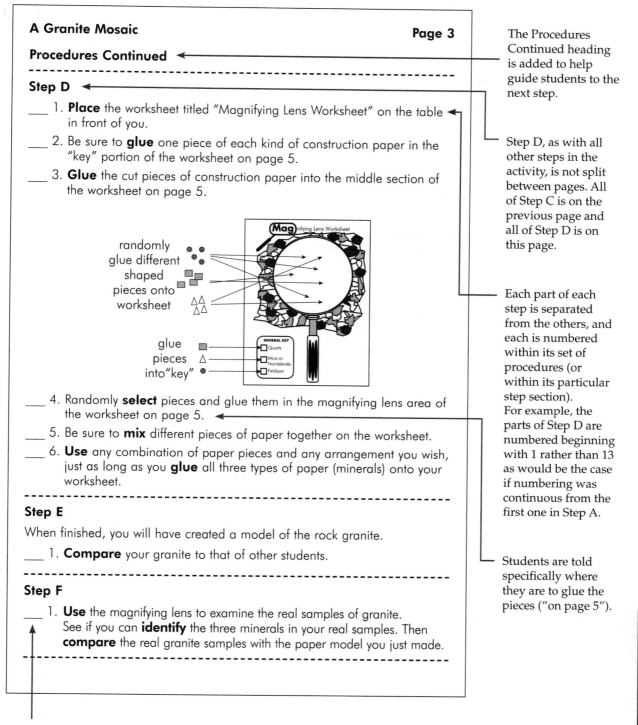

randomly glue different shaped pieces onto worksheet

glue pieces into "key"

MINERAL KEY
Quartz
Mica or Hornblende
Feldspar

___ 4. Randomly **select** pieces and glue them in the magnifying lens area of the worksheet on page 5. ◄

___ 5. Be sure to **mix** different pieces of paper together on the worksheet.

___ 6. **Use** any combination of paper pieces and any arrangement you wish, just as long as you **glue** all three types of paper (minerals) onto your worksheet.

- -

Step E

When finished, you will have created a model of the rock granite.

___ 1. **Compare** your granite to that of other students.

- -

Step F

___ 1. **Use** the magnifying lens to examine the real samples of granite. See if you can **identify** the three minerals in your real samples. Then **compare** the real granite samples with the paper model you just made.

- -

The Procedures Continued heading is added to help guide students to the next step.

Step D, as with all other steps in the activity, is not split between pages. All of Step C is on the previous page and all of Step D is on this page.

Each part of each step is separated from the others, and each is numbered within its set of procedures (or within its particular step section). For example, the parts of Step D are numbered beginning with 1 rather than 13 as would be the case if numbering was continuous from the first one in Step A.

Students are told specifically where they are to glue the pieces ("on page 5").

For each Procedure step, the particular step (Step A, Step B) is highlighted (or made bold) to stand out better for students.

A Granite Mosaic Page 4

Questions

1. In what way(s) was your granite the same as that created by other students?

2. In what way(s) was your granite different from that created by other students?

3. Describe how your paper "granite" was similar to and different from the real samples of granite you examined in Procedure Step F.

4. Were all the samples of granite you examined the same?

   a. If yes, explain in what way were they the same.

   b. If not, how were they different?

5. Why do you think one granite can form so it contains different amounts of minerals compared to another granite?

Standards Addressed

NSES Content Standard D (NRC, p. 134); *NSES* Inquiry Standard A (p. 122)

Source

National Wildlife Federation (1988). Mineral mosaics. *Geology: The active earth, Ranger Rick's nature scope.* Washington, DC: Author.

This new section of questions is clearly identified so it is not easily confused with the earlier procedures' sections.

White space now appears between the questions so students can write their answers in the spaces. This helps avoid translational or transcription errors that can occur when students must rewrite questions on another sheet of paper, or correlate written answers with their respective questions.

The content and inquiry standards from the *National Science Education Standards* (NRC, 1996) are provided to help guide teachers. This information typically appears on a teacher page that the student does not see. Since this activity does not include a teacher page, the information is placed here to avoid confusing the student at the beginning where the introduction and vocabulary appear.

The source from which the activity idea was derived is included at the bottom of the last page before the student worksheet.

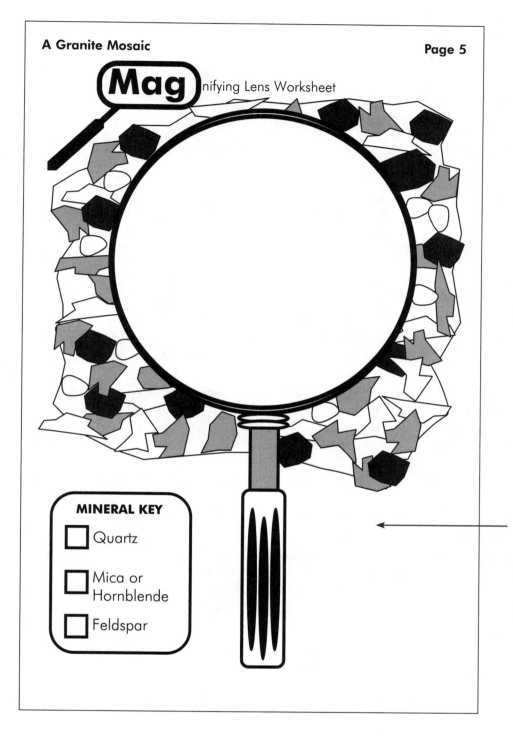

A Granite Mosaic

Page 5

Magnifying Lens Worksheet

MINERAL KEY

☐ Quartz

☐ Mica or Hornblende

☐ Feldspar

The student worksheet size is maintained rather than reduced to save space. This page is also easily separated from the rest of the activity to help students complete it (without having to flip pages back and forth).

THE BOUNCING BALL

Objectives

After completing this activity, the student should be able to

1. construct a graph with two variables, and
2. predict future outcomes based on interpretations of graphed data.

Materials

| 1 roll of masking tape | 3 rubber balls (3 different types) | 3 colored pencils |
| 1 meterstick | 1 sheet of graph paper | 1 pencil |

Procedures

A. Take Rubber Ball A and the meterstick. Stand the meterstick upright on the table (or floor) so that the 0-cm end is against the tabletop (or floor). The meterstick should be at a right angle (or perpendicular) to the tabletop. One partner should hold the meterstick in place. As an alternative, you may wish to simply hold the meterstick against the wall while keeping its 0-cm end against the floor.

B. Hold Ball A so that it is even with the 10-cm mark of the meterstick. The ball should not touch the meterstick.

C. Drop Ball A and let it bounce. As this is done, a partner should carefully observe the ball and try to determine how high Ball A bounces (in cm). Record this measurement as bounce height in Table 1 (on next page).

D. Now hold Ball A at the 20-cm level and drop it. Measure the bounce height for Ball A when it is dropped from the 20-cm level.

E. Repeat these procedures for drop heights of 30, 40, 50, 80, and 100 cm. Be sure to record your data in Table 1.

F. Repeat all the above procedures but this time use Ball B.

G. Now repeat all the procedures again, but use Ball C.

H. Using the data in Table 1, graph the data for Ball A. Drop height should be on the horizontal axis and bounce height should be on the vertical axis. Be sure to label each axis.

I. Next graph the data for Balls B and C. Use different colors or different types of lines for each ball (so you can tell them apart from each other and apart from the line for Ball A).

Questions

1. Using the graph you constructed, predict the height that Ball A will bounce if it is dropped from a height of 75 cm.

2. How high do you think Ball A will bounce if you drop it from a height of 120 cm? Explain why you think this.

3. Did all three balls bounce the same amounts (did each have the same bounce height for a given drop height)?

4. What is the average difference (in cm) of bounce height of Ball B compared to Ball A? Of Ball C compared to Ball A? Of Ball B compared to Ball C?

5. Knowing the information from Question 4, if you only have Ball A available, how high do you expect Ball C to bounce if you drop it from a height of 120 cm?

6. What could be a reason for any differences in bounce heights for the three balls?

The Bouncing Ball

Table 1

Drop Ht (cm)	Ball A Bounce Ht (cm)	Ball B Bounce Ht (cm)	Ball C Bounce Ht (cm)
10			
20			
30			
40			
50			
80			
100			

The Bouncing Ball

Page 3

THE BOUNCING BALL

Rationale

Imagine that one day you go into an electronics store to purchase a VCR.
In the store, you find Brand A and Brand B, but not Brand C. From what you've read, you know that Brand C is very similar to Brand A, but you have not actually seen Brand A before. You take a videotape and place it first in Brand A and later in Brand B so you can compare how the two VCRs operate. From this information, you may be able to infer how Brand C will also operate. Then you can make a decision about which VCR you will probably purchase.

In the situation described in the above paragraph, you collected data about one or two objects and applied that information to find out information about other objects. You may be faced with similar situations at different times in your life. In this activity, you will do a similar thing, but you will collect data about different balls. You will analyze the data, and make some decisions based on your data.

Vocabulary

axis	graph	perpendicular
centimeter	height	predict
cm	horizontal	vertical
bounce height	horizontal axis	vertical axis
drop height	meterstick	

Objectives

After completing this activity, the student should be able to

1. **collect and record** data from an experiment,

2. **construct** a graph with two variables, and

3. **predict** future outcomes based on interpretations of graphed data.

Materials

1 roll of masking tape
3 rubber balls (3 different types)
3 colored pencils (red, green, blue)

1 pencil
1 meterstick
1 sheet of graph paper

The Bouncing Ball   Page 2

Procedures

- -

Step A

___ 1. **Get** the RED BALL and the meterstick.

___ 2. **Stand** the meterstick upright on the table (or floor) so that the 0-centimeter end is against the tabletop (or floor).

___ 3. **Make sure** the meterstick is at a right angle (or perpendicular) to the tabletop.

___ 4. Have one partner **hold** the meterstick in place.

___ 5. As an alternative, simply **hold** the meterstick against the wall while keeping its 0-centimeter end against the floor.

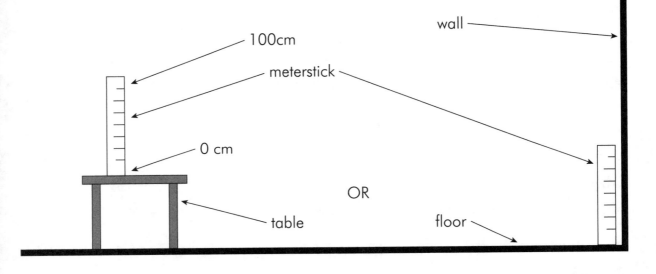

- -

Step B

___ 1. **Hold** the RED BALL so that it is even with the 10-centimeter mark of the meterstick.

___ 2. **Do not allow** the ball to touch the meterstick.

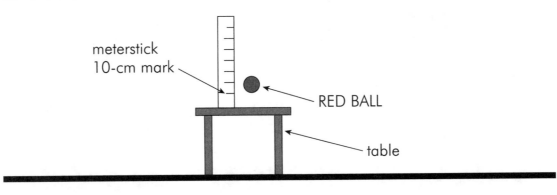

The Bouncing Ball

Procedures Continued

- -

Step C

___ 1. **Drop** the RED BALL and let it bounce.

___ 2. **Watch** while a partner determines how high in centimeters the RED BALL bounces.

___ 3. **Record** this measurement as bounce height in Table 1 (located at the **bottom of page 5** of this activity).

- -

Step D

___ 1. **Hold** the RED BALL at the 20-centimeter level and drop it.

___ 2. **Measure** the bounce height for the RED BALL when it drops from the 20-centimeter level.

___ 3. **Record** the measurement as bounce height in Table 1 (at the bottom of page 5).

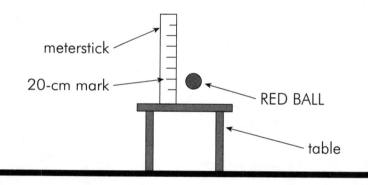

meterstick

20-cm mark

RED BALL

table

- -

Step E

___ 1. **Repeat** these procedures for drop heights of 40, 60, 80, and 100 centimeters.

___ 2. Be sure to **record** your data in Table 1 (on page 5).

- -

Step F

___ 1. **Repeat** all the above procedures but this time use the GREEN BALL.

- -

Step G

___ 1. **Repeat** all the procedures again, but use the BLUE BALL.

The Bouncing Ball   Page 4

Procedures Continued

Step H

___ 1. Using the data in Table 1, **graph the data** for the RED BALL.
    ___ a. **Use** the graph paper that is on the last page of this activity (on page 6).
    ___ b. **Graph** drop height on the horizontal axis.
    ___ c. **Graph** bounce height on the vertical axis.
    ___ d. Be sure to **label each axis**.

Step I

___ 1. **Graph** the data for the GREEN BALL.

___ 2. **Use** a green marker or pencil to draw the graph line for the GREEN BALL.

___ 3. **Draw** the green line on the same graph as you used for the RED BALL.

___ 4. **Graph** the data for the BLUE BALL.

___ 5. **Use** a blue marker or pencil to draw the graph line for the BLUE BALL.

___ 6. **Draw** the blue line on the same graph as you used for the RED BALL.

Questions

1. **Using the graph** you made, **predict** the height that the RED BALL will bounce if it drops from a height of 75 centimeters. After you have made your prediction, test it by dropping the RED BALL from 75 centimeters. How close was your prediction to the real result?

2. How high to you think the RED BALL will bounce if you drop it from a height of 120 centimeters? Explain why you think this.

The Bouncing Ball

Questions Continued

- -

3. Did all three balls bounce the same amounts (did each have the same bounce height for a given drop height)?

4. Knowing the information from Question 4, if you only had the RED BALL available, how high do you expect the GREEN BALL to bounce if you drop it from a height of 120 centimeters?

5. What could be a reason for any differences in bounce heights for the three balls?

Table 1

Drop Height (cm)	RED BALL Bounce Height (cm)	BLUE BALL Bounce Height (cm)	GREEN BALL Bounce Height (cm)
10			
20			
30			
40			
50			
80			
100			

The Bouncing Ball

Drop Height vs. Bounce Height of Balls

Bounce Height (in cm)

100
90
80
70
60
50
40
30
20
10
0

0 10 20 30 40 50 60 70 80 90 100

Drop Height (in cm)

Standards Addressed

NSES Content Standard B (NRC, p. 127); *NSES* Inquiry Standard A (p. 123)

Source

American Association for the Advancement of Science (1961). *Science: A process approach, Grade 3 Module 48.* Washington, DC: Author.

THE BOUNCING BALL

Rationale

Imagine that one day you go into an electronics store to purchase a VCR. In the store, you find Brand A and Brand B, but not Brand C. From what you've read, you know that Brand C is very similar to Brand A, but you have not actually seen Brand A before. You take a videotape and place it first in Brand A and later in Brand B so you can compare how the two VCRs operate. From this information, you may be able to infer how Brand C will also operate. Then you can make a decision about which VCR you will probably purchase.

In the situation described in the above paragraph, you collected data about one or two objects and applied that information to find out information about other objects. You may be faced with similar situations at different times in your life. In this activity, you will do a similar thing, but you will collect data about different balls. You will analyze the data, and make some decisions based on your data.

Vocabulary

axis	graph	perpendicular
centimeter	height	predict
cm	horizontal	vertical
bounce height	horizontal axis	vertical axis
drop height	meterstick	

Objectives

After completing this activity, the student should be able to

1. **collect and record** data from an experiment,
2. **construct** a graph with two variables, and
3. **predict** future outcomes based on interpretations of graphed data.

Materials

1 roll of masking tape	1 pencil
3 rubber balls (3 different types)	1 meterstick
3 colored pencils (red, green, blue)	1 sheet of graph paper

This Rationale section is added so that students see some reason for doing the activity, and better understand how the activity relates to the world around them.

The font of the lettering changed to avoid having letters with tails (such as at the bottom of *t*) or curlicues, which prove problematic for some students in their reading.

Vocabulary words that arise in this activity are added. Although some students may not need the help of having these words highlighted, others may benefit by first understanding them prior to doing the activity.

Verbs in the directions given to students are highlighted to help guide students.

- Although the sample shown here is reduced in size, the print size used on the page is no smaller than 12 point.

- Efforts are made to provide more white space and avoid cluttered appearances.

- Margins on all sides are not reduced.

- The activity is photocopied and not reproduced on ditto or mimeograph, both of which sometimes prove difficult for students to read.

- Directions are simplified, with shorter, more direct wording.

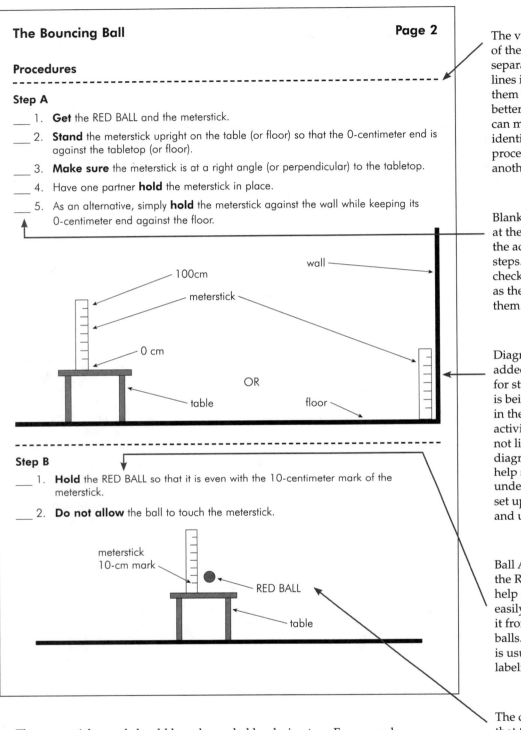

The Bouncing Ball   **Page 2**

Procedures

- -

Step A

___ 1. **Get** the RED BALL and the meterstick.

___ 2. **Stand** the meterstick upright on the table (or floor) so that the 0-centimeter end is against the tabletop (or floor).

___ 3. **Make sure** the meterstick is at a right angle (or perpendicular) to the tabletop.

___ 4. Have one partner **hold** the meterstick in place.

___ 5. As an alternative, simply **hold** the meterstick against the wall while keeping its 0-centimeter end against the floor.

100cm

meterstick

wall

0 cm

OR

table

floor

- -

Step B

___ 1. **Hold** the RED BALL so that it is even with the 10-centimeter mark of the meterstick.

___ 2. **Do not allow** the ball to touch the meterstick.

meterstick
10-cm mark

RED BALL

table

The various steps of the activity are separated by dotted lines in order for them to stand out better. Students can more easily identify one set of procedures from another.

Blanks now appear at the left margin of the activity's various steps. Students can check off each step as they complete them.

Diagrams are added to illustrate for students what is being described in the text of the activity. Although not life size, these diagrams should help students better understand how to set up the equipment and use it.

Ball A is renamed the RED BALL to help students more easily distinguish it from the other balls. Color-coding is usually better than labeling items.

The diagram shows that the bottom of the red ball should be at the 10-centimeter mark, from where it is to be dropped.

- The metersticks used should be color-coded by decimeters. For example, the first decimeter may be lined on the edge with a thin strip of yellow tape. The second decimeter may be lined on the edge with a thin strip of red tape. Other decimeters are color-coded in similar ways. This aids students in spotting the balls' bounce heights more effectively.

The Bouncing Ball   Page 3

Procedures Continued

- -

Step C

___ 1. **Drop** the RED BALL and let it bounce.

___ 2. **Watch** while a partner determines how high in centimeters the RED BALL bounces.

___ 3. **Record** this measurement as bounce height in Table 1 (located at the **bottom of page 5** of this activity).

- -

Step D

___ 1. **Hold** the RED BALL at the 20-centimeter level and drop it.

___ 2. **Measure** the bounce height for the RED BALL when it drops from the 20-centimeter level.

___ 3. **Record** the measurement as bounce height in Table 1 (at the bottom of page 5).

meterstick

20-cm mark

RED BALL

table

- -

Step E

___ 1. **Repeat** these procedures for drop heights of 40, 60, 80, and 100 centimeters.

___ 2. Be sure to **record** your data in Table 1 (on page 5).

- -

Step F

___ 1. **Repeat** all the above procedures but this time use the GREEN BALL.

- -

Step G

___ 1. **Repeat** all the procedures again, but use the BLUE BALL.

The Procedures Continued heading is added to help guide students to the next step.

Step C, as with all other steps in the activity, is not split between pages. All of Step B is on the previous page while all of Step C is on this page.

Each part of each step is separated from the others, and each is numbered within its set of procedures rather than continuing from the numbering started in the previous step (i.e., parts in Step D begin with 1 rather than 4, as would be the case if numbering was continued from Step C).

The parenthetical statement is added to direct students to the location of Table 1, where they are told to record their data.

For each Procedure step, the particular step is highlighted (or made bold) to stand out better to students.

The Bouncing Ball   Page 4

Procedures Continued

- -

Step H

___ 1. Using the data in Table 1, **graph the data** for the RED BALL.
  ___ a. **Use** the graph paper that is on the last page of this activity (on page 6).
  ___ b. **Graph** drop height on the horizontal axis.
  ___ c. **Graph** bounce height on the vertical axis.
  ___ d. Be sure to **label each axis**.

- -

Step I

___ 1. **Graph** the data for the GREEN BALL.

___ 2. **Use** a green marker or pencil to draw the graph line for the GREEN BALL.

___ 3. **Draw** the green line on the same graph as you used for the RED BALL.

___ 4. **Graph** the data for the BLUE BALL.

___ 5. **Use** a blue marker or pencil to draw the graph line for the BLUE BALL.

___ 6. **Draw** the blue line on the same graph as you used for the RED BALL.

- -

Questions

1. **Using the graph** you made, **predict** the height that the RED BALL will bounce if it drops from a height of 75 centimeters. After you have made your prediction, test it by dropping the RED BALL from 75 centimeters. How close was your prediction to the real result?

2. How high to you think the RED BALL will bounce if you drop it from a height of 120 centimeters? Explain why you think this.

Verbs continue to be highlighted in each direction as appropriate.

The students are told exactly where to find the graph paper they are to use for the data they record in Table 1 (on page 5).

Ball 2 is renamed GREEN BALL. The actual ball used should be green.

Ball 3 is renamed BLUE BALL, and the ball should be blue.

As with the Procedures sections and steps, the Questions section is separated from the others. Each question is provided ample white space and room for student answers. Verbs are highlighted where appropriate.

Ball names (RED BALL, GREEN BALL, BLUE BALL) are put in capital letters to help students more easily identify the things of focus in the question.

The Bouncing Ball   **Page 5**

Questions Continued ◄─────────────────────────────────────

----

3. Did all three balls bounce the same amounts (did each have the same bounce height for a given drop height)?

4. Knowing the information from Question 4, if you only had the RED BALL available, how high do you expect the GREEN BALL to bounce if you drop it from a height of 120 centimeters?

5. What could be a reason for any differences in bounce heights for the three balls?

Table 1

Drop Height (cm)	RED BALL Bounce Height (cm)	BLUE BALL Bounce Height (cm)	GREEN BALL Bounce Height (cm)
10			
20			
30			
40			
50			
80			
100			

The highlighted header informs students that the Question section continues onto this page.

The table in which students are to record data is placed by itself and exactly where students are told it will be when reading Procedure Step D, Part 3. The table is also not embedded in the text of the activity on page 3, where students will have to constantly flip pages back and forth to find it.

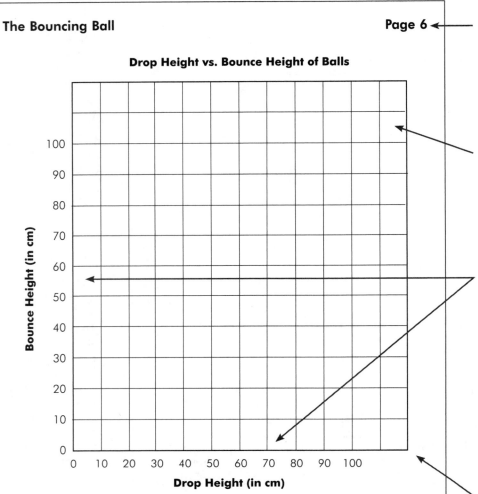

The Bouncing Ball   **Page 6**

Drop Height vs. Bounce Height of Balls

Bounce Height (in cm)

Drop Height (in cm)

The graph is located on the last page, exactly where students are told it will be located (on page 4, beginning in Step H).

The graph paper grid is larger than normal, but still fits within the range of data students will likely collect (and it all still fits on a single page).

The graph grid's axes are prepared ahead of time and labeled for the student. Similarly, scale units are premarked for students.

Students should use colored markers (pencils, pens, etc.) for their graphs. Red markers should be used for RED BALL data, green markers for GREEN BALL data, and blue markers for BLUE BALL data. Other data can be made with black marker, or other colors as desired or needed.

Standards Addressed

NSES Content Standard B (NRC, p. 127); *NSES* Inquiry Standard A (p. 123)

Source

American Association for the Advancement of Science (1961). *Science: A process approach, Grade 3 Module 48.* Washington, DC: Author.

The standards addressed in this activity are included here. They are typically placed on a teacher's page, but since this activity does not have one, the standards are identified here. In addition, the source of the activity is provided.

TESTING FOR SUGARS

Introduction

How can you tell if something contains sugar? Can you tell by simply looking at it or tasting it? Sometimes it isn't safe to taste substances, so we need to rely on a test other than taste. In this activity, you will use Benedict's solution to test for the presence of simple sugars. Benedict's solution is blue in color, but when mixed with sugar and heated, it colors—from yellow to deep red. This change in color is considered a *positive test* for simple sugar.

Materials

Benedict's solution	bread (various types)	potato
milk	cornstarch	Karo syrup (clear)
5 test tubes (Pyrex)	1 25 mL graduated cylinder	1 500 mL beaker
distilled water	1 medicine dropper	1 hot plate
1 test tube holder	1 test tube rack	beaker tongs
1 hot pad	paper towels	

Procedures

A. Prepare a hot water bath. You do this by filling the 500-mL beaker to about 2/3 full with water and placing the beaker on the hot plate. The pouring lip of the beaker should be pointed away from you and anyone else. Turn on the hot plate and bring the water in the beaker to a gentle boil.

B. Place 5 mL of Karo syrup in a clean test tube. Add 5 mL of Benedict's solution.

C. Carefully hold the test tube with the test tube holder and lower the test tube into the hot water. Position the test tube so its opening points away from you and anyone else. See Figure 1.

   NOTE: Be sure to wear your safety goggles and lab apron!

D. Allow the test tube to "cook" for a minute or two. Record the color change that occurs in Table 1.

E. As soon as there is a definite color change in the test tube, remove it from the beaker by using the test tube holder, and place the test tube in the test tube rack.

   NOTE: Benedict's solution will change from blue to other colors when in the presence of sugars and then heated. The more sugar that is present, the more the color changes. Colors for relatively low amounts of simple sugars will be light green to yellow, and those for higher concentrations of sugars will be deep red. See Figure 2.

F. Repeat Procedures A–E for each of the other test substances (potato, milk, bread, cornstarch).

Figure 1   Hot Water Bath Set-Up

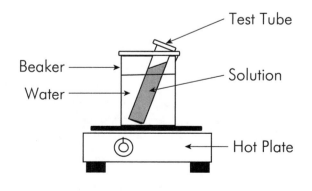

Testing for Sugars

Page 2

Figure 2 Positive Sugar Test Colors*

None   **Low** ←   → **High**
                    Sugar Concentration

Questions

1. Which of the test substances contained simple sugars?
2. List the substances in order of least to most sugar content. How could you tell the sugar contents?

Extension

Test other substances, or other varieties of the substances tested in this activity (e.g., whole milk as compared to skim milk).

Source

Abraham, N., Beidleman, R. G., Moore, J. A., Moores, M., & Utley, W. J. (1970). *Interaction of man & the biosphere: Inquiry in life science.* Chicago: Rand McNally.

Table 1

Test Substance	Observations and Color Changes
Karo syrup	
Cornstarch	
Milk	
Potato	
Bread	

* If students have a color copy , the squares in Figure 2 would show blue, green, yellow, dark yellow, light orange, dark orange, and red.

TESTING FOR SUGARS

Rationale

Have you ever wondered why tree leaves turn so many bright colors in the autumn? Part of the answer is because of the chlorophylls in the leaves. Another part of the answer is the sugars that the leaves produce as food for the tree. How can you tell if something contains sugar? Can you tell by simply looking at it or tasting it? Sometimes it isn't safe to taste substances, so we need to rely on a test other than taste. We wouldn't want to taste tree leaves!

In this activity, you will explore one way of testing for sugars in substances.

Objective

When finished with the activity, the student should be able to

1. explain how to conduct a test for sugar content in a material.

Vocabulary

Benedict's solution

water bath

test tube rack

positive test

test tube holder

concentrations

Materials

safety goggles

Benedict's solution

potato

cornstarch

distilled water

5 test tubes

1 test tube holder

1 500-milliliter beaker (Pyrex)

1 hot plate

paper towels

lab apron

bread (various types)

milk

Karo syrup (clear)

1 medicine dropper

1 test tube rack

1 25-milliliter graduated cylinder

beaker tongs

1 hot pad

Testing for Sugars   **Page 2**

Procedures

- -

Step A

___ 1. **Get** the 500-milliliter beaker.

___ 2. **Fill** the beaker with water to the 300-milliliter mark.

___ 3. **Place** the beaker on the hot plate.

> **CAUTION:** The pouring lip of the beaker should be pointed away from you and anyone else.

> **CAUTION:** Boiling water is very HOT and will burn you. Do not move the beaker when it has boiling water in it!

___ 4. **Turn on** the hot plate and bring the water in the beaker to a gentle boil.

- -

Step B

___ 1. **Using** the graduated cylinder, **place** 5 milliliters of Karo syrup in a clean test tube. Then **clean** the graduated cylinder before using it again.

___ 2. Using the graduated cylinder, **add** 5 milliliters of Benedict's solution to the test tube with the Karo syrup. **Clean** the graduated cylinder.

___ 3. Carefully **hold** the test tube with the test tube holder and **gently lower** the test tube into the hot water.

___ 4. **Position** the test tube so its opening points away from you and anyone else. See Figure 1 below.

> **NOTE:** Be sure to **wear** your safety goggles and lab apron!

Figure 1   Hot Water Bath Set-Up

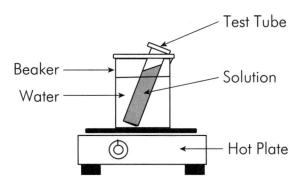

Testing for Sugars

Page 3

Step B (continued)

___ 5. **Allow** the test tube to "cook" for two minutes.

___ 6. Carefully **observe** what happens to the liquid in the test tube as it heats up.

___ 7. As soon as there is a definite color change in the test tube, **remove** it from the beaker by **using** the test tube holder. **Place** the test tube in the test tube rack to cool.

> **NOTES**
> - Benedict's solution will change from blue to other colors when in the presence of sugars and then heated.
> - The more sugar that is present, the more the color changes.
> - Colors for relatively low amounts of simple sugars will be light green to yellow, and those for higher concentrations of sugars will be deep red. See Figure 2 below.

___ 8. **Record** the color change that occurs in Table 1 on page 6.

Figure 2 Positive Sugar Test Colors

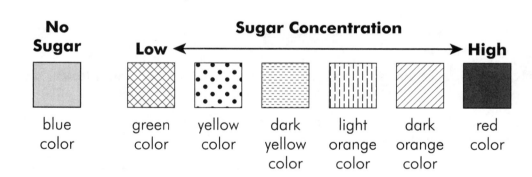

No Sugar	Sugar Concentration					
	Low					High
blue color	green color	yellow color	dark yellow color	light orange color	dark orange color	red color

Testing for Sugars   Page 4

Step C

___ 1. **Add** a small piece of potato and add 5 milliliters of Benedict's solution to another clean test tube.

___ 2. Carefully **hold** the test tube with the test tube holder and gently lower the test tube into the hot water.

___ 3. **Position** the test tube so its opening points away from you and anyone else. See Figure 1 on page 2.

> **NOTE:** Be sure to **wear** your safety goggles and lab apron!

___ 4. **Allow** the test tube to "cook" for two minutes.

___ 5. Carefully **observe** what happens to the liquid in the test tube as it heats up.

___ 6. As soon as there is a definite color change in the test tube, **remove** it from the beaker by **using** the test tube holder. **Place** the test tube in the test tube rack to cool.

___ 7. **Record** the color change that occurs in Table 1 on page 6.

Step D

___ 1. **Add** 5 milliliters of milk and add 5 milliliters of Benedict's solution to another clean test tube.

___ 2. Carefully **hold** the test tube with the test tube holder and gently **lower** the test tube into the hot water.

___ 3. **Position** the test tube so its opening points away from you and anyone else. See Figure 1 on page 2.

> **NOTE:** Be sure to **wear** your safety goggles and lab apron!

___ 4. **Allow** the test tube to "cook" for two minutes.

___ 5. Carefully **observe** what happens to the liquid in the test tube as it heats up.

___ 6. As soon as there is a definite color change in the test tube, **remove** it from the beaker by **using** the test tube holder. **Place** the test tube in the test tube rack to cool.

___ 7. **Record** the color change that occurs in Table 1 on page 6.

Testing for Sugars

Page 5

Step E

___ 1. **Add** a small piece of bread and add 5 milliliters of Benedict's solution to another clean test tube.

___ 2. Carefully **hold** the test tube with the test tube holder and gently lower the test tube into the hot water.

___ 3. **Position** the test tube so its opening points away from you and anyone else. See Figure 1 on page 2.

> **NOTE:** Be sure to **wear** your safety goggles and lab apron!

___ 4. **Allow** the test tube to "cook" for two minutes.

___ 5. Carefully **observe** what happens to the liquid in the test tube as it heats up.

___ 6. As soon as there is a definite color change in the test tube, **remove** it from the beaker by **using** the test tube holder. **Place** the test tube in the test tube rack to cool.

___ 7. **Record** the color change that occurs in Table 1 on page 6.

Step F

___ 1. **Add** a small amount of cornstarch and add 5 milliliters of Benedict's solution to another clean test tube.

___ 2. Carefully **hold** the test tube with the test tube holder and gently **lower** the test tube into the hot water.

___ 3. **Position** the test tube so its opening points away from you and anyone else. See Figure 1 on page 2.

> **NOTE:** Be sure to **wear** your safety goggles and lab apron!

___ 4. **Allow** the test tube to "cook" for two minutes.

___ 5. Carefully **observe** what happens to the liquid in the test tube as it heats up.

___ 6. As soon as there is a definite color change in the test tube, **remove** it from the beaker by **using** the test tube holder. **Place** the test tube in the test tube rack to cool.

___ 7. **Record** the color change that occurs in Table 1 on page 6.

Upper-Elementary Biological Science Activity
Revised Activity: Testing for Sugars

Testing for Sugars   **Page 6**

Table 1

Test Substance	Observations and Color Changes
Karo syrup	
Potato	
Milk	
Bread	
Cornstarch	

Questions

1. Which of the test substances contained simple sugars?

2. List the substances in order of least to most sugar content.

3. How could you tell the amount (or concentration) of sugar in each one?

4. What other substances could you test for sugar content? Explain why you think those substances might contain sugar.

Standards Addressed

NSES Content Standard C (NRC, p. 156); *NSES* Inquiry Standard A (p. 122)

Source

Abraham, N., Beidleman, R. G., Moore, J. A., Moores, M., & Utley, W. J. (1970). *Interaction of man & the biosphere: Inquiry in life science.* Chicago: Rand McNally.

TESTING FOR SUGARS

Rationale

Have you ever wondered why tree leaves turn so many bright colors in the autumn? Part of the answer is because of the chlorophylls in the leaves. Another part of the answer is the sugars that the leaves produce as food for the tree. How can you tell if something contains sugar? Can you tell by simply looking at it or tasting it? Sometimes it isn't safe to taste substances, so we need to rely on a test other than taste. We wouldn't want to taste tree leaves!

In this activity, you will explore one way of testing for sugars in substances.

Objective

When finished with the activity, the student should be able to

1. explain how to conduct a test for sugar content in a material.

Vocabulary

Benedict's solution	positive test
water bath	test tube holder
test tube rack	concentrations

Materials

safety goggles	lab apron
Benedict's solution	bread (various types)
potato	milk
cornstarch	Karo syrup (clear)
distilled water	1 medicine dropper
5 test tubes	1 test tube rack
1 test tube holder	1 25-milliliter graduated cylinder
1 500-milliliter beaker (Pyrex)	beaker tongs
1 hot plate	1 hot pad
paper towels	

The Introduction header changed to Rationale, and expanded to make it more applicable to students' life experiences.

Vocabulary is added to help students focus on important terms used in the activity.

Additional white space is now embedded between the items in the materials list so the list isn't so overwhelming to the student's eye.

Although not readily apparent in this example, the font has been changed. A straight font without curlicue tails is used, and the font size increased to 14 point.

Testing for Sugars   Page 2

Procedures

- -

Step A ←

____ 1. **Get** the 500-milliliter beaker.

____ 2. **Fill** the beaker with water to the 300-milliliter mark.

____ 3. **Place** the beaker on the hot plate.

> **CAUTION:** The pouring lip of the beaker should be pointed away from you and anyone else.

> **CAUTION:** Boiling water is very HOT and will burn you. Do not move the beaker when it has boiling water in it!

____ 4. **Turn on** the hot plate and bring the water in the beaker to a gentle boil.

- -

Step B

____ 1. **Using** the graduated cylinder, **place** 5 milliliters of Karo syrup in a clean test tube. Then **clean** the graduated cylinder before using it again.

____ 2. Using the graduated cylinder, **add** 5 milliliters of Benedict's solution to the test tube with the Karo syrup. **Clean** the graduated cylinder.

____ 3. Carefully **hold** the test tube with the test tube holder and **gently lower** the test tube into the hot water.

____ 4. **Position** the test tube so its opening points away from you and anyone else. See Figure 1 below.

> **NOTE:** Be sure to **wear** your safety goggles and lab apron!

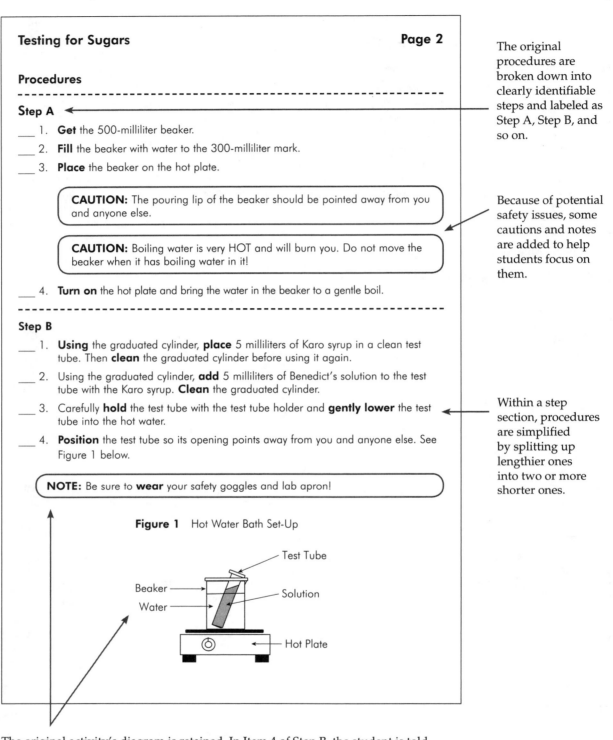

Figure 1 Hot Water Bath Set-Up

Test Tube

Beaker

Water

Solution

Hot Plate

The original procedures are broken down into clearly identifiable steps and labeled as Step A, Step B, and so on.

Because of potential safety issues, some cautions and notes are added to help students focus on them.

Within a step section, procedures are simplified by splitting up lengthier ones into two or more shorter ones.

The original activity's diagram is retained. In Item 4 of Step B, the student is told specifically where to look for the figure being discussed.

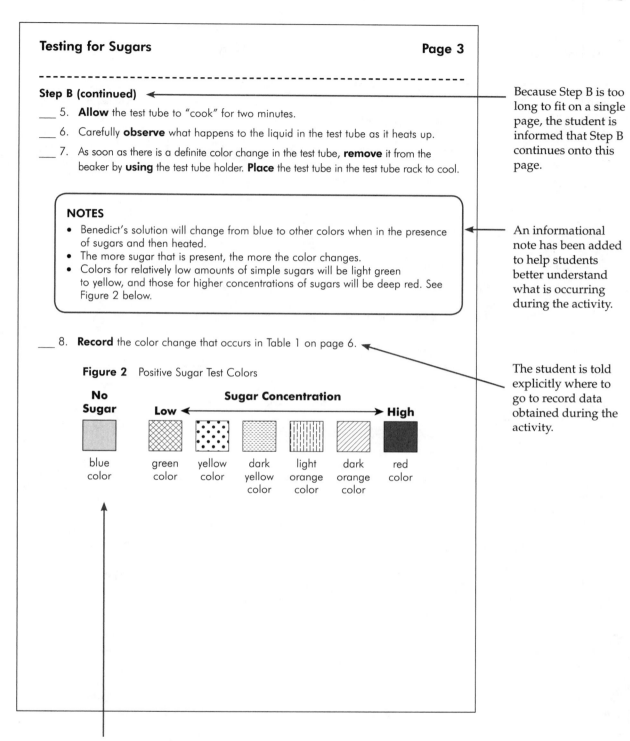

Testing for Sugars   **Page 3**

- -

Step B (continued) ◄─────

___ 5. **Allow** the test tube to "cook" for two minutes.

___ 6. Carefully **observe** what happens to the liquid in the test tube as it heats up.

___ 7. As soon as there is a definite color change in the test tube, **remove** it from the beaker by **using** the test tube holder. **Place** the test tube in the test tube rack to cool.

> **NOTES**
> - Benedict's solution will change from blue to other colors when in the presence of sugars and then heated.
> - The more sugar that is present, the more the color changes.
> - Colors for relatively low amounts of simple sugars will be light green to yellow, and those for higher concentrations of sugars will be deep red. See Figure 2 below.

___ 8. **Record** the color change that occurs in Table 1 on page 6.

Figure 2   Positive Sugar Test Colors

No Sugar		Sugar Concentration				
	Low ◄				► High	
blue color	green color	yellow color	dark yellow color	light orange color	dark orange color	red color

Because Step B is too long to fit on a single page, the student is informed that Step B continues onto this page.

An informational note has been added to help students better understand what is occurring during the activity.

The student is told explicitly where to go to record data obtained during the activity.

The original activity's Figure 2 is modified to include the addition of color labels for each of the color boxes. As in the diagram here, even if the student's handout is in black and white, the color labels serve as a useful guide for what students should see. If the handout is done in color, the color labels will still help students more easily identify and name the colors they see.

In addition, the low to high concentration arrow is now at the top of the figure to help avoid confusing its text with the color labels.

Testing for Sugars   **Page 4**

Step C

___ 1. **Add** a small piece of potato and add 5 milliliters of Benedict's solution to another clean test tube.

___ 2. Carefully **hold** the test tube with the test tube holder and gently lower the test tube into the hot water.

___ 3. **Position** the test tube so its opening points away from you and anyone else. See Figure 1 on page 2.

> **NOTE:** Be sure to **wear** your safety goggles and lab apron!

___ 4. **Allow** the test tube to "cook" for two minutes.

___ 5. Carefully **observe** what happens to the liquid in the test tube as it heats up.

___ 6. As soon as there is a definite color change in the test tube, **remove** it from the beaker by **using** the test tube holder. **Place** the test tube in the test tube rack to cool.

___ 7. **Record** the color change that occurs in Table 1 on page 6.

Step D

___ 1. **Add** 5 milliliters of milk and add 5 milliliters of Benedict's solution to another clean test tube.

___ 2. Carefully **hold** the test tube with the test tube holder and gently **lower** the test tube into the hot water.

___ 3. **Position** the test tube so its opening points away from you and anyone else. See Figure 1 on page 2.

> **NOTE:** Be sure to **wear** your safety goggles and lab apron!

___ 4. **Allow** the test tube to "cook" for two minutes.

___ 5. Carefully **observe** what happens to the liquid in the test tube as it heats up.

___ 6. As soon as there is a definite color change in the test tube, **remove** it from the beaker by **using** the test tube holder. **Place** the test tube in the test tube rack to cool.

___ 7. **Record** the color change that occurs in Table 1 on page 6.

Dashed lines now separate each of the sections for steps. The area between dashed lines comprises a single step of the activity. This helps students focus on one section, or step, at a time.

At the risk of repetition, instructions are repeated in each step section rather than having a single procedure that tells students to repeat Procedures A–E and then listing the other substances to test. The retooled version helps students better follow what they are expected to do.

Students are referred to the specific page on which Figure 1 appears. Some teachers may desire to insert the same figure on each page to help guide students.

Testing for Sugars   **Page 5**

- -

Step E

___ 1. **Add** a small piece of bread and add 5 milliliters of Benedict's solution to another clean test tube.

___ 2. Carefully **hold** the test tube with the test tube holder and gently lower the test tube into the hot water.

___ 3. **Position** the test tube so its opening points away from you and anyone else. See Figure 1 on page 2.

> **NOTE:** Be sure to **wear** your safety goggles and lab apron!

___ 4. **Allow** the test tube to "cook" for two minutes.

___ 5. Carefully **observe** what happens to the liquid in the test tube as it heats up.

___ 6. As soon as there is a definite color change in the test tube, **remove** it from the beaker by **using** the test tube holder. **Place** the test tube in the test tube rack to cool.

___ 7. **Record** the color change that occurs in Table 1 on page 6.

- -

Step F

___ 1. **Add** a small amount of cornstarch and add 5 milliliters of Benedict's solution to another clean test tube.

___ 2. Carefully **hold** the test tube with the test tube holder and gently **lower** the test tube into the hot water.

___ 3. **Position** the test tube so its opening points away from you and anyone else. See Figure 1 on page 2.

> **NOTE:** Be sure to **wear** your safety goggles and lab apron!

___ 4. **Allow** the test tube to "cook" for two minutes.

___ 5. Carefully **observe** what happens to the liquid in the test tube as it heats up.

___ 6. As soon as there is a definite color change in the test tube, **remove** it from the beaker by **using** the test tube holder. **Place** the test tube in the test tube rack to cool.

___ 7. **Record** the color change that occurs in Table 1 on page 6.

Blank lines now appear to the left of each procedure. Students can check off blanks as they complete procedures. This helps students keep better track of what they have completed and what they have remaining to do.

Safety notes continue with each step.

Key action verbs are now highlighted (put in boldface) to emphasize actions to students.

Additional white space now appears between procedures. This helps the page be less busy to the eye, and helps students read it more easily.

Testing for Sugars   **Page 6**

Table 1

Test Substance	Observations and Color Changes
Karo syrup	
Potato	
Milk	
Bread	
Cornstarch	

The data table changed and now lists the test substances in the same order as students are asked to test them throughout the procedural steps of the activity. In addition, extra space allows students to write in their observations.

Questions

1. Which of the test substances contained simple sugars?

2. List the substances in order of least to most sugar content.

3. How could you tell the amount (or concentration) of sugar in each one?

4. What other substances could you test for sugar content? Explain why you think those substances might contain sugar.

Spaces for answers beneath each question help alleviate problems students may have with transferring the questions to a sheet of notebook paper, or with confusing which answers go with which questions.

Standards Addressed

NSES Content Standard C (NRC, p. 156); *NSES* Inquiry Standard A (p. 122)

Source

Abraham, N., Beidleman, R. G., Moore, J. A., Moores, M., & Utley, W. J. (1970). *Interaction of man & the biosphere: Inquiry in life science.* Chicago: Rand McNally.

The questions are slightly modified to make them clearer. Additionally, a fourth question replaces the extensions component in the original activity. If desired, students can proceed to investigate other substances they might list in their answer for Question 4. Question 4 also goes further by asking students to use higher-level thinking to "explain" their answers.

RADIOACTIVE DATING AND HALF-LIFE

Introduction

Many of the events of the geologic past have only been given a definite date since the discovery of a material to tell time with naturally radioactive materials. A rock or other material receives its maximum charge, or radioactive isotopes (forms of elements that give off radiation), at the time of their formation. Since the change from the radioactive form to a nonradioactive form occurs when each atom gives off radiation, the amount of radiation and the number of radioactive atoms in the materials lessens as time passes. For each type of radioactive atom, the rate of change occurs at a known rate called the **half-life**. Therefore, if we know how many radioactive atoms are present now, and can measure the number of atoms produced by radioactive atoms that have changed to nonradioactive forms, we can (a) predict how many radioactive atoms were originally present, and (b) measure the time that has passed since the material was originally formed.

Materials

1 shoe box   50 pennies   2 sheets of graph paper

Procedures

1. You will receive a tray with 50 pennies (count them—you are responsible for the correct number being present). Place all the coins that *face up* in the shoe box. These represent radioactive atoms. Place the lid on the shoe box and shake for a short period of time (three or four good shakes). Be sure to hold the lid on securely as you shake the box! This shaking represents one half-life. Remove the lid and remove all pennies that *face down*. Count the number of pennies remaining in the tray. Record this number as "Time Period 1" ("Time Period 0" was the 50 pennies you started with before shaking the tray) in Table 1. You may have to redraw Table 1 on the back of this page to get all your data on it. Repeat this procedure without returning any pennies to the shoe box, and *record the number of coins left that face up*. Repeat again and again until none are left that face up.

2. Replace all 50 pennies in the tray and repeat Procedure 1. Add together the number of coins that face up for each time period to represent what would have happened if you had used 100 pennies (i.e., add the first "Time Period 1" to the second "Time Period 1" to get a total for "Time Period 1"). Be sure to record your TOTAL in Table 1. You may need to redraw Table 1 on the back of this page to have enough room for your data.

3. Prepare a graph as follows: Along the vertical edge (long edge) on the graph paper, label the scale "Percent Radioactivity Remaining" and let each square equal 2%. Label the horizontal scale as "Time Periods" and let 2 squares equal 1 time period.

4. Make a second graph exactly like the first, except this graphed line will represent what would happen if the pennies had behaved in a *perfect* manner and the correct number of pennies had changed each time (exactly 50% each time). Note: you may use a different color and plot this line on Graph 1.

Radioactive Dating and Half-Life   Page 2

Table 1

Time Period	Number Remaining 1st 50 Pennies	Number Remaining 2nd 50 Pennies	Number Remaining Total Pennies
0	50	50	100
1			
2			

Questions

1. Each time period on your graph could be called a "half-life." Define "half-life."

2. What percent of the original radioactive material would remain after

    (a) one half-life?   (b) two half-lives?   (c) four half-lives?   (d) five half-lives?

3. Suppose each half-life was 1,600 years. How many years must pass before the amount of radioactive material is reduced to 25%?

4. If the half-life is 40 minutes, how much radioactive material will remain after 200 minutes?

RADIOACTIVE DATING AND HALF-LIFE

Introduction

A rock receives its maximum amount of radioactive isotopes at the time it forms. An isotope is a form of an element that gives off radiation. The isotope of an element will change to a nonradioactive form when each atom gives off radiation. The amount of radiation and the number of radioactive atoms in the rock lessens as time passes. This change occurs at a known rate. This rate is called the **half-life**.

Rationale

If we know how many radioactive atoms are present now, and can measure the number of atoms produced by radioactive atoms that have changed to nonradioactive forms, we can predict how many radioactive atoms were originally present. We can also calculate the time that has passed since the material was originally formed.

In this activity, you will use pennies to simulate radioactive decay. The pennies represent atoms. When they flip over, that represents radioactive decay. You will use this information to determine the half-life of the set of pennies.

Objectives

After completing this activity, you should be able to

1. **define** what is meant by "half-life,"

2. **determine** the half-life of a set of pennies,

3. **make** a graph of pennies' half-life,

4. **use** the graph to **predict** the amount of radioactive material, and

5. **use** the half-life graph to **determine** the amount of time that passed since a material was originally formed.

Vocabulary

atom	element	half-life
isotopes	radioactive decay	

Materials

1 shoe box	100 pennies	2 sheets of graph paper

Radioactive Dating and Half-Life   Page 2

Procedures

- -

Step A

___ 1. **Get** a container of 100 pennies.

___ 2. **Count** the pennies to **be sure** you have all 100.

___ 3. **Get** the shoe box and remove the lid.

___ 4. **Put** the pennies in the shoe box.

___ 5. **Place** all the pennies so their face side is up.

___ 6. **Put** the lid on the shoe box.

___ 7. **Pick up** the shoe box, and **hold** the lid on tight.

___ 8. **Shake** the shoe box up and down with three or four good shakes.

> **NOTE:** The shaking of the shoe box represents one half-life.

___ 9. **Put** the shoe box on the table and remove the lid.

___ 10. **Look** into the shoe box at the pennies.

___ 11. **Remove** all the pennies that have flipped over and that now face down. See Figure 1 below.

___ 12. **Count** the number of pennies remaining in the shoe box.

___ 13. **Record** this number of pennies in Table 1 on page 5.

> **NOTE:** "Time Period 0" was when you had 100 pennies all that face up before you shook the shoe box.

Figure 1

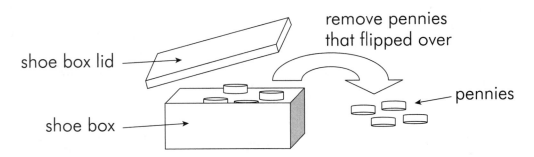

shoe box lid

remove pennies that flipped over

pennies

shoe box

Radioactive Dating and Half-Life   **Page 3**

- -

Step B

___ 1. **Repeat** the procedures, but now **use** only the pennies remaining in the shoe box.

___ 2. **Put** the lid on the shoe box.

___ 3. **Pick up** the shoe box, and **hold** the lid on tight.

___ 4. **Shake** the shoe box up and down with three or four good shakes.

> **NOTE:** The shaking of the shoe box represents one half-life.

___ 5. **Put** the shoe box on the table and remove the lid.

___ 6. **Look** into the shoe box at the pennies.

___ 7. **Remove** all the pennies that have flipped over and that now face down.

___ 8. **Count** the number of pennies remaining in the shoe box.

___ 9. **Record** this number of pennies in Table 1 on page 5.

- -

Step C

___ 1. **Repeat** the procedures described in Steps A and B.
Each time, be sure to **remove** the pennies that have flipped over.
Each time, be sure to **record** your data in Table 1 on page 5.

___ 2. **Continue** repeating the procedures until you have no pennies left that face up in the shoe box.

- -

Step D

___ 1. **Use** the data in Table 1 to **make** a graph. Go to page 6.

___ 2. **Make** a *second* line on the graph.

- This second graphed line will represent what would happen if the pennies had behaved in a *perfect* manner and the correct number of pennies had changed each time (exactly 50% each time, or exactly half the pennies flip over each time).

- **Make** this second line in a different color than the first line you graphed.

Radioactive Dating and Half-Life   **Page 4**

Questions

1. Each time period on your graph could be called a "half-life." Define "half-life."

2. What percent of the original radioactive material would remain after

   (a) one half-life?

   (b) two half-lives?

   (c) four half-lives?

   (d) five half-lives?

3. Suppose each half-life was 1,600 years. How many years must pass before the amount of radioactive material is reduced to 25%?

4. If the half-life is 40 minutes, how much radioactive material will remain after 200 minutes?

Upper-Elementary Earth Science Activity
Revised Activity: Radioactive Dating and Half-Life

Standards Addressed

NSES Grades 5–8 Content Standard D (NRC, p. 160); *NSES* Grades 9–12 Content Standard B (p. 178) and D (p. 189); *NSES* Grades 5–8 Inquiry Standard A (pp. 145, 148); *NSES* Grades 9–12 Inquiry Standard A (pp. 175–176)

Source

American Geological Institute. (1973). Section 15–4: Investigating radioactive decay rates. *Investigating the earth.* Boston: Houghton-Mifflin.

Radioactive Dating and Half-Life   **Page 5**

Table 1

Time Period #	TOTAL 100 (Number of Pennies Remaining in Box)
0	100
1	
2	
3	
4	
5	
6	
7	
8	
9	
10	
11	
12	
13	
14	
15	
16	
17	
18	

NOTE: You may not need all 18 lines in the data table. You may need more. If you need more, simply add more on the back of this page.

Radioactive Dating and Half-Life

Half-Life Graph of Pennies

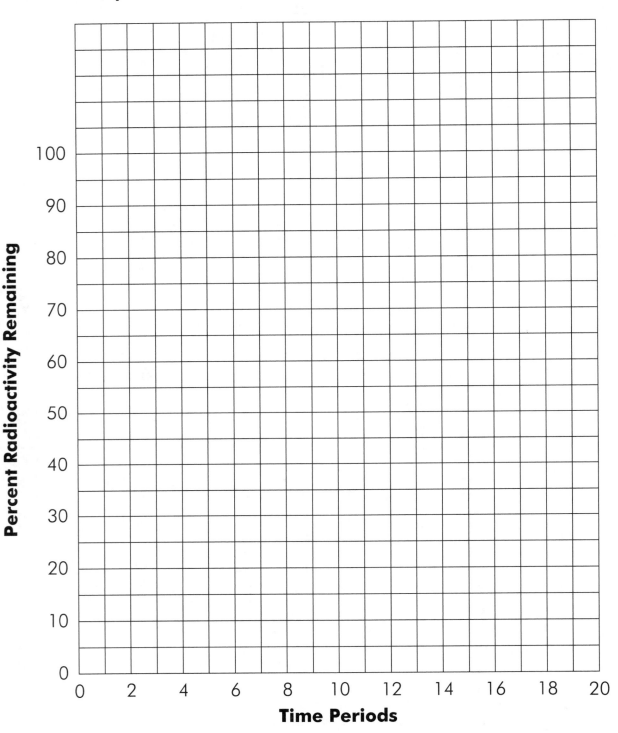

RADIOACTIVE DATING AND HALF-LIFE

Introduction

A rock receives its maximum amount of radioactive isotopes at the time it forms. An isotope is a form of an element that gives off radiation. The isotope of an element will change to a nonradioactive form when each atom gives off radiation. The amount of radiation and the number of radioactive atoms in the rock lessens as time passes. This change occurs at a known rate. This rate is called the **half-life**.

For this activity, including both an Introduction section and a Rationale section now provides more clarity to set the stage for the student.

Rationale

If we know how many radioactive atoms are present now, and can measure the number of atoms produced by radioactive atoms that have changed to nonradioactive forms, we can predict how many radioactive atoms were originally present. We can also calculate the time that has passed since the material was originally formed.

In this activity, you will use pennies to simulate radioactive decay. The pennies represent atoms. When they flip over, that represents radioactive decay. You will use this information to determine the half-life of the set of pennies.

Objectives

After completing this activity, you should be able to

1. **define** what is meant by "half-life,"
2. **determine** the half-life of a set of pennies,
3. **make** a graph of pennies' half-life,
4. **use** the graph to **predict** the amount of radioactive material, and
5. **use** the half-life graph to **determine** the amount of time that passed since a material was originally formed.

Vocabulary

atom	element	half-life
isotopes	radioactive decay	

Vocabulary terms are identified and inserted to help students.

Materials

1 shoe box	100 pennies	2 sheets of graph paper

- Although not clear on this copy, the font changed to one having few serifs and enlarged to 14-point size.

Radioactive Dating and Half-Life   **Page 2**

Procedures

- -

Step A

____ 1.   **Get** a container of 100 pennies.

____ 2.   **Count** the pennies to **be sure** you have all 100.

____ 3.   **Get** the shoe box and remove the lid.

____ 4.   **Put** the pennies in the shoe box.

____ 5.   **Place** all the pennies so their face side is up.

____ 6.   **Put** the lid on the shoe box.

____ 7.   **Pick up** the shoe box, and **hold** the lid on tight.

____ 8.   **Shake** the shoe box up and down with three or four good shakes.

> **NOTE:** The shaking of the shoe box represents one half-life.

____ 9.   **Put** the shoe box on the table and remove the lid.

____ 10. **Look** into the shoe box at the pennies.

____ 11. **Remove** all the pennies that have flipped over and that now face down. See Figure 1 below.

____ 12. **Count** the number of pennies remaining in the shoe box.

____ 13. **Record** this number of pennies in Table 1 on page 5.

> **NOTE:** "Time Period 0" was when you had 100 pennies all that face up before you shook the shoe box.

Figure 1

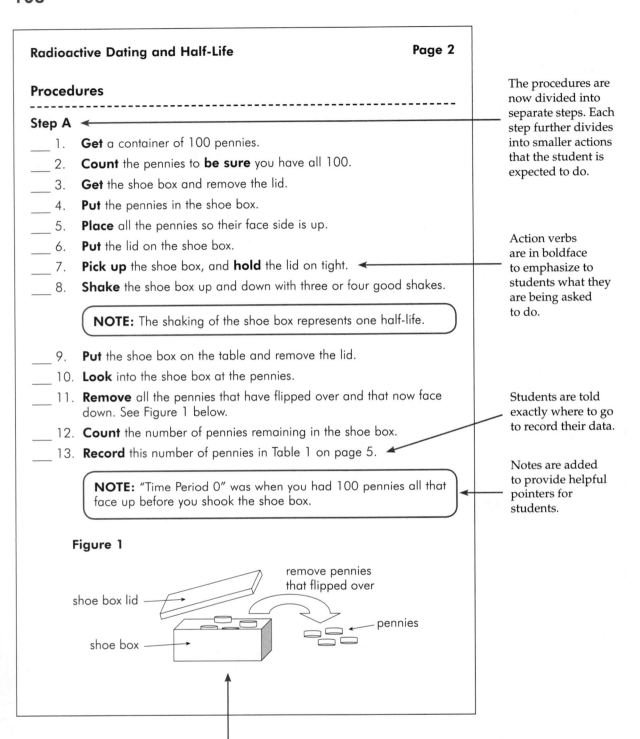

The procedures are now divided into separate steps. Each step further divides into smaller actions that the student is expected to do.

Action verbs are in boldface to emphasize to students what they are being asked to do.

Students are told exactly where to go to record their data.

Notes are added to provide helpful pointers for students.

A figure helps students visualize what they are being asked to do in the procedural steps of the activity.

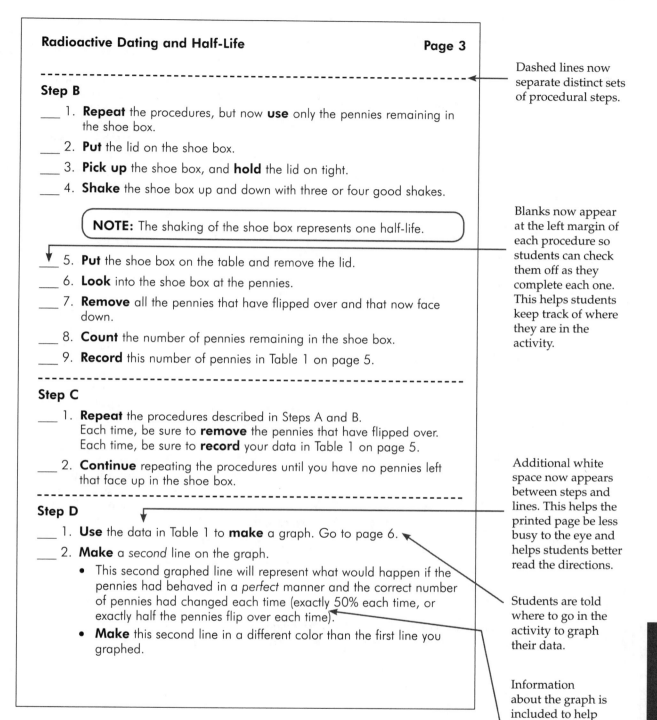

Radioactive Dating and Half-Life   **Page 3**

- ← Dashed lines now separate distinct sets of procedural steps.

Step B

___ 1. **Repeat** the procedures, but now **use** only the pennies remaining in the shoe box.

___ 2. **Put** the lid on the shoe box.

___ 3. **Pick up** the shoe box, and **hold** the lid on tight.

___ 4. **Shake** the shoe box up and down with three or four good shakes.

> **NOTE:** The shaking of the shoe box represents one half-life.

___ 5. **Put** the shoe box on the table and remove the lid.

___ 6. **Look** into the shoe box at the pennies.

___ 7. **Remove** all the pennies that have flipped over and that now face down.

___ 8. **Count** the number of pennies remaining in the shoe box.

___ 9. **Record** this number of pennies in Table 1 on page 5.

- -

Step C

___ 1. **Repeat** the procedures described in Steps A and B.
Each time, be sure to **remove** the pennies that have flipped over.
Each time, be sure to **record** your data in Table 1 on page 5.

___ 2. **Continue** repeating the procedures until you have no pennies left that face up in the shoe box.

- -

Step D

___ 1. **Use** the data in Table 1 to **make** a graph. Go to page 6.

___ 2. **Make** a *second* line on the graph.

- This second graphed line will represent what would happen if the pennies had behaved in a *perfect* manner and the correct number of pennies had changed each time (exactly 50% each time, or exactly half the pennies flip over each time).

- **Make** this second line in a different color than the first line you graphed.

Blanks now appear at the left margin of each procedure so students can check them off as they complete each one. This helps students keep track of where they are in the activity.

Additional white space now appears between steps and lines. This helps the printed page be less busy to the eye and helps students better read the directions.

Students are told where to go in the activity to graph their data.

Information about the graph is included to help guide students. In the original, students were asked to make a second graph. In this revision, the idea is to make the graphed lines on the same grid for easier comparison of data.

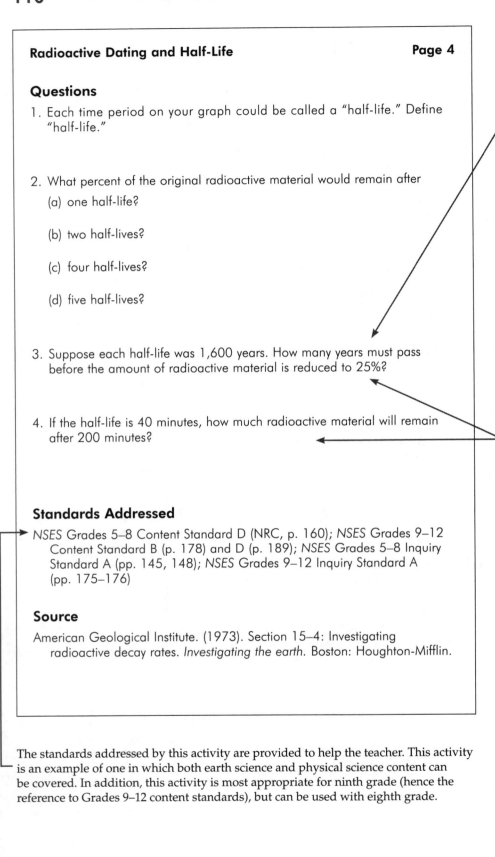

Radioactive Dating and Half-Life   **Page 4**

Questions

1. Each time period on your graph could be called a "half-life." Define "half-life."

2. What percent of the original radioactive material would remain after

   (a) one half-life?

   (b) two half-lives?

   (c) four half-lives?

   (d) five half-lives?

3. Suppose each half-life was 1,600 years. How many years must pass before the amount of radioactive material is reduced to 25%?

4. If the half-life is 40 minutes, how much radioactive material will remain after 200 minutes?

Standards Addressed

NSES Grades 5–8 Content Standard D (NRC, p. 160); *NSES* Grades 9–12 Content Standard B (p. 178) and D (p. 189); *NSES* Grades 5–8 Inquiry Standard A (pp. 145, 148); *NSES* Grades 9–12 Inquiry Standard A (pp. 175–176)

Source

American Geological Institute. (1973). Section 15–4: Investigating radioactive decay rates. *Investigating the earth*. Boston: Houghton-Mifflin.

The questions are clarified, and additional space now allows students to write their answers immediately following each question. This helps reduce the likelihood that students will make errors in transcription or with correlating answers on a different sheet of paper.

Questions 3 and 4 may require prompts from the teacher. Teachers may need to show students how to prepare a table that shows half-lives in one column with corresponding percentages of radioactive material in the second column, and then use that table to answer the questions.

The standards addressed by this activity are provided to help the teacher. This activity is an example of one in which both earth science and physical science content can be covered. In addition, this activity is most appropriate for ninth grade (hence the reference to Grades 9–12 content standards), but can be used with eighth grade.

Upper-Elementary Earth Science Activity
Annotated Revised Activity: Radioactive Dating and Half-Life

Radioactive Dating and Half-Life   **Page 5**

Table 1

Time Period #	TOTAL 100 (Number of Pennies Remaining in Box)
0	100
1	.
2	
3	
4	
5	
6	
7	
8	
9	
10	
11	
12	
13	
14	
15	
16	
17	
18	

NOTE: You may not need all 18 lines in the data table. You may need more. If you need more, simply add more on the back of this page.

The data table expanded and its format is clarified. In addition, enough lines now appear on the table so that most students' data can be accommodated here. The spaces in the data table allow students to more easily record their data. Table column headings also now clarify what data should be entered into the table.

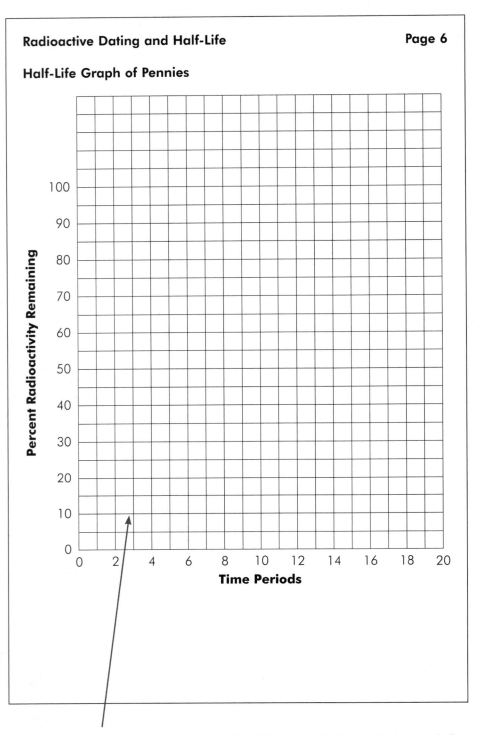

Radioactive Dating and Half-Life Page 6

Half-Life Graph of Pennies

In the original activity, students were simply told to graph their data. In the retooled version, a grid with labeled axes is provided to help students. In the original, the graph axes can prove to be particularly difficult for students to make (especially determining the units for spacing purposes).

MYSTERY POWDERS

Grade Level

This activity is designed for upper-elementary levels (Grades 3–6).

Topic Area

Chemistry and describing and analyzing the properties of matter.

Rationale

The purpose of this activity is to provide students an opportunity to inquire about the observable properties of some common household powders and to investigate some physical and chemical tests for each one.

Concepts

Common household materials have different physical properties and react in certain ways with other substances (i.e., chemicals).

Thinking and Process Skills

Observing and describing properties of materials. Recording and communicating observations. Classifying or sorting the powders on a test mat. Developing proper lab techniques to ensure safety and avoid contamination. Manipulating variables. Collecting and analyzing data. Communicating results. Reflecting on experiences through writing and discussion.

Tools of Science

Learning how to use a magnifying glass.

Materials (per student or per group)

1 test mat (plastic)	1 sheet black of construction paper	1 magnifying lens per student
1 tray	2 sheets of waxed paper	5 toothpicks
1 dropper bottle of vinegar	1 sheet white paper	5 wood splints
1 dropper bottle of water	1 dropper bottle of iodine	1 marker/pencil
1 candle or other heat source	1 clothespin (spring type)	5 aluminum foil squares (5 × 5 cm)
1 slice of bread (white) or 1 white saltine cracker		
1 set of five white powders in cups (baking powder, baking soda, cornstarch, salt, granulated sugar)		

Procedures

A. Identifying Physical Properties

1. Provide the set of white powders to students. Be sure each cup is marked with a number so they can be easily identified later.

2. Have students examine the powders. Be sure to discuss proper safety procedures, such as not tasting anything unless the teacher says it is okay to do so. Demonstrate safe tasting procedures, safe smelling procedures, etc.

Mystery Powders

3. Be sure students record their observations in a chart. After some time examining the powders, give students the magnifying lenses and let them continue examining the powders. When students are finished, have them share their observations. Lead them to answer the following questions if they are not already offered by students:

   a. How are the powders alike?
   b. How are the powders different?
   c. Do all the powders feel the same? Describe how they feel.
   d. Does any powder have an odor? Describe any odors.
   e. Are all the powders the same shade of white?
   f. Can you list three properties of each powder? What are they?
   g. Can you list more than three properties of each powder? What are they?
   h. Are all the powders really powders?

4. Allow students to speculate about what they think each powder may be.

5. Consider allowing students to bring in known powders from home to compare with the mystery powders. This may help students begin to identify what each powder is. If you do this, be sure students bring their powders in either their original containers or in containers with clearly marked labels identifying what the powder is. After comparisons, any powders remaining unidentified should be referred to by their cup numbers.

6. Have students place the white paper on the desk and draw circles on the paper. Each circle should be about the size of a quarter. Then, have students place a sheet of wax paper over the white paper. This will be the test mat. An alternative is to prepare paper test mats in advance and have them laminated.

7. Explain to students they are to use the test mat and wooden splints with the powders. The wooden splints can be used as scoops to place small samples of powder on the test mat.

B. Testing the Effects of Water

8. Have students investigate the effect of water on each of the powders. Be sure students write down their observations. (Students may use toothpicks to stir the water into each powder. Be sure students use a clean toothpick for each powder so as to not contaminate one with the other.) Questions you might ask can include:

   a. What happens to each powder when you put a few drops of water on it? What happened when you put a large amount of water on the powder?
   b. Did each powder mix with water? Which ones did and which ones didn't?
   c. Did any of the powders disappear in water? Which one(s)?
   d. Did you use the same amount of powder each time? Is this important?

(**Note:** Baking soda, baking powder, salt, and sugar are soluble in water. Cornstarch is not.)

9. Have students place their wet powders on a tray and store the trays overnight. The next day, have students again examine the powders and record their observations.

C. Testing the Effects of Heat

10. Provide students with a heat sources. A small candle supported by a lump of clay will provide sufficient heat to test the powders.

11. Discuss safety procedures when using heat sources and/or open flames. Discuss the importance of testing only dry powders to avoid spattering, and not testing any powders that have been mixed with any liquid.

12. Have students take the aluminum foil and make it into the shape of a bowl. Clamp the clothespin onto one edge of the aluminum bowl. Adjust the clothespin so it is like a panhandle. Demonstrate how this is done.

13. Have students place a small sample of one powder in one aluminum bowl and heat it. Have students observe what happens to the powder and record their observations. Students should heat the powders until no more change occurs—approximately several minutes. Be sure

Mystery Powders   **Page 3**

to alert students to not set the hot aluminum bowl on top of anything that will burn (even though it should cool off quickly). Then have students repeat the same procedure with each of the other powders.

(**Note:** Baking soda seems to remain unchanged; salt snaps and crackles; cornstarch turns brown and smells like burnt toast; sugar melts and bubbles and may smoke and might smell like caramel, burns brown and/or black, and finally hardens.)

D. Testing the Effects of Iodine

14. Have students make a clean test mat. Be sure the circles are numbered to correspond with the numbers of the powders. Have one extra circle for a small piece of bread or a cracker.

15. Have students place a few drops of iodine on the piece of bread. Note the results (the bread or cracker should turn dark blue or black). Explain to students this is a "positive" test for starch.

16. Have students place small samples of each powder on the powders' respective circles. Be sure students use about the same amounts of powder for each.

17. Let students drop several drops of iodine on each powder. Have them record any observations they make.

18. As a safety note, be sure to tell students to NOT taste anything with which iodine has been mixed.

(**Note:** Starch will turn dark blue/black when iodine is added to it. The more starch in the substance being tested, the darker the blue/black will appear.)

E. Testing the Effects of Vinegar

19. Have students obtain a clean test mat. Be sure the circles are numbered to correspond with the numbers of the powders. Have one extra circle for a small sample of baking soda.

20. Have students place a few drops of vinegar on the baking soda. Note the results (the baking soda should bubble and fizz). Explain to students this is a "positive" test for baking soda.

21. Have students place small samples of each powder on the powders' respective circles. Be sure students use about the same amounts of powder for each.

22. Let students drop several drops of vinegar on each powder. Have them record any observations they make.

23. If students don't offer all the observations you desire, consider asking the following questions:
    a. What happens when you put a few drops of vinegar on each powder?
    b. Did any powder react more than the others? If so, which one?
    c. Do you think powders that dissolved in water will also dissolve in vinegar? Explain why you think so.
    d. Which powder do you think will take the least amount of vinegar to dissolve? The most vinegar? How can you find out?
    e. How can vinegar be used to distinguish baking soda from other powders?

F. Discussing Physical and Chemical Properties

24. Discuss with students the difference between chemical and physical properties of a substance.

25. Discuss with students the difference between chemical and physical changes. (In a physical change, the original material may be altered in its shape or size, but it remains the same material. In a chemical change, the original material becomes something different.)

(**Note:** Changes such as cornstarch turning dark when iodine is added or baking soda bubbling or fizzing when vinegar is added are examples of chemical changes. The dissolving of sugar or salt in water are examples of physical changes.)

Source

Elementary Science Study. (1974). *Mystery powders.* New York: McGraw-Hill.

Mystery Powders

Mystery Powders

Powder	Observations of Powder	Mixed With Water	Powder When Heated	Powder With Iodine	Powder With Vinegar
1					
2					
3					
4					
5					

MYSTERY POWDERS

Rationale

Suppose you are in a friend's kitchen and have a recipe you want to make. As you begin to look in the cupboard for ingredients, you notice that your friend has placed all the spices and baking supplies in plastic containers with lids, but didn't save the original packages. Your friend also forgot to label each container. Before you begin making your recipe, you need to determine what is in the containers, so how can you determine what is in them?

The purpose of this activity is to provide you an opportunity to inquire about the observable properties of some common household powders and to investigate some physical and chemical tests for each one. The results of your investigation should then make it possible for you to identify the powders.

Standards Addressed

NSES Grades K–4 Content Standard B (NRC, p. 127) and K–4 Inquiry Standard A (pp. 122–123); or *NSES* Grades 5–8 Content Standard B (p. 154) and Inquiry Standard A (pp. 145–148)

Vocabulary

physical property   chemical property   technique   iodine   vinegar

Objectives

After completing this activity, the student should be able to

1. **use** simple tests on common household materials to **determine** their properties,
2. **follow** proper lab techniques to ensure safety and avoid contamination,
3. **collect** and **analyze** data and **communicate** results, and
4. **draw conclusions** about the identity of common materials based on simple tests.

Materials (per student or per group)

1 test mat (black, plastic)

1 dropper bottle of vinegar

1 dropper bottle of distilled water

1 candle or other heat source

1 magnifying lens

1 marker or pencil

5 aluminum foil squares (5 cm x 5 cm)

2 sheets of waxed paper

1 sheet of white paper

1 dropper bottle of iodine solution

1 clothespin (spring type)

5 toothpicks

safety goggles

1 slice of bread (white) or 1 white saltine cracker

1 set of five white powders in cups (baking powder, baking soda, cornstarch, salt, granulated sugar)

Mystery Powders

Page 2

Procedures

Step A: Identifying Physical Properties of Powders

___ 1. **Get** the set of five cups of white powders. Be sure each cup is **marked with a number** so you can easily identify each cup later.

___ 2. **Select** one cup of powder and examine it.

___ 3. To examine the powder, **put** your test mat on the table. **Put** a small sample of the powder on the test mat. **Use** a toothpick to pull powder from the cup onto the mat. You may want to **use** the magnifying lens and other materials to make observations.

> **IMPORTANT NOTES!**
> - Be sure to **wear** your safety goggles.
> - **DO NOT taste** anything unless the teacher tells you it is okay to do so.
> - **Use** proper technique for smelling any of the powders.
> - **Wash** your hands thoroughly if you get powders on them.
> - **Clean up** any powder you might spill on the tabletop.

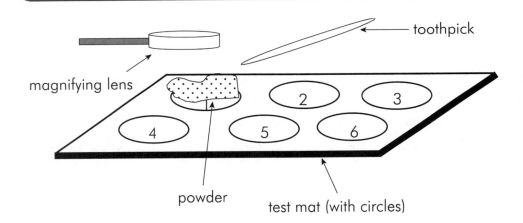

toothpick

magnifying lens

powder

test mat (with circles)

___ 4. **Write** your observations about the powder in Observation Table 1 on the last page of this activity (page 9).

___ 5. **Pick** a second powder and **examine** it. Be sure to **write** your observations in Table 1 on page 9.

___ 6. **Select** a third powder and **examine** it. Be sure to **write** your observations in Table 1 on page 9.

___ 7. **Get** the fourth powder and **examine** it. **Write** your observations in Table 1.

___ 8. **Get** the fifth powder and **examine** it. **Write** your observations in Table 1 (page 9).

___ 9. When you are finished examining all the powders, **clean** your mat as the teacher tells you.

Mystery Powders   **Page 3**

QUESTIONS about Step A: Physical Properties of Powders

Read each of the following questions. Then write your answers in the spaces below each question.

a. How are the powders alike?

b. How are the powders different?

c. Do all the powders feel the same? Describe how they feel.

d. Does any powder have an odor? Describe any odors.

e. Are all the powders the same shade of white?

f. Can you list three properties of each powder? What are they?

g. Are all the powders really powders? Explain why you think this.

h. What do you think each powder is? (For example, what is Powder 1?) Why do you think this?

Mystery Powders   **Page 4**

- -

Step B: Testing the Effects of Water on the Powders

___ 1. **Pick** one of the powders and put a small sample of it on your testing mat.

___ 2. **Add** 4–5 drops of water to the powder. **Use** a toothpick to stir the water into the powder.

___ 3. **Write** your observations about the powder in Table 1 on page 9.

___ 4. **Pick** a second powder and **put** a small sample of it on your testing mat.

___ 5. **Add** 4–5 drops of water to the second powder. **Use** a toothpick to stir the water into the powder.

___ 6. **Write** your observations about the second powder in Table 1 on page 9.

___ 7. Now, **repeat** Procedures 4, 5, and 6 for a third powder.

___ 8. **Pick** a fourth powder and **repeat** Procedures 4, 5, and 6.

___ 9. **Take** the fifth powder and **repeat** Procedures 4, 5, and 6.

___ 10. Do not clean your testing mat. **Put** your name on it and place the mat where your teacher tells you. Tomorrow, **make** more observations about each powder that had water added to it. Be sure to **record** your observations in Table 1 on page 9.

QUESTIONS about Step B: Testing the Effects of Water on the Powders

Read each of the following questions. Then write your answers in the spaces below each question.

a. What happens to each powder when you put a few drops of water on it?

b. Did each powder mix with water?

c. Which ones did and which ones didn't mix with water?

d. Did any of the powders disappear in water? If so, which one(s)?

e. Why might it be important to use the same amount of powder each time?

Mystery Powders **Page 5**

Step C: Testing the Effects of Heat on Powders

___ 1. **Obtain** a heat source. This might be a small candle supported by a lump of clay.

> **CAUTION**: If you use a candle, be very careful with the flame. Keep your fingers, clothing, and hair away from the flame. Do not throw matches into the trash. Test only dry powders. Do not heat any powders that have been mixed with any liquid. Always wear your eye goggles!

___ 2. **Get** the small piece of aluminum foil and **make** it into the shape of a bowl.

___ 3. **Take** the clothespin and make it **pinch** one edge of the foil bowl. **Adjust** the clothespin so it is like a panhandle.

___ 4. **Place** a small sample of the first powder in the aluminum foil bowl.

___ 5. **Light** the candle, and then **pick up** the aluminum foil bowl by using only the clothespin handle.

___ 6. **Carefully hold** the aluminum foil bowl over the candle flame to heat the powder inside the foil bowl. You may need to **hold** the foil bowl over the flame for several minutes.

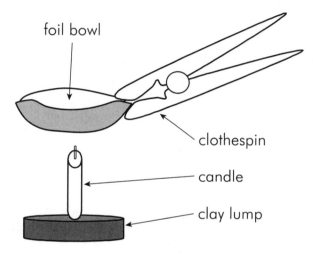

foil bowl

clothespin

candle

clay lump

> **CAUTION:** Do not touch the foil bowl or the powder with your fingers! It will be hot. Do not look directly down into the foil bowl at the powder.

___ 7. **Observe** what happens to the powder in the foil bowl. When you are finished heating the powder, **put** the foil bowl on a hot pad to cool.

___ 8. **Record** your observations in Table 1 on page 9.

___ 9. **Get** a new piece of aluminum foil, and **get** the second powder.

___ 10. **Repeat** Procedures 2, 3, 4, 5, 6, and 7 for the second powder.

___ 11. **Take** the third powder and **repeat** Procedures 2, 3, 4, 5, 6, and 7.

___ 12. **Take** the fourth powder and **repeat** Procedures 2, 3, 4, 5, 6, and 7.

___ 13. **Take** the fifth powder and **repeat** Procedures 2, 3, 4, 5, 6, and 7.

Mystery Powders   **Page 6**

Step D: Testing the Effects of Iodine on Powders

___ 1. **Get** a clean testing mat. Be sure the circles on the testing mat are numbered. The mat should have one circle for each powder, plus one extra circle.

___ 2. **Put** a small piece of bread or cracker in the extra circle on the testing mat.

___ 3. **Take** the bottle of iodine and **add** 3 drops to the bread or cracker.

> **CAUTION:** Be sure to wear your eye goggles at all times. Wear plastic gloves when using iodine. Wear a lab apron when using iodine. If you get iodine on you, tell the teacher and wash it immediately. Do NOT taste any of the bread, cracker, or iodine!

___ 4. **Note** that the result of adding the iodine to the bread or cracker is a positive test for starch. Substances containing starch will turn dark when iodine is added.

___ 5. **Place** a small sample of the first powder in Circle 1 on your testing mat.

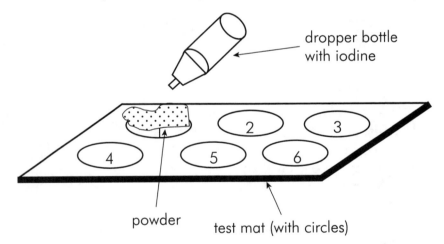

dropper bottle with iodine

powder   test mat (with circles)

___ 6. **Add** 3 drops of iodine to the powder. **Record** your observations in Table 1 on page 9.

___ 7. **Get** a small sample of the second powder and **put** it in Circle 2 on your mat.

___ 8. **Add** 3 drops of iodine to the second powder. **Record** your observations in Table 1 on page 9.

___ 9. **Get** a small sample of the third powder, **put** it in Circle 3, and **add** 3 drops of iodine to it. **Record** your observations in Table 1 on page 9.

___ 10. **Get** a small sample of the fourth powder, **put** it in Circle 4, and **add** 3 drops of iodine to it. **Record** your observations in Table 1 on page 9.

___ 11. **Get** a small sample of the fifth powder, **put** it in Circle 5, and **add** 3 drops of iodine to it. **Record** your observations in Table 1 on page 9.

Mystery Powders

QUESTIONS for Step D: Testing the Effects of Iodine on Powders

Read each of the following questions. Then write your answers in the spaces below each question.

a. Which powder or powders turned dark blue-black when you added iodine?

b. Which powder or powders did not turn dark blue-black when iodine was added?

c. Based on your testing results, which powder or powders probably contain starch? Explain why you think so.

- -

Step E: Testing the Effects of Vinegar

___ 1. **Get** a clean testing mat. Be sure the circles on the testing mat are numbered. The mat should have one circle for each powder, plus one extra circle.

> **CAUTION:** Be sure to wear your eye goggles at all times. Wear plastic gloves when using vinegar. Wear a lab apron when using vinegar. If you get vinegar on you, tell the teacher and wash it immediately. Do NOT taste any of the materials!

___ 2. **Note** how the vinegar will fizz and bubble when it is added to a substance like chalk or lime. This fizzing is a positive test for the main ingredient in the lime: calcium carbonate.

___ 3. **Place** a small sample of the first powder in Circle 1 on your testing mat.

___ 4. **Add** 3 drops of vinegar to the powder. **Record** your observations in Table 1.

___ 5. **Get** a small sample of the second powder and **put** it in Circle 2 on your mat.

___ 6. **Add** 3 drops of vinegar to the second powder. **Record** your observations in Table 1 on page 9.

Mystery Powders   **Page 8**

Procedures: Step E: Testing the Effects of Vinegar (continued)

___ 7. **Get** a small sample of the third powder, **put** it in Circle 3, and **add** 3 drops of vinegar to it. **Record** your observations in Table 1 on page 9.

___ 8. **Get** a small sample of the fourth powder, **put** it in Circle 4, and **add** 3 drops of vinegar to it. **Record** your observations in Table 1 on page 9.

___ 9. **Get** a small sample of the fifth powder, **put** it in Circle 5, and **add** 3 drops of vinegar to it. **Record** your observations in Table 1 on page 9.

QUESTIONS for Step E: Testing the Effects of Vinegar on Powders

Read each of the following questions. Then write your answers in the spaces below each question.

a. What happens when you put a few drops of vinegar on each powder?

b. Did any powder react more with vinegar than the others? If so, which one?

c. Do you think powders that dissolved in water will also dissolve in vinegar? Explain why you think so.

d. Which powder do you think will take the least amount of vinegar to dissolve? The most vinegar? How can you find out?

e. How can vinegar be used to distinguish baking soda from other powders?

Sources

Delta Education. (1986). *Mystery powders teacher's guide.* Nashua, NH: Author.
Elementary Science Study. (1974). *Mystery powders.* New York: McGraw-Hill.

Mystery Powders

Page 9

Table 1

Mystery Powders

Powder	Observations of Powder	Mixed With Water	Powder When Heated	Powder With Iodine	Powder With Vinegar
1					
2					
3					
4					
5					

MYSTERY POWDERS

Rationale

Suppose you are in a friend's kitchen and have a recipe you want to make. As you begin to look in the cupboard for ingredients, you notice that your friend has placed all the spices and baking supplies in plastic containers with lids, but didn't save the original packages. Your friend also forgot to label each container. Before you begin making your recipe, you need to determine what is in the containers, so how can you determine what is in them?

The purpose of this activity is to provide you an opportunity to inquire about the observable properties of some common household powders and to investigate some physical and chemical tests for each one. The results of your investigation should then make it possible for you to identify the powders.

Standards Addressed

NSES Grades K–4 Content Standard B (NRC, p. 127) and K–4 Inquiry Standard A (pp. 122–123); or *NSES* Grades 5–8 Content Standard B (p. 154) and Inquiry Standard A (pp. 145–148)

Vocabulary

physical property   chemical property   technique   iodine   vinegar

Objectives

After completing this activity, the student should be able to

1. **use** simple tests on common household materials to **determine** their properties,
2. **follow** proper lab techniques to ensure safety and avoid contamination,
3. **collect** and **analyze** data and **communicate** results, and
4. **draw conclusions** about the identity of common materials based on simple tests.

Materials (per student or per group)

1 test mat (black, plastic)	2 sheets of waxed paper
1 dropper bottle of vinegar	1 sheet of white paper
1 dropper bottle of distilled water	1 dropper bottle of iodine solution
1 candle or other heat source	1 clothespin (spring type)
1 magnifying lens	5 toothpicks
1 marker or pencil	safety goggles
5 aluminum foil squares (5 cm x 5 cm)	1 slice of bread (white) or 1 white saltine cracker

1 set of five white powders in cups (baking powder, baking soda, cornstarch, salt, granulated sugar)

The Rationale section is expanded and explained more thoroughly.

The applicable science standards are identified, with standards for both Grades K–4 and Grades 5–8 specified. If teachers use the simpler form of the activity for lower-elementary levels, the Grades K–4 standards apply. The fuller version of the activity addresses the Grades 5–8 standards.

Vocabulary words are introduced.

Verbs in the objectives and directions given to students are in boldface to help guide students.

- The font of the lettering changed to avoid letters with tails, which prove problematic for students in their reading.

- Although the sample shown here is reduced in size, the print size used on the page is no smaller than 12 point.

- More white space is included to avoid a cluttered appearance.

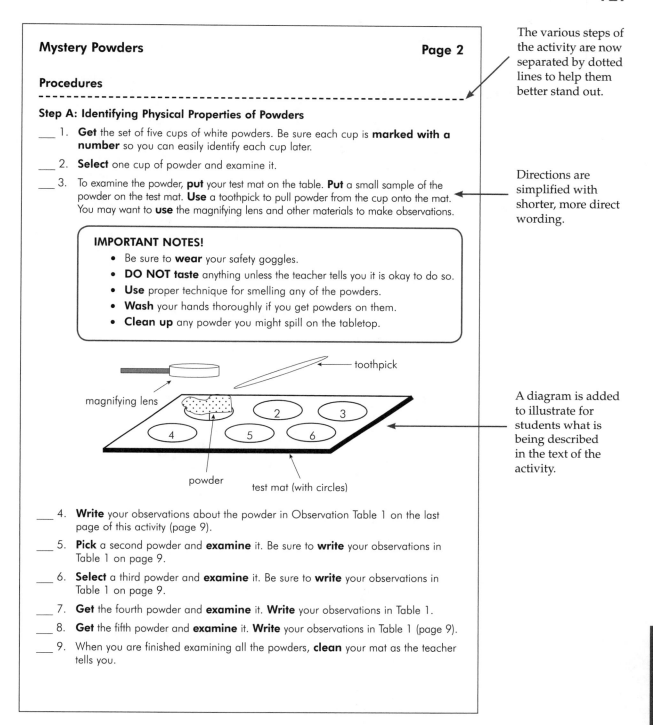

Mystery Powders   **Page 2**

Procedures
- -

Step A: Identifying Physical Properties of Powders

___ 1. **Get** the set of five cups of white powders. Be sure each cup is **marked with a number** so you can easily identify each cup later.

___ 2. **Select** one cup of powder and examine it.

___ 3. To examine the powder, **put** your test mat on the table. **Put** a small sample of the powder on the test mat. **Use** a toothpick to pull powder from the cup onto the mat. You may want to **use** the magnifying lens and other materials to make observations.

> **IMPORTANT NOTES!**
> - Be sure to **wear** your safety goggles.
> - **DO NOT taste** anything unless the teacher tells you it is okay to do so.
> - **Use** proper technique for smelling any of the powders.
> - **Wash** your hands thoroughly if you get powders on them.
> - **Clean up** any powder you might spill on the tabletop.

toothpick

magnifying lens

powder

test mat (with circles)

___ 4. **Write** your observations about the powder in Observation Table 1 on the last page of this activity (page 9).

___ 5. **Pick** a second powder and **examine** it. Be sure to **write** your observations in Table 1 on page 9.

___ 6. **Select** a third powder and **examine** it. Be sure to **write** your observations in Table 1 on page 9.

___ 7. **Get** the fourth powder and **examine** it. **Write** your observations in Table 1.

___ 8. **Get** the fifth powder and **examine** it. **Write** your observations in Table 1 (page 9).

___ 9. When you are finished examining all the powders, **clean** your mat as the teacher tells you.

The various steps of the activity are now separated by dotted lines to help them better stand out.

Directions are simplified with shorter, more direct wording.

A diagram is added to illustrate for students what is being described in the text of the activity.

- Blanks now appear at the left margin of the activity's steps so students can check off each one as they complete them.

Mystery Powders   **Page 3**

QUESTIONS about Step A: Physical Properties of Powders ◄

Read each of the following questions. Then write your answers in the spaces below each question.

a. How are the powders alike? ◄

b. How are the powders different?

c. Do all the powders feel the same? Describe how they feel.

d. Does any powder have an odor? Describe any odors.

e. Are all the powders the same shade of white?

f. Can you list three properties of each powder? What are they?

g. Are all the powders really powders? Explain why you think this.

h. What do you think each powder is? (For example, what is Powder 1?) Why do you think this?

A heading is added to indicate what is on this page.

Questions now appear immediately following the steps of the activity to which they apply. Space is provided for students to answer each question.

Mystery Powders   **Page 4**

- -

Step B: Testing the Effects of Water on the Powders ←

___ 1.   **Pick** one of the powders and put a small sample of it on your testing mat.

___ 2.   **Add** 4–5 drops of water to the powder. **Use** a toothpick to stir the water into the powder.

___ 3.   **Write** your observations about the powder in Table 1 on page 9.

___ 4.   **Pick** a second powder and **put** a small sample of it on your testing mat.

___ 5.   **Add** 4–5 drops of water to the second powder. **Use** a toothpick to stir the water into the powder.

___ 6.   **Write** your observations about the second powder in Table 1 on page 9.

___ 7.   Now, **repeat** Procedures 4, 5, and 6 for a third powder.

___ 8.   **Pick** a fourth powder and **repeat** Procedures 4, 5, and 6.

___ 9.   **Take** the fifth powder and **repeat** Procedures 4, 5, and 6.

___ 10. Do not clean your testing mat. **Put** your name on it and place the mat where your teacher tells you. Tomorrow, **make** more observations about each powder that had water added to it. Be sure to **record** your observations in Table 1 on page 9. ←

QUESTIONS about Step B: Testing the Effects of Water on the Powders

Read each of the following questions. Then write your answers in the spaces below each question.

a. What happens to each powder when you put a few drops of water on it?

b. Did each powder mix with water?

c. Which ones did and which ones didn't mix with water?

d. Did any of the powders disappear in water? If so, which one(s)?

e. Why might it be important to use the same amount of powder each time?

For each procedure step, the particular step (Step A, Step B) is highlighted (or made bold) to better stand out for students.

Students are told where to record the data they collect.

Each part of each step is separated from the others, and each is numbered within its set of procedures. This limits confusion and also allows the teacher to separate parts of the activity for use on multiple class sessions as needed. The teacher can ask students to place a mark in the procedure blank each time the procedure is done.

Mystery Powders   **Page 5**

- -

Step C: Testing the Effects of Heat on Powders

___ 1. **Obtain** a heat source. This might be a small candle supported by a lump of clay.

> **CAUTION**: If you use a candle, be very careful with the flame. Keep your fingers, clothing, and hair away from the flame. Do not throw matches into the trash. Test only dry powders. Do not heat any powders that have been mixed with any liquid. Always wear your eye goggles!

___ 2. **Get** the small piece of aluminum foil and **make** it into the shape of a bowl.

___ 3. **Take** the clothespin and make it **pinch** one edge of the foil bowl. **Adjust** the clothespin so it is like a panhandle.

___ 4. **Place** a small sample of the first powder in the aluminum foil bowl.

___ 5. **Light** the candle, and then **pick up** the aluminum foil bowl by using only the clothespin handle.

___ 6. **Carefully hold** the aluminum foil bowl over the candle flame to heat the powder inside the foil bowl. You may need to **hold** the foil bowl over the flame for several minutes.

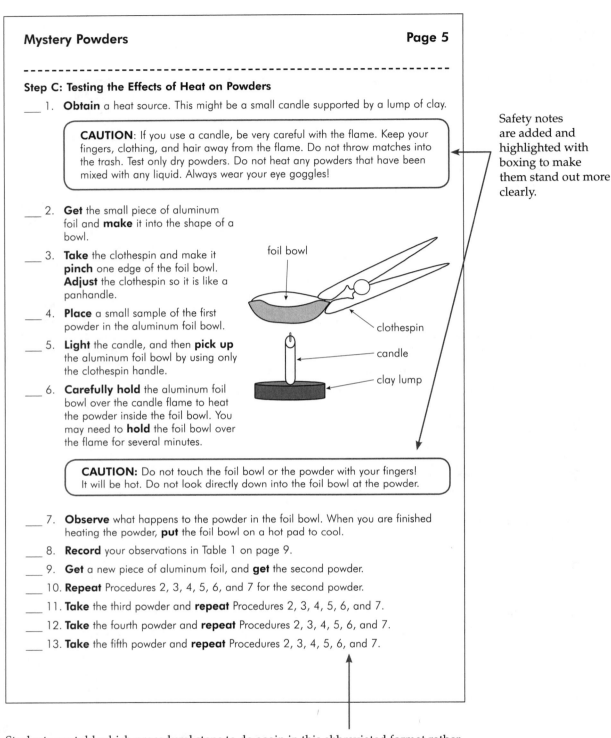

foil bowl

clothespin

candle

clay lump

> **CAUTION:** Do not touch the foil bowl or the powder with your fingers! It will be hot. Do not look directly down into the foil bowl at the powder.

___ 7. **Observe** what happens to the powder in the foil bowl. When you are finished heating the powder, **put** the foil bowl on a hot pad to cool.

___ 8. **Record** your observations in Table 1 on page 9.

___ 9. **Get** a new piece of aluminum foil, and **get** the second powder.

___ 10. **Repeat** Procedures 2, 3, 4, 5, 6, and 7 for the second powder.

___ 11. **Take** the third powder and **repeat** Procedures 2, 3, 4, 5, 6, and 7.

___ 12. **Take** the fourth powder and **repeat** Procedures 2, 3, 4, 5, 6, and 7.

___ 13. **Take** the fifth powder and **repeat** Procedures 2, 3, 4, 5, 6, and 7.

Safety notes are added and highlighted with boxing to make them stand out more clearly.

Students are told which procedural steps to do again in this abbreviated format rather than lengthening the activity pages through inserting repeats of each individual step.

Mystery Powders   **Page 6**

- -

Step D: Testing the Effects of Iodine on Powders

___ 1. **Get** a clean testing mat. Be sure the circles on the testing mat are numbered. The mat should have one circle for each powder, plus one extra circle.

___ 2. **Put** a small piece of bread or cracker in the extra circle on the testing mat.

___ 3. **Take** the bottle of iodine and **add** 3 drops to the bread or cracker.

> **CAUTION:** Be sure to wear your eye goggles at all times. Wear plastic gloves when using iodine. Wear a lab apron when using iodine. If you get iodine on you, tell the teacher and wash it immediately. Do NOT taste any of the bread, cracker, or iodine!

___ 4. **Note** that the result of adding the iodine to the bread or cracker is a positive test for starch. Substances containing starch will turn dark when iodine is added.

___ 5. **Place** a small sample of the first powder in Circle 1 on your testing mat.

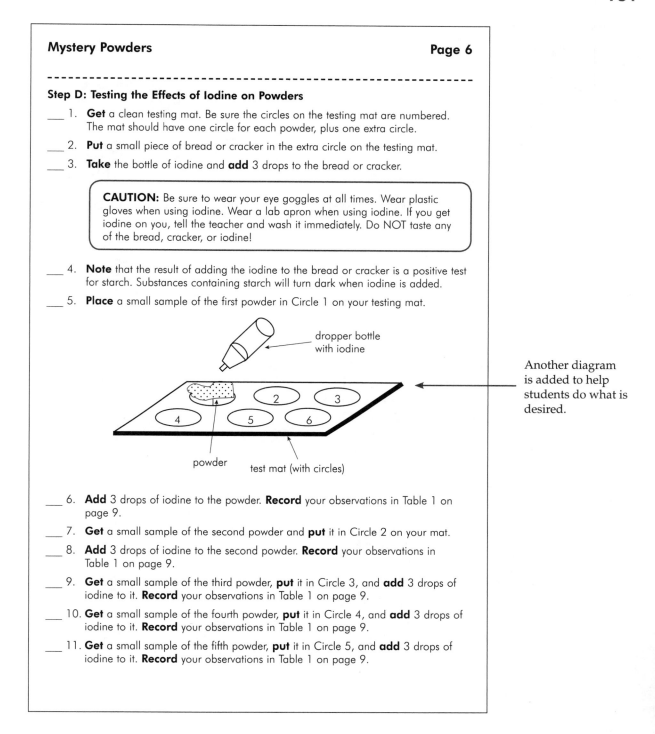

dropper bottle with iodine

powder   test mat (with circles)

Another diagram is added to help students do what is desired.

___ 6. **Add** 3 drops of iodine to the powder. **Record** your observations in Table 1 on page 9.

___ 7. **Get** a small sample of the second powder and **put** it in Circle 2 on your mat.

___ 8. **Add** 3 drops of iodine to the second powder. **Record** your observations in Table 1 on page 9.

___ 9. **Get** a small sample of the third powder, **put** it in Circle 3, and **add** 3 drops of iodine to it. **Record** your observations in Table 1 on page 9.

___ 10. **Get** a small sample of the fourth powder, **put** it in Circle 4, and **add** 3 drops of iodine to it. **Record** your observations in Table 1 on page 9.

___ 11. **Get** a small sample of the fifth powder, **put** it in Circle 5, and **add** 3 drops of iodine to it. **Record** your observations in Table 1 on page 9.

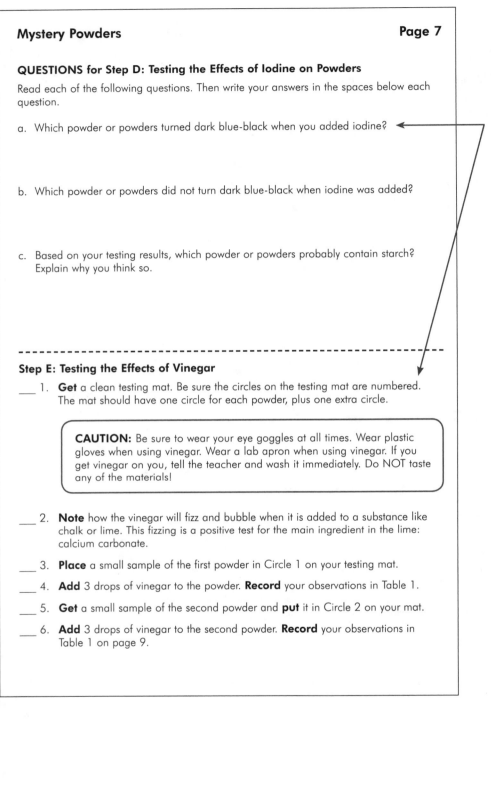

Mystery Powders   **Page 7**

QUESTIONS for Step D: Testing the Effects of Iodine on Powders

Read each of the following questions. Then write your answers in the spaces below each question.

a. Which powder or powders turned dark blue-black when you added iodine?

b. Which powder or powders did not turn dark blue-black when iodine was added?

c. Based on your testing results, which powder or powders probably contain starch? Explain why you think so.

- -

Step E: Testing the Effects of Vinegar

___ 1. **Get** a clean testing mat. Be sure the circles on the testing mat are numbered. The mat should have one circle for each powder, plus one extra circle.

> **CAUTION:** Be sure to wear your eye goggles at all times. Wear plastic gloves when using vinegar. Wear a lab apron when using vinegar. If you get vinegar on you, tell the teacher and wash it immediately. Do NOT taste any of the materials!

___ 2. **Note** how the vinegar will fizz and bubble when it is added to a substance like chalk or lime. This fizzing is a positive test for the main ingredient in the lime: calcium carbonate.

___ 3. **Place** a small sample of the first powder in Circle 1 on your testing mat.

___ 4. **Add** 3 drops of vinegar to the powder. **Record** your observations in Table 1.

___ 5. **Get** a small sample of the second powder and **put** it in Circle 2 on your mat.

___ 6. **Add** 3 drops of vinegar to the second powder. **Record** your observations in Table 1 on page 9.

Each question is separated from the other questions, and identified with a letter rather than a number that could get confused with a procedure step.

Mystery Powders   **Page 8**

- -

Procedures: Step E: Testing the Effects of Vinegar (continued) ←

___ 7. **Get** a small sample of the third powder, **put** it in Circle 3, and **add** 3 drops of vinegar to it. **Record** your observations in Table 1 on page 9.

___ 8. **Get** a small sample of the fourth powder, **put** it in Circle 4, and **add** 3 drops of vinegar to it. **Record** your observations in Table 1 on page 9.

___ 9. **Get** a small sample of the fifth powder, **put** it in Circle 5, and **add** 3 drops of vinegar to it. **Record** your observations in Table 1 on page 9.

QUESTIONS for Step E: Testing the Effects of Vinegar on Powders

Read each of the following questions. Then write your answers in the spaces below each question.

a. What happens when you put a few drops of vinegar on each powder?

b. Did any powder react more with vinegar than the others? If so, which one?

c. Do you think powders that dissolved in water will also dissolve in vinegar? Explain why you think so.

d. Which powder do you think will take the least amount of vinegar to dissolve? The most vinegar? How can you find out?

e. How can vinegar be used to distinguish baking soda from other powders?

Sources

Delta Education. (1986). *Mystery powders teacher's guide*. Nashua, NH: Author.
Elementary Science Study. (1974). *Mystery powders*. New York: McGraw-Hill.

The highlighted header informs the student that the Procedures section continues onto this page.

Upper-Elementary Physical Science Activity
Annotated Revised Activity: Mystery Powders

Mystery Powders   **Page 9**

Table 1

Mystery Powders

Powder	Observations of Powder	Mixed With Water	Powder When Heated	Powder With Iodine	Powder With Vinegar
1					
2					
3					
4					
5					

The table in which students are to record data now appears by itself and exactly where students are told it will be when reading the activity's procedures. The data table can be separated from the rest of the activity so students can fill in data beside the pages with the directions for each activity step, rather than having to constantly flip back to the end.

CONCLUSION

Throughout this chapter, examples of science activities were provided in different forms: the original version, a revised version that follows the guidelines and suggestions from Chapter 3, and then a revised version with annotations to specifically indicate what revisions were made and rationales for why they were done. Activity samples included a broad range of science disciplines, from biological to earth to physical sciences; and a range of grade levels, from primary up through middle school. Although more examples could be provided, the ones included in this chapter should be sufficient models to help teachers in their attempts to apply the guidelines to activities from their own classrooms. To help keep such application attempts manageable, teachers may first wish to revise smaller or shorter activities until they are practiced in the process, or they may prefer to revise certain portions of larger activities rather than the entire activities. Whatever course of action taken, the teacher must remember that these revising protocols are to help with the delivery of inquiry-based instruction, not to replace it.

5

Revising Science Assessments

INTRODUCTION

The purpose of this chapter is to illustrate how the revision suggestions in Chapter 3 can actually be applied to science assessments. Recalling Chapter 3, many of the suggestions for making revisions apply to both science activities and assessments, but there are some that are more appropriate for only assessments. The examples in this chapter highlight these particular suggestions. They show specific ways to change the format of questions, and how to provide specific directions to guide students through the assessment at various points in an assessment's pages.

High-quality assessment plans include multiple and varied types of assessments. Although there are many possible components that could be included in an assessment plan, many can include some combination of traditional testing along with performance assessing. Both can help teachers determine what their students know, and the performance assessing can help teachers go further to find out what their students can do. The performance aspect fits better with inquiry-based instruction, because it usually involves hands-on aspects requiring problem solving and presentation of results.

This chapter includes four assessments to illustrate how they can be revised. As in Chapter 4 for revising activities, each original assessment is provided and then followed by its revised version plus an annotated version that highlights significant aspects of the changes made, with rationale. The first assessment, Understanding Oceans, is a traditional one and typical of those found in many teacher's guides from published curricula. It includes the usual multiple-choice and matching items one expects to see in such tests. The remaining three sample assessments are all performance based, and begin with one for the primary level and progress up through the middle-school level. The second assessment is a primary-grade (Grades 1–2) performance assessment on using attribute blocks. The third, originally called Batteries and Bulbs, is a middle-elementary level performance-based assessment based on the activity developed by the *Elementary Science Study* (*ESS*) (Education Development Center, 1960). Teachers have revised this in various ways over the years of its use. Here, the Batteries and Bulbs assessment is renamed as Electric Circuits. Finally, the fourth sample assessment is an upper-elementary (middle school) performance assessment on density.

Sharing the multiple performance assessment examples is necessary in order to show revisions in one that are not appropriate or possible in the others. An example of one of these revisions is the formula template used in the Density performance-based assessment but not applicable to the Electric Circuits assessment. Another example of this is the use of life-sized figures for attribute blocks in the revised version of the assessment, whereas the other revised assessments do not include life-sized images.

VIGNETTE WITH MRS. SIMONS

Rosa seemed to progress easily through her class activities, and didn't seem to have much trouble with reading her class books. From Mrs. Simons's perspective, Rosa seemed to be doing as well as any of the other fifth-grade students. Then came the day of the test. Rosa's performance was dismal. Mrs. Simons was taken aback, because she was convinced Rosa knew the information. When Mrs. Simons talked with Rosa, she learned that Rosa had studied diligently for the test, but evidently had difficulty correctly marking her answers. The test was taken from the textbook publisher's supplemental teacher materials packet, so Mrs. Simons concluded that the way the test was formatted on the page must have had something to do with Rosa's performance. Consequently, Mrs. Simons decided she should revise the test, keeping the same set of questions, but reformatting them so the questions, possible answers, and answer formats would be less confusing.

The assessment samples that follow show how test questions can be revised to accomplish what Mrs. Simons desired. (Note that this is in the absence of an IEP for Rosa, which may or may not be drafted at this point in time.) By remembering the suggested guidelines from Chapter 3 and building on the revision process with the science activities from Chapter 4, Mrs. Simons and other teachers hopefully will see how those suggestions pertinent to assessments can be applied to both performance-based and traditional forms of assessment.

Name: _____

CHAPTER 12 TEST

Understanding Oceans

Read each question below. Below each question are answers. Choose the best answer for each question. Write the letter for your answer in the blank at the left of the question.

_____ 1. The place beyond the continental shelf where the ocean floor has a steep drop is called the

      a. continental slope   c. trench

      b. plain   d. tide

_____ 2. The top part of an ocean wave is called the

      a. tide   c. crest

      b. trough   d. breaker

_____ 3. The bottom part of an ocean wave is called the

      a. tide   c. crest

      b. trough   d. breaker

_____ 4. Black rocks on the ocean floor, called _____, contain many minerals.

      a. resources   c. salt

      b. nodules   d. lumps

_____ 5. The oceans on the east and west sides of the U.S. are the

      a. Indian and Atlantic Oceans   d. Pacific and Atlantic Oceans

      b. Pacific and Arctic Oceans   e. Arctic and Indian Oceans

      c. Arctic and Atlantic Oceans   f. None of the above

_____ 6. Which of the following is not true of the Alvin deep sea submersible?

      a. It looks like an insect.   d. It can dive as deep as 700 meters.

      b. Two people can fit inside it.   e. It has its own air supply.

      c. It was replaced by diving suits.

_____ 7. We get two sources of energy from the ocean. They are

      a. oil and tides   d. lumps and tides

      b. breakers and salt   e. lumps and oil

      c. salt and oil

_____ 8. Salt in the oceans comes from

      a. dead fish that settle to the bottom   c. heavy tropical rains

      b. dissolved minerals washed off the land   d. waste from deep sea submarines

_____ 9. Deep underwater canyons are most likely found on this part of the ocean floor.

      a. continental slope   c. ocean plain

      b. continental shelf   d. ocean ridges

Chapter 12 Test

_____ 10. A large chain of underwater mountains in the Atlantic Ocean is called the
  a. Mid-Atlantic rise
  b. Mid-Atlantic slope
  c. Mid-Atlantic trench
  d. Mid-Atlantic ridge

_____ 11. A giant wave that can destroy whole towns is a
  a. tide
  b. tsunami
  c. teriyaki
  d. breaker

_____ 12. What causes ocean tides?
  a. breakers
  b. tsunami
  c. continental rises
  d. the moon

_____ 13. How many ocean tides are there every 24 hours?
  a. one
  b. two
  c. three
  d. four
  e. none of the above

_____ 14. The name of the large current next to the Atlantic coast of the U.S. is the
  a. South Stream
  b. Gulf Stream
  c. Eastern Current
  d. Slope Current

_____ 15. Which of the following is not an ocean resource?
  a. electricity
  b. fish
  c. nodules
  d. natural gas
  e. oil

Write the term that does not belong in each group below. Write the term in the blank to the left of each question.

_____ 1. plain, high tide, continental slope, trench

_____ 2. nodules, tide, current, wave

_____ 3. breaker, trough, resource, crest

_____ 4. fish, minerals, natural gas, plain

Chapter 12 Test   Page 3

Write the letter of the term that best matches the definition. Not all the terms will be used.

_____ 1. A rise in the level of ocean water   a. tide

_____ 2. A river of water in the ocean   b. low tide

_____ 3. A useful material taken from the earth   c. breaker

_____ 4. The bottom of the ocean floor   d. Alvin

_____ 5. The edge of a continent that is underwater   e. oceanographer

_____ 6. A drop in the level of ocean water   f. continental shelf

_____ 7. A deep, narrow slit in the ocean floor   g. trench

_____ 8. A falling wave   h. high tide

_____ 9. A change in the level of ocean water   i. plain

       j. current

       k. resource

Newspapers near the coasts sometimes print tide charts like the one below. Notice that in the chart there are two high tides and two low tides for each day. Use the chart to answer the next two questions.

Table of Tides			
	Friday	**Saturday**	**Sunday**
Low Tide	12:42 AM	1:14 AM	1:49 AM
High Tide	6:48 AM	7:49 AM	8:14 AM
Low Tide	2:05 PM	2:40 PM	3:15 PM
High Tide	7:05 PM	7:40 PM	8:05 PM

_____ 1. Suppose you want to go sailing on Saturday. Sailing is best when the water is deepest. What time would you go sailing on Saturday?

     a. 7:49 AM   d. 2:40 PM

     b. 1:14 AM   e. Both answers a and c

     c. 7:40 PM   f. Both answers b and d

_____ 2. If you wanted to collect seashells on the beach on Sunday, when should you go?

     a. 8:14 PM   d. 8:05 PM

     b. 1:49 AM   e. 3:15 PM

     c. 8:14 AM

Name: _____

CHAPTER 12 TEST

Understanding Oceans

Read each question carefully. Below each question are answers. Choose the best answer for each question. Use your pencil to **circle your answer**. Your answers will tell the teacher some things you know about oceans.

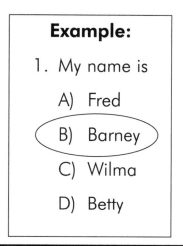

Example:

1. My name is

    A) Fred

    B) Barney

    C) Wilma

    D) Betty

---

1. The place beyond the continental shelf where the ocean floor has a steep drop is called the

    A) continental slope

    B) ocean plain

    C) trench

    D) tide

2. Deep underwater canyons are most likely found on the

    A) continental slope

    B) continental shelf

    C) ocean plain

    D) ocean ridges

Chapter 12 Test   **Page 2**

---

3. A large chain of underwater mountains in the Atlantic Ocean is called the

   A) Mid-Atlantic rise

   B) Mid-Atlantic slope

   C) Mid-Atlantic trench

   D) Mid-Atlantic ridge

4. The oceans on the east and west sides of the U.S. are the

   A) Indian and Atlantic Oceans

   B) Pacific and Arctic Oceans

   C) Arctic and Atlantic Oceans

   D) Pacific and Atlantic Oceans

5. The top part of an ocean wave is called the

   A) tide

   B) trough

   C) crest

   D) breaker

6. The bottom part of an ocean wave is called the

   A) tide

   B) trough

   C) crest

   D) breaker

Chapter 12 Test   **Page 3**

7. A giant wave that can destroy whole towns is a
   A) tide
   B) tsunami
   C) teriyaki
   D) breaker

8. What causes ocean tides?
   A) breakers
   B) tsunami
   C) continental rises
   D) the moon's gravity

9. How many ocean tides are there every 24 hours?
   A) one
   B) two
   C) three
   D) four

10. The name of the large current next to the U.S. Atlantic coast of the U.S. is the
    A) South Stream
    B) Gulf Stream
    C) Eastern Current
    D) Slope Current

Chapter 12 Test   **Page 4**

11. Black rocks on the ocean floor that contain many minerals are called
    A) resources
    B) nodules
    C) salt
    D) lumps

12. Which of the following is an ocean resource?
    A) electricity
    B) gravity
    C) nodules
    D) currents

13. Salt in the oceans comes from
    A) dead fish that settle to the bottom
    B) dissolved minerals washed off the land
    C) heavy tropical rains
    D) waste from deep sea submersibles

14. Two sources of energy we get from the ocean are
    A) oil and tides
    B) breakers and oil
    C) salt and oil
    D) lumps and tides

Chapter 12 Test **Page 5**

15. Which of the following is true about the deep sea submersible named Alvin?

    A) It looks like an insect.

    B) One person can fit inside it.

    C) It was replaced by diving suits.

    D) It has its own air supply.

STOP!

Check with the teacher before doing the next section.

You will find four groups of terms below. Each group's terms are about oceans. You are going to show your understanding of how the terms go together. Find the term that does not fit with the other terms in each group. In each group, **circle the term** that does not fit.

Example			
Group 0:	carrots	corn	(chicken)	peas

Group 1:	plain	high tide	ridge	trench
Group 2:	nodules	tide	current	wave
Group 3:	breaker	trough	resource	crest
Group 4:	fish	minerals	natural gas	plain

Chapter 12 Test   Page 6

> ### STOP!
> Check with the teacher before doing the next section.

Newspapers often print a tide table like the one below. Notice that the chart shows two high tides and two low tides for each day. Use the **Table of Tides** to answer the **next two questions**. **Circle the answers** you choose.

Table of Tides			
	Friday	Saturday	Sunday
Low Tide	12:42 AM	1:14 AM	1:49 AM
High Tide	6:48 AM	7:49 AM	8:14 AM
Low Tide	2:05 PM	2:40 PM	3:15 PM
High Tide	7:05 PM	7:40 PM	8:05 PM

1. Suppose you want to go sailing on Saturday. Sailing is best when the water is deepest. What time would you go sailing on Saturday?

   A) 7:49 AM

   B) 1:14 AM

   C) 7:40 PM

   D) 2:40 PM

> Continue to Question 2 on the next page.

Chapter 12 Test   **Page 7**

---

2. If you wanted to collect seashells on the beach on Sunday, when should you go?

   A) 8:14 PM

   B) 1:49 AM

   C) 8:14 AM

   D) 3:15 PM

> **STOP!**
>
> Check with the teacher before doing the next section.

You will find some descriptions in Column A. In Column B are the names that match the descriptions. You need to show that you know the names for the things that are described. **Draw a line to connect** each description with its name.

Example

Column A	Column B
1. An orange vegetable	apple
2. A red fruit	carrot

Column A   **Column B**

1. A rise in the level of ocean water   tide

2. A river of water in the ocean   low tide

3. A falling wave   high tide

4. A drop in the level of ocean water   breaker

5. A change in the level of ocean water   current

Chapter 12 Test   Page 8

You will find some descriptions in Column A. In Column B are the names that match the descriptions. You need to show that you know the names for the things that are described. **Draw a line to connect** each description with its name.

Example

Column A   **Column B**

1. An orange vegetable   apple

2. A red fruit   carrot

Column A   **Column B**

1. The bottom of the ocean floor   plain

2. The edge of a continent that is under water   resource

3. A deep narrow slit in the ocean floor   trench

4. A material taken from the earth   continental shelf

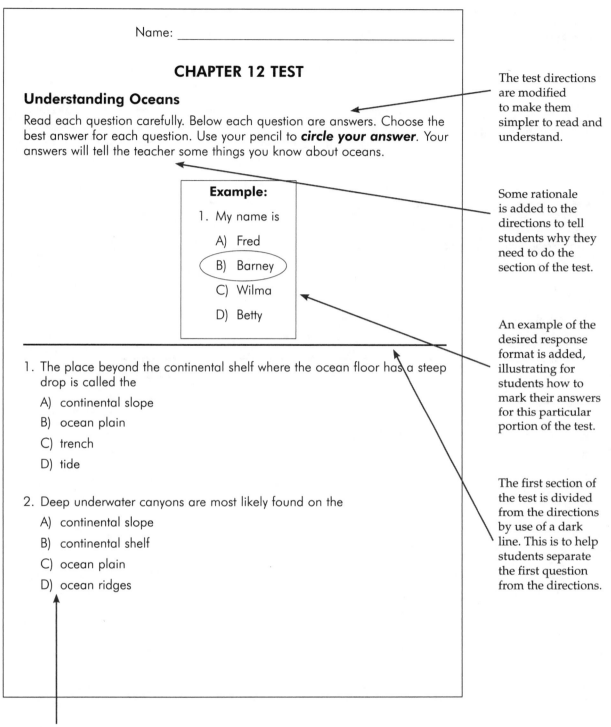

Name: _____

CHAPTER 12 TEST

Understanding Oceans

Read each question carefully. Below each question are answers. Choose the best answer for each question. Use your pencil to **circle your answer**. Your answers will tell the teacher some things you know about oceans.

> **Example:**
>
> 1. My name is
>   - A) Fred
>   - (B) Barney
>   - C) Wilma
>   - D) Betty

1. The place beyond the continental shelf where the ocean floor has a steep drop is called the
   - A) continental slope
   - B) ocean plain
   - C) trench
   - D) tide

2. Deep underwater canyons are most likely found on the
   - A) continental slope
   - B) continental shelf
   - C) ocean plain
   - D) ocean ridges

The test directions are modified to make them simpler to read and understand.

Some rationale is added to the directions to tell students why they need to do the section of the test.

An example of the desired response format is added, illustrating for students how to mark their answers for this particular portion of the test.

The first section of the test is divided from the directions by use of a dark line. This is to help students separate the first question from the directions.

The multiple-choice question format changed from the compressed to the expanded format in which the choices are "stacked" one on top of the other. This helps students more easily differentiate between the question stem and the foils, and between foils.

Traditional Science Assessment
Annotated Revised Assessment: Understanding Oceans

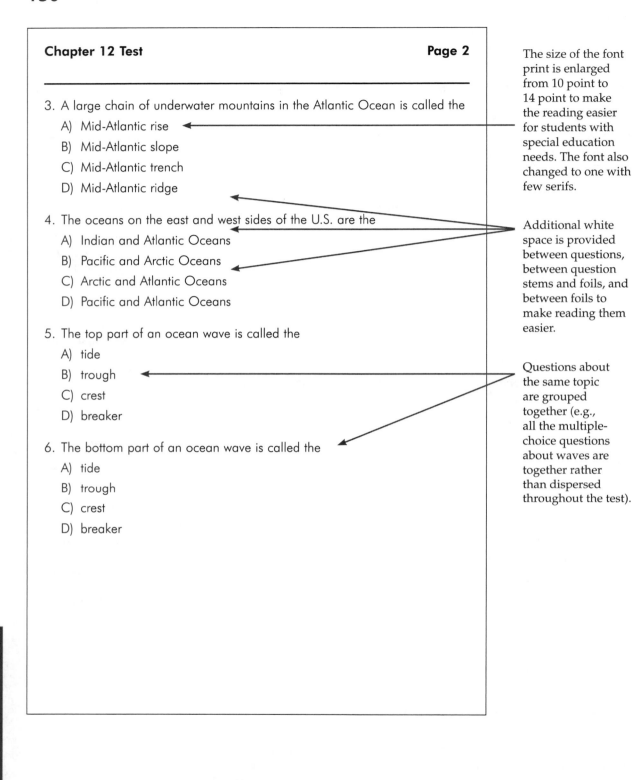

Chapter 12 Test   **Page 2**

3. A large chain of underwater mountains in the Atlantic Ocean is called the
   A) Mid-Atlantic rise
   B) Mid-Atlantic slope
   C) Mid-Atlantic trench
   D) Mid-Atlantic ridge

4. The oceans on the east and west sides of the U.S. are the
   A) Indian and Atlantic Oceans
   B) Pacific and Arctic Oceans
   C) Arctic and Atlantic Oceans
   D) Pacific and Atlantic Oceans

5. The top part of an ocean wave is called the
   A) tide
   B) trough
   C) crest
   D) breaker

6. The bottom part of an ocean wave is called the
   A) tide
   B) trough
   C) crest
   D) breaker

The size of the font print is enlarged from 10 point to 14 point to make the reading easier for students with special education needs. The font also changed to one with few serifs.

Additional white space is provided between questions, between question stems and foils, and between foils to make reading them easier.

Questions about the same topic are grouped together (e.g., all the multiple-choice questions about waves are together rather than dispersed throughout the test).

Chapter 12 Test Page 3

7. A giant wave that can destroy whole towns is a

A) tide

B) tsunami

C) teriyaki

D) breaker

8. What causes ocean tides?

A) breakers

B) tsunami

C) continental rises

D) the moon's gravity

9. How many ocean tides are there every 24 hours?

A) one

B) two

C) three

D) four

10. The name of the large current next to the U.S. Atlantic coast of the U.S. is the

A) South Stream

B) Gulf Stream

C) Eastern Current

D) Slope Current

The test identification (Chapter 12 Test) is been retained on each page, but is separated from the test questions by a dark line. This should help students not confuse the heading with the questions.

The foils' letter designations changed from a. to A) to help students not confuse the letter with the foil answer that follows to its right.

Foils such as "all of the above" or "none of the above" no longer appear. This may require changing some of the foils, or even breaking a single question into two or more questions. This was Question 13 from the original version of the test, which included an answer "E. None of the above." Inclusion of response foils like these are poorly designed and can be confusing to students.

Additional space now appears between the foils' letter designations and the foil answers to help students not confuse the letter with the foil answer that follows it.

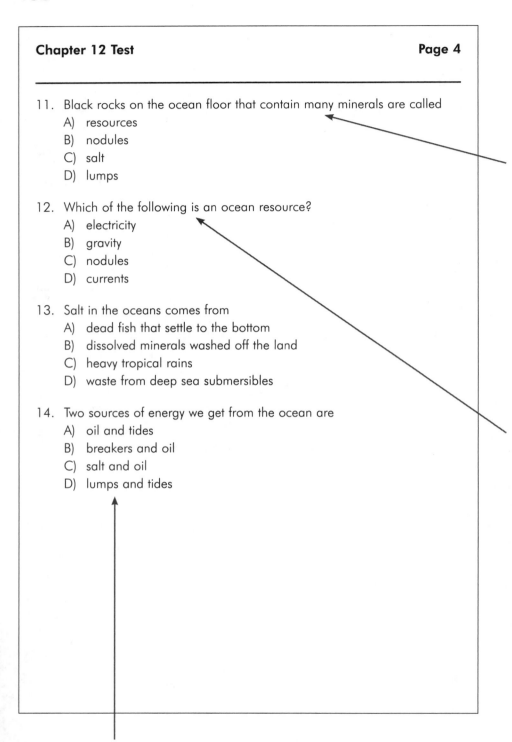

Chapter 12 Test   **Page 4**

11. Black rocks on the ocean floor that contain many minerals are called
    A) resources
    B) nodules
    C) salt
    D) lumps

12. Which of the following is an ocean resource?
    A) electricity
    B) gravity
    C) nodules
    D) currents

13. Salt in the oceans comes from
    A) dead fish that settle to the bottom
    B) dissolved minerals washed off the land
    C) heavy tropical rains
    D) waste from deep sea submersibles

14. Two sources of energy we get from the ocean are
    A) oil and tides
    B) breakers and oil
    C) salt and oil
    D) lumps and tides

Question stems containing blanks in their middles (where the foils need to be inserted when read in order to make sense of the phrase) are reworded. All questions are now in a format in which the reading of the foils follows the stem. This was Question 4 on the original version of the test.

Question stems containing "not" are omitted. The original question is rephrased and worded as a positive statement, requiring a change in the foils as well. This was Question 15 on the original version of the test. Such changes help students more clearly understand what is being asked and assess their knowledge rather than their ability to decipher reading.

The number of possible responses, or foils, for each question reduced to a maximum of four. Questions containing more than four foils tend to confuse students. A second similar question can be provided that includes the other foils if desired, but the total number of foils per question should be limited to four.

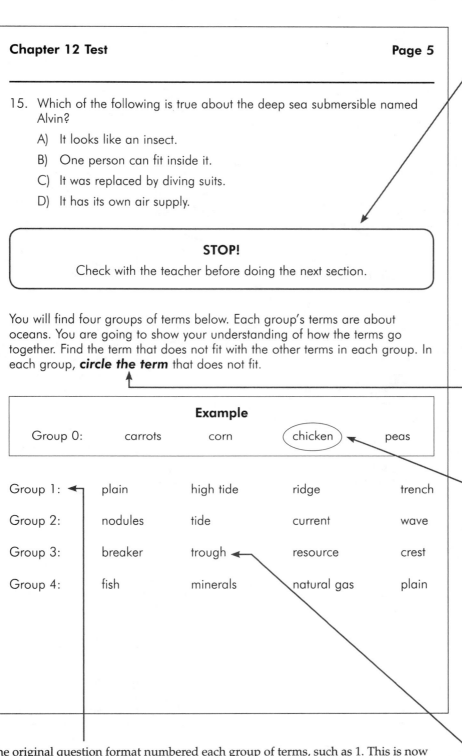

Chapter 12 Test   **Page 5**

15. Which of the following is true about the deep sea submersible named Alvin?

   A) It looks like an insect.

   B) One person can fit inside it.

   C) It was replaced by diving suits.

   D) It has its own air supply.

> **STOP!**
> Check with the teacher before doing the next section.

You will find four groups of terms below. Each group's terms are about oceans. You are going to show your understanding of how the terms go together. Find the term that does not fit with the other terms in each group. In each group, **_circle the term_** that does not fit.

> **Example**
> Group 0:   carrots   corn   (chicken)   peas

Group 1:   plain   high tide   ridge   trench

Group 2:   nodules   tide   current   wave

Group 3:   breaker   trough   resource   crest

Group 4:   fish   minerals   natural gas   plain

The student is provided cues to check with the teacher prior to continuing. This allows the teacher an opportunity to check the student's work to ensure the student is doing what the test requires. Hence, the teacher ensures the student is being tested on topic knowledge rather than how to take a test.

Verbs with directions, as well as important portions of the directions, are highlighted in bold and/or underlined to attract the student's attention.

Students are instructed to circle their answers rather than write them into blanks or transfer them onto separate answer sheets. This avoids translational errors that students with special needs often make.

The original question format numbered each group of terms, such as 1. This is now clarified as Group 1 to help students avoid confusion between the item designation and the grouping of terms.

The original question format had large blanks to the left of each group of terms, in which students were to write the term that did not fit the others. The format changes here so students need only circle the odd term. This avoids translation difficulties that some students encounter.

Chapter 12 Test   **Page 6**

> ## STOP!
> Check with the teacher before doing the next section.

Newspapers often print a tide table like the one below. Notice that the chart shows two high tides and two low tides for each day. Use the **Table of Tides** to answer the **next two questions**. **Circle the answers** you choose.

Table of Tides			
	Friday	Saturday	Sunday
Low Tide	12:42 AM	1:14 AM	1:49 AM
High Tide	6:48 AM	7:49 AM	8:14 AM
Low Tide	2:05 PM	2:40 PM	3:15 PM
High Tide	7:05 PM	7:40 PM	8:05 PM

1. Suppose you want to go sailing on Saturday. Sailing is best when the water is deepest. What time would you go sailing on Saturday?

   A) 7:49 AM

   B) 1:14 AM

   C) 7:40 PM

   D) 2:40 PM

   > Continue to Question 2 on the next page.

The phrasing in the directions and illustration are now congruent. Rather than referring to the "tide chart" in the directions and to the "tide table" in the illustration, both are identified by the same title.

The table is larger so it is at least the same size font as the rest of the test. This makes its contents easier for students to read.

Preferably, both questions dealing with the Table of Tides should be on the same page. However, due to the size of the print, the size of the table, and the expanded format of the questions, the second question needs to be move to the next page. This situation should be avoided whenever possible because doing so could cause errors in students' thinking—disconnecting the second question on the following page from the table to which it refers.

Each section of the test is separate from the other sections in a distinct manner. This reduces student confusion about what questions are grouped by similar topics, and helps students keep the response modes necessary for each set of questions separate.

Students are alerted that the second question to this question set is on the next page.

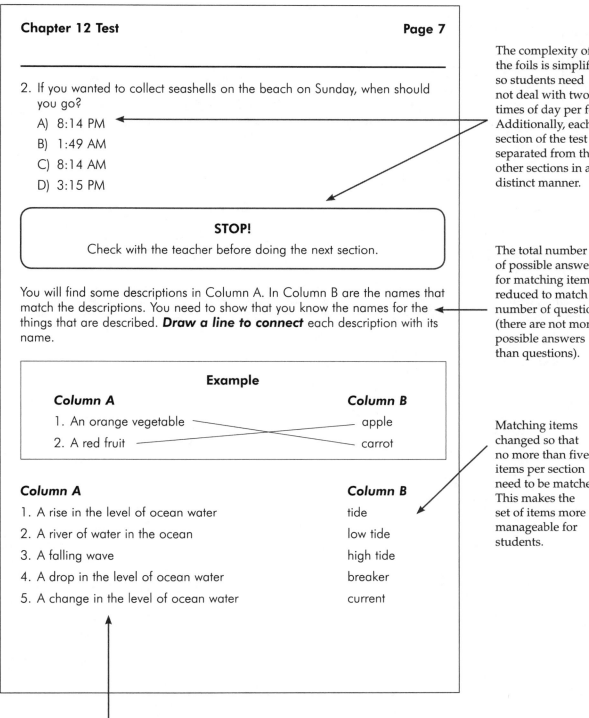

Chapter 12 Test **Page 7**

2. If you wanted to collect seashells on the beach on Sunday, when should you go?

A) 8:14 PM

B) 1:49 AM

C) 8:14 AM

D) 3:15 PM

STOP!
Check with the teacher before doing the next section.

You will find some descriptions in Column A. In Column B are the names that match the descriptions. You need to show that you know the names for the things that are described. ***Draw a line to connect*** each description with its name.

Example

Column A	*Column B*
1. An orange vegetable	apple
2. A red fruit	carrot

Column A

1. A rise in the level of ocean water

2. A river of water in the ocean

3. A falling wave

4. A drop in the level of ocean water

5. A change in the level of ocean water

Column B

tide

low tide

high tide

breaker

current

The complexity of the foils is simplified so students need not deal with two times of day per foil. Additionally, each section of the test is separated from the other sections in a distinct manner.

The total number of possible answers for matching items reduced to match the number of questions (there are not more possible answers than questions).

Matching items changed so that no more than five items per section need to be matched. This makes the set of items more manageable for students.

Matching items are reorganized so that items about similar topics are grouped together rather than being dispersed throughout a larger set of matching items. This helps the student focus more clearly on what the teacher wishes to assess.

Chapter 12 Test   **Page 8**

You will find some descriptions in Column A. In Column B are the names that match the descriptions. You need to show that you know the names for the things that are described. **_Draw a line to connect_** each description with its name.

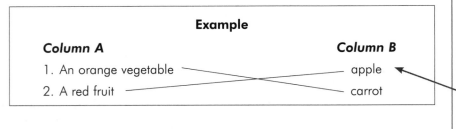

Example

Column A	Column B
1. An orange vegetable	apple
2. A red fruit	carrot

Column A

1. The bottom of the ocean floor
2. The edge of a continent that is under water
3. A deep narrow slit in the ocean floor
4. A material taken from the earth

Column B

plain

resource

trench

continental
   shelf

Rationale is included with each section of the test to help students understand why they are being asked the questions.

An example of the desired response format is added, illustrating for students how to mark their answers for this particular portion of the test. Having students respond in such a manner helps avoid translation errors that can occur when writing answers in blanks or on separate answer sheets.

Hyphenated words are avoided since they may cause difficulties for students with special needs. Also, in this case, the term "continental shelf" was too long to keep on a single line, so the term continues on a second line, and it is indented to help students recognize it as a continuance rather than as an entirely new term.

- True-false questions are also avoided because they prove difficult for students with special education needs.

- Fill-in-the-blank questions are avoided because they prove difficult for students. Often, such questions fail to provide students enough information for them to put the blanks into context and determine what should go into the blanks.

ATTRIBUTE BLOCKS

KEY

Grades	1–2
Concept(s)	object, material, property, patterns, serial ordering
Process Skill(s)	observing and classifying

1. Compare your work station with the picture to the right. Be sure you have each thing that is shown in the picture. If you do not have everything, ask your teacher. When you are done with this station, be sure each thing is back in its place.

2. Pick up one block. Draw a picture of the block.

What you should have. Where it should be.

block

cards

pencil

3. Name two properties of the block that you drew.

4. Look at the pattern of blocks below. Tell what blocks you need to complete the pattern.

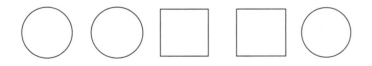

5. Look at the circle diagram with blocks in it. Find a card that matches the characteristic of all the blocks in the circle. Write down what the card says.

Attribute Blocks   Page 2

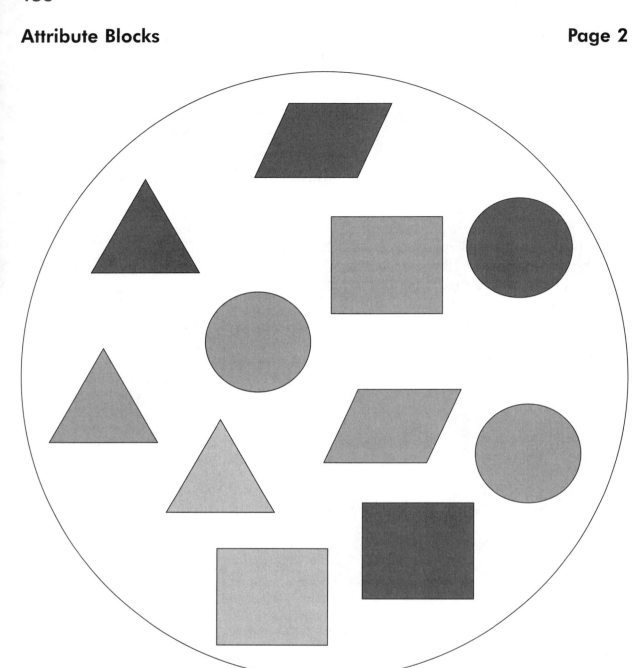

ATTRIBUTE BLOCKS

Name: _____

1. **Look** at the box below. You should have the things shown in the box. If you do not, **tell** the teacher.

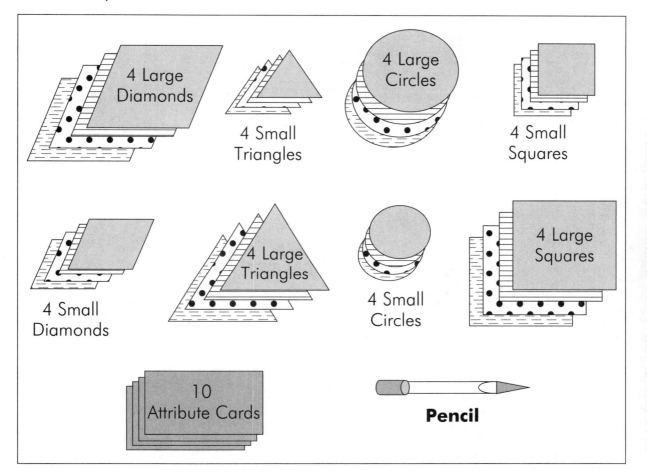

4 Large Diamonds

4 Small Triangles

4 Large Circles

4 Small Squares

4 Small Diamonds

4 Large Triangles

4 Small Circles

4 Large Squares

10 Attribute Cards

Pencil

2. **Pick up** one block. **Draw** a picture of it in the space below.

3. **Name** two attributes of the block that you drew.

Attribute 1: _____

Attribute 2: _____

Go to next page.

Attribute Blocks   **Page 2**

- -

4. **Look** at the pattern of blocks below. **Tell** what blocks you need to complete the pattern.

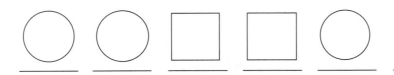

5. **Look** at the big circle below. **Put** the attribute blocks in it. **Match** the blocks with the shapes in the circle.

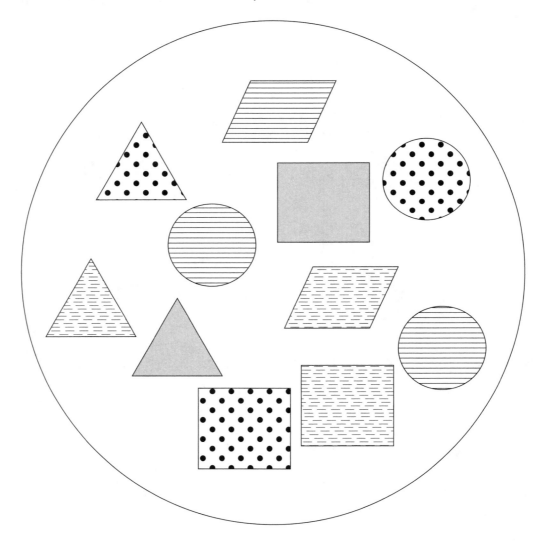

6. What is the attribute that is the same for all the blocks? **Find** a card to match that attribute. **Write** the attribute in the space below.

The attribute is: _____

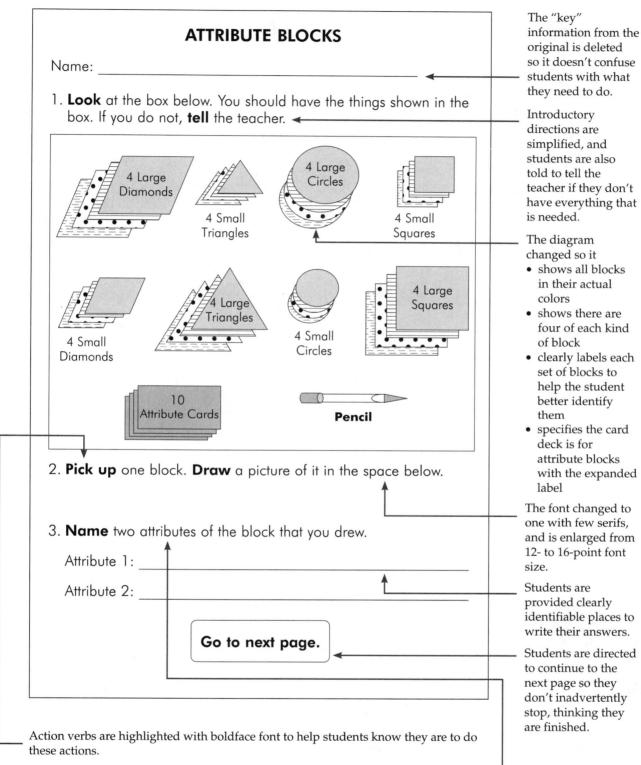

ATTRIBUTE BLOCKS

Name: _____

1. **Look** at the box below. You should have the things shown in the box. If you do not, **tell** the teacher.

4 Large Diamonds

4 Small Triangles

4 Large Circles

4 Small Squares

4 Small Diamonds

4 Large Triangles

4 Small Circles

4 Large Squares

10 Attribute Cards

Pencil

2. **Pick up** one block. **Draw** a picture of it in the space below.

3. **Name** two attributes of the block that you drew.

Attribute 1: _____

Attribute 2: _____

Go to next page.

The "key" information from the original is deleted so it doesn't confuse students with what they need to do.

Introductory directions are simplified, and students are also told to tell the teacher if they don't have everything that is needed.

The diagram changed so it
- shows all blocks in their actual colors
- shows there are four of each kind of block
- clearly labels each set of blocks to help the student better identify them
- specifies the card deck is for attribute blocks with the expanded label

The font changed to one with few serifs, and is enlarged from 12- to 16-point font size.

Students are provided clearly identifiable places to write their answers.

Students are directed to continue to the next page so they don't inadvertently stop, thinking they are finished.

Action verbs are highlighted with boldface font to help students know they are to do these actions.

The original term "properties" changed to "attributes" to provide consistency with other terms in the assessment.

Primary-Level Performance-Based Science Assessment
Annotated Revised Assessment: Attribute Blocks

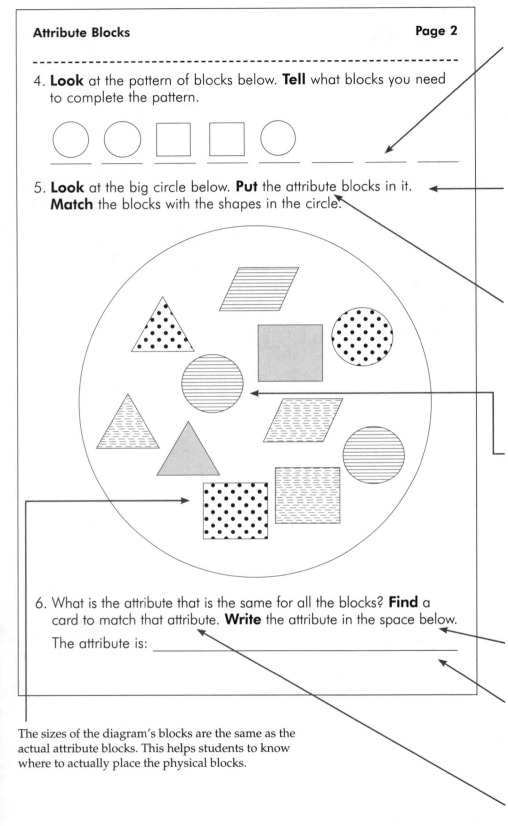

Attribute Blocks   **Page 2**

- -

4. **Look** at the pattern of blocks below. **Tell** what blocks you need to complete the pattern.

5. **Look** at the big circle below. **Put** the attribute blocks in it. **Match** the blocks with the shapes in the circle.

6. What is the attribute that is the same for all the blocks? **Find** a card to match that attribute. **Write** the attribute in the space below.

   The attribute is: _____

Blank spaces are provided so students can see that there should be one shape per space, and see that there are three spaces for them to draw blocks.

Directions are clarified for students, and include telling students specifically where to look for the diagram.

The term "characteristics" is replaced with "attributes" so it is consistent with phrasing and terms in the other parts of the assessment.

The shapes in the diagram are patterned to distinguish the actual colors of the attribute blocks rather than relying on gray-scale shadings. This will help students relate the actual blocks better to the diagram.

This tells students clearly where to write their answers.

A blank space is provided for students to write in their answers.

Item 6 is split from the original Item 5 to help students better understand what they are being asked to do.

The sizes of the diagram's blocks are the same as the actual attribute blocks. This helps students to know where to actually place the physical blocks.

Name: _____

STATION: MAKING OBSERVATIONS AND INFERENCES WITH AN ELECTRIC CIRCUIT

Grades: 4–6

Process Skill(s): observing and inferring

Concept(s): conductors, complete circuit, closed circuit, open circuit, series circuit

Do you have the items in the diagram?

1. Be sure your circuit (3 wires, bulb, bulb holder, battery, and battery holder) is set up as shown in the diagram.
2. Use this OPEN circuit to find the hidden conductors in the puzzle card.
3. Test the combinations and record a **"Y"** for each combination that lights the bulb. Record an **"N"** for each combination that doesn't light the bulb.

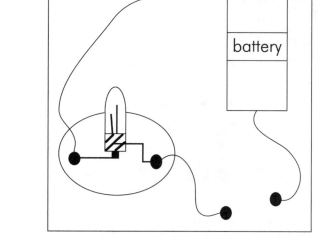

(OBSERVATIONS)

Use as many spaces as needed.

Combinations Tested												
Response of Bulb (**Y** or **N**)												

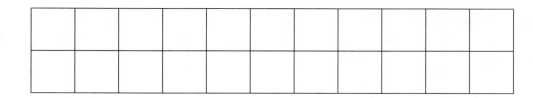

(INFERENCES)

4. From your observations, make inferences about where the wires are in your puzzle card. You may have more than one inference to explain your observations. Use the spaces below to record your inference and two alternate inferences.

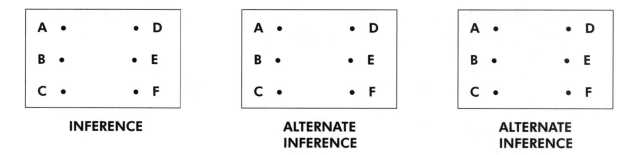

INFERENCE	**ALTERNATE INFERENCE**	**ALTERNATE INFERENCE**

Name: _____

STATION: MAKING OBSERVATIONS AND INFERENCES WITH AN ELECTRIC CIRCUIT

> **Grades:** 4–6   **Process Skill(s):** observing and inferring
>
> **Concept(s):** conductors, complete circuit, closed circuit, open circuit, series circuit

Look at the diagram to the right. You should have all the items shown in the diagram. If you do not, **tell the teacher** before going further.

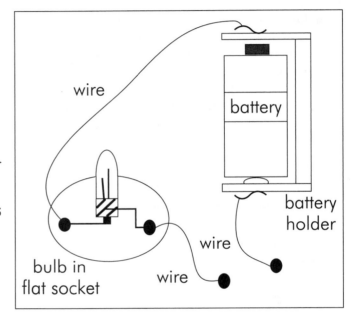

1. Be sure your circuit is set up as shown in the diagram. The circuit should include three wires, one bulb, one bulb holder, one battery, and one battery holder.

2. **Identify the type of circuit** shown in the diagram: Below is a list of terms used to describe circuits. **Circle the term or terms** that describe the circuit.

    CLOSED   OPEN   SERIES   PARALLEL   COMPLETE

3. **Use the circuit** to find the hidden conductors in the puzzle card. Here is what you should do:

    a) The puzzle-card circuit has six contact points. Each contact point is labeled with a letter. You will need to **decide which contact points are connected** with one another by a conductor.

> **Go to the next page!**

STATION: Electric Circuits

Page 2

----

b) **Write** in Table 1 any combinations of contact points you need to try. (Hint: You should only **use two** contact points for one combination.)

EXAMPLE
Testing contact points B and F

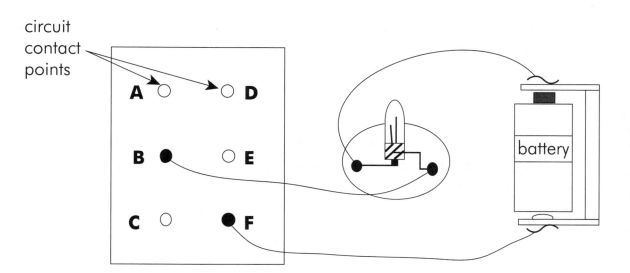

circuit contact points

c) If any contact points are connected by a conductor, the lightbulb will turn on. If they are not connected, the lightbulb will not turn on.

d) If a combination of contact points causes the light to turn on, **mark Table 1** with a "Y" for "yes." If the light does not turn on, **mark Table 1** with a "N" for "no." Table 1 is on top of page 3.

EXAMPLE

Combination Tested	A & D	B & F	
Bulb Turned On? (**Y** or **N**)	Y	N	

Go to the next page!

STATION: Electric Circuits   Page 3

----

e) Table 1 may not have enough spaces for you to mark. If you need more spaces, **make another table** in the space below Table 1.

Table 1

Combination Tested						
Bulb Turned On? (**Y** or **N**)						

4. From your observations, **make inferences** about where the wires are located in your puzzle card. **Draw your inferences** of where the wires are in the puzzle card. Do your drawing on the puzzle-card diagrams below. You may have more than one inference to explain your observations.

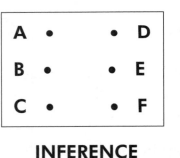

INFERENCE

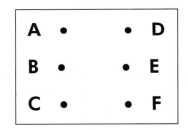

ALTERNATE INFERENCE

ALTERNATE INFERENCE

Name: _____

STATION: MAKING OBSERVATIONS
AND INFERENCES WITH AN ELECTRIC CIRCUIT

The information for the teacher is visually offset from the rest of the assessment.

Grades: 4–6   **Process Skill(s):** observing and inferring

Concept(s): conductors, complete circuit, closed circuit, open circuit, series circuit

Look at the diagram to the right. You should have all the items shown in the diagram. If you do not, **tell the teacher** before going further.

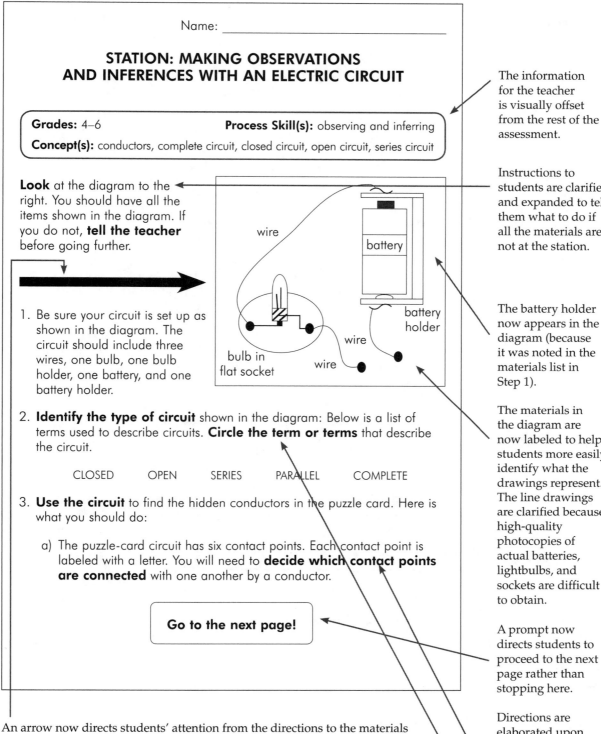

Instructions to students are clarified and expanded to tell them what to do if all the materials are not at the station.

The battery holder now appears in the diagram (because it was noted in the materials list in Step 1).

1. Be sure your circuit is set up as shown in the diagram. The circuit should include three wires, one bulb, one bulb holder, one battery, and one battery holder.

2. **Identify the type of circuit** shown in the diagram: Below is a list of terms used to describe circuits. **Circle the term or terms** that describe the circuit.

    CLOSED   OPEN   SERIES   PARALLEL   COMPLETE

3. **Use the circuit** to find the hidden conductors in the puzzle card. Here is what you should do:

    a) The puzzle-card circuit has six contact points. Each contact point is labeled with a letter. You will need to **decide which contact points are connected** with one another by a conductor.

    Go to the next page!

The materials in the diagram are now labeled to help students more easily identify what the drawings represent. The line drawings are clarified because high-quality photocopies of actual batteries, lightbulbs, and sockets are difficult to obtain.

A prompt now directs students to proceed to the next page rather than stopping here.

Directions are elaborated upon and expanded, yet appear in simpler form for better student understanding.

An arrow now directs students' attention from the directions to the materials diagram.

Step 2 now asks students to identify the terms that apply to the circuit (rather than giving the information to students).

- The original observations table is shorter and appears on another page where it is more appropriate for the sequence of steps students are to follow.

- The original inferences table was deleted, because students are asked to indicate their inferences on the puzzle-card diagrams on page 3.

STATION: Electric Circuits   **Page 2**

Directions are separated from the assessment identification by a thick line to reduce student confusion between the two.

b) **Write** in Table 1 any combinations of contact points you need to try. (Hint: You should only **use two** contact points for one combination.)

EXAMPLE
Testing contact points B and F

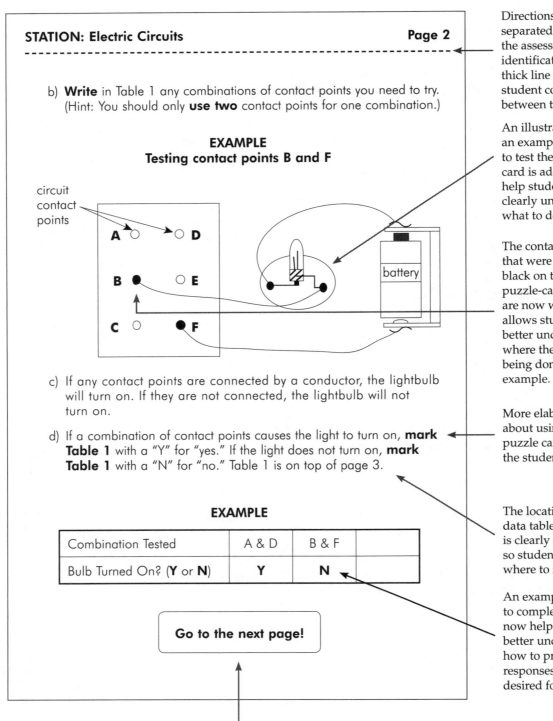

circuit contact points

An illustration of an example of how to test the puzzle card is added to help students more clearly understand what to do.

The contact points that were originally black on the original puzzle-card diagram are now white. This allows students to better understand where the testing is being done in this example.

c) If any contact points are connected by a conductor, the lightbulb will turn on. If they are not connected, the lightbulb will not turn on.

d) If a combination of contact points causes the light to turn on, **mark Table 1** with a "Y" for "yes." If the light does not turn on, **mark Table 1** with a "N" for "no." Table 1 is on top of page 3.

More elaboration about using the puzzle card helps the students.

The location of the data table (Table 1) is clearly designated so students know where to find it.

EXAMPLE

Combination Tested	A & D	B & F	
Bulb Turned On? (**Y** or **N**)	Y	N	

An example of how to complete Table 1 now helps students better understand how to provide their responses in the desired format.

Go to the next page!

A prompt now directs students to proceed to the next page rather than stopping here.

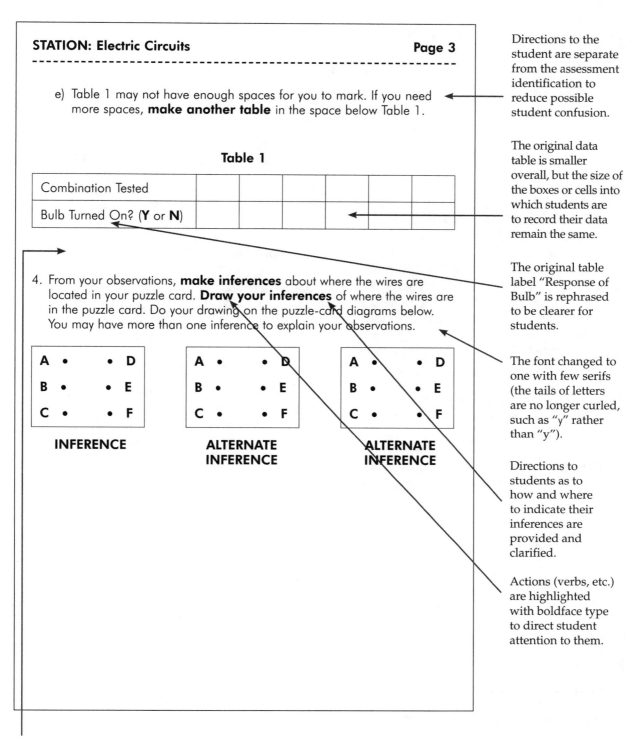

STATION: Electric Circuits Page 3

---

e) Table 1 may not have enough spaces for you to mark. If you need more spaces, **make another table** in the space below Table 1.

Table 1

Combination Tested						
Bulb Turned On? (**Y** or **N**)						

4. From your observations, **make inferences** about where the wires are located in your puzzle card. **Draw your inferences** of where the wires are in the puzzle card. Do your drawing on the puzzle-card diagrams below. You may have more than one inference to explain your observations.

A •   • D
B •   • E
C •   • F

INFERENCE

A •   • D
B •   • E
C •   • F

ALTERNATE INFERENCE

A •   • D
B •   • E
C •   • F

ALTERNATE INFERENCE

Directions to the student are separate from the assessment identification to reduce possible student confusion.

The original data table is smaller overall, but the size of the boxes or cells into which students are to record their data remain the same.

The original table label "Response of Bulb" is rephrased to be clearer for students.

The font changed to one with few serifs (the tails of letters are no longer curled, such as "y" rather than "y").

Directions to students as to how and where to indicate their inferences are provided and clarified.

Actions (verbs, etc.) are highlighted with boldface type to direct student attention to them.

Extra space is provided for students to continue recording their data if needed.

DENSITY

KEY
Grades   6–8
Concept(s)   mass, volume, density
Process Skill(s) measuring, using numbers,
                     observing, predicting

What You Should Have & Where It Should Be

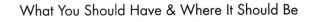

1. Compare your work station with the diagram to the right. Be sure each item is present in its location as shown on the diagram. When you complete this station's activities, be sure each item is placed back where it belongs at this work station.

balance & masses   100 ml graduated cylinder   bottle of water

metric ruler

metal cube

paper towels

Work Station Diagram

2. Determine the mass of the metal cube. Record its mass in the blank below:

   a. Cube Mass: _____

3. Determine the volume of the metal cube. Record its volume in the blank below:

   a. Cube Volume: _____

4. Calculate the density of the metal cube. Record its density in the blank to the right: _____

   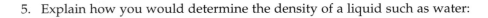

   _____

5. Explain how you would determine the density of a liquid such as water:

   _____

   _____

   _____

   _____

   _____

6. Now determine the actual density of water: _____

7. Explain why the metal cube would probably sink in water while a wooden cube would probably float in water:

   _____

   _____

   _____

PLEASE BE SURE THE WORK STATION AREA IS *CLEAN* AND DRY, AND THAT EVERYTHING IS PUT BACK IN ITS PLACE BEFORE YOU LEAVE.

DENSITY

Name: _____

In this assessment, you will show what you know about mass, volume, and density. You will be observing, measuring, using numbers, and predicting. Read each question carefully. Then, write your answers in the spaces provided for them.

- -

BEFORE YOU BEGIN

Look at the diagram to the right. ➡

- Compare the diagram to your work area.
- Be sure each item shown in the diagram is also at your work area.
- Each thing should be in its own place, just like it is in the diagram.
- If something is missing, let the teacher know now.

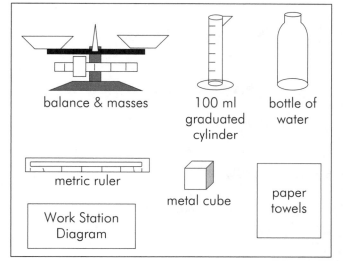

- -

PROCEDURES

Step A

___ 1. Determine the mass of the metal cube.

___ 2. Record the mass of the metal cube in this space ➡ ____

- -

Step B

___ 1. Determine the volume of the metal cube.

___ 2. Record the volume of the metal cube in this space ➡ ____

> **Continue to the next page.**

Density   **Page 2**

PROCEDURES Continued

- -

Step C

___ 1. Calculate the density of the metal cube. Remember the density
formula for the calculation:

density = mass divided by volume

$$\text{density} = \frac{\text{mass}}{\text{volume}} \qquad d = \frac{m}{v}$$

metal cube **mass** (from Step A) =

metal cube **volume** (from Step B) =

- -

QUESTION

a. **Explain** how you would determine the density of a liquid such as
water:

_____

_____

_____

_____

_____

_____

┌───┐
│   │
│   **Continue to the next page.**   │
│   │
└───┘

Density **Page 3**

Step D

___ 1. Determine the actual density of water. Follow the procedure you explained in the question on page 2. Be sure to show your work in the space below.

Mass of water = _____

Volume of water = _____

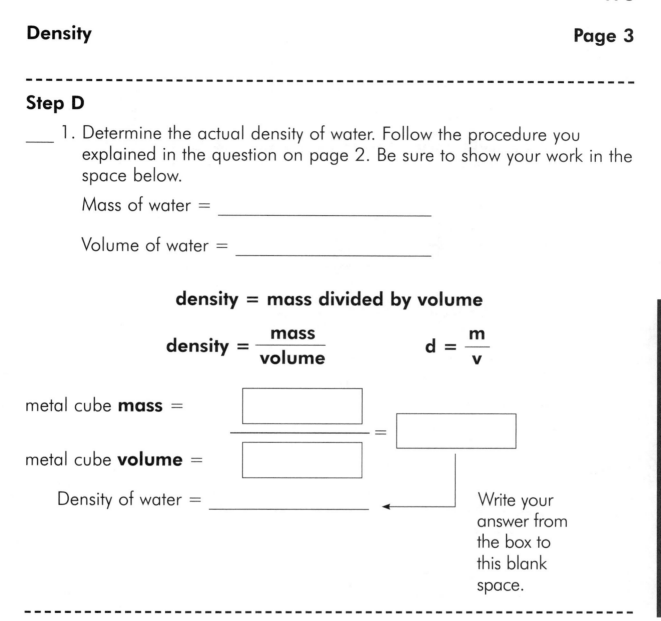

density = mass divided by volume

$$\text{density} = \frac{\text{mass}}{\text{volume}} \qquad d = \frac{m}{v}$$

metal cube **mass** =

$$\frac{\boxed{}}{\boxed{}} = \boxed{}$$

metal cube **volume** =

Density of water = _____

Write your answer from the box to this blank space.

QUESTION

b. **Explain** why the metal cube would probably sink in water while a wooden cube would probably float in water:

_____

_____

_____

YOU ARE NOW FINISHED. PLEASE BE SURE THE WORK STATION AREA IS *CLEAN* AND DRY, AND THAT EVERYTHING IS PUT BACK IN ITS PLACE BEFORE YOU LEAVE.

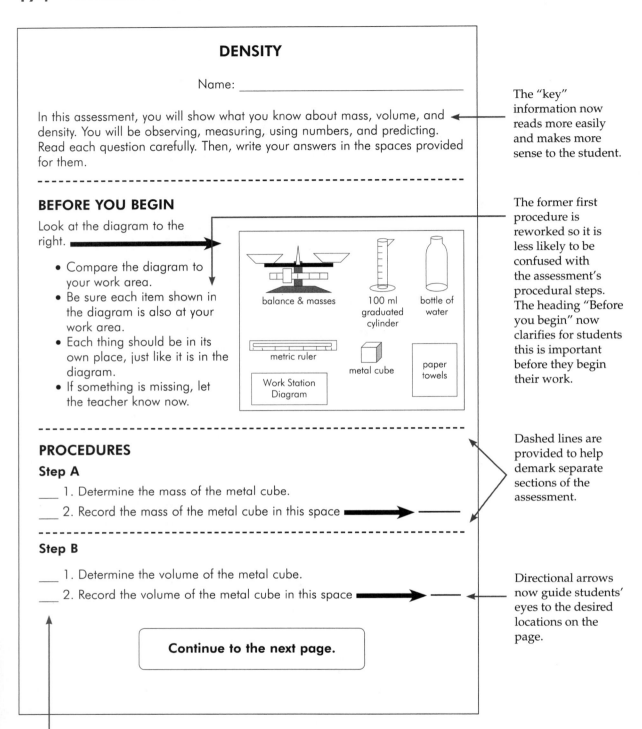

DENSITY

Name: _____

In this assessment, you will show what you know about mass, volume, and density. You will be observing, measuring, using numbers, and predicting. Read each question carefully. Then, write your answers in the spaces provided for them.

The "key" information now reads more easily and makes more sense to the student.

BEFORE YOU BEGIN

Look at the diagram to the right.

- Compare the diagram to your work area.
- Be sure each item shown in the diagram is also at your work area.
- Each thing should be in its own place, just like it is in the diagram.
- If something is missing, let the teacher know now.

balance & masses

100 ml graduated cylinder

bottle of water

metric ruler

metal cube

paper towels

Work Station Diagram

The former first procedure is reworked so it is less likely to be confused with the assessment's procedural steps. The heading "Before you begin" now clarifies for students this is important before they begin their work.

PROCEDURES

Step A

____ 1. Determine the mass of the metal cube.

____ 2. Record the mass of the metal cube in this space ⟶ ____

Dashed lines are provided to help demark separate sections of the assessment.

Step B

____ 1. Determine the volume of the metal cube.

____ 2. Record the volume of the metal cube in this space ⟶ ____

Continue to the next page.

Directional arrows now guide students' eyes to the desired locations on the page.

Blanks now appear to the left of each procedural step so the assessment format is more consistent with the format used for activities.

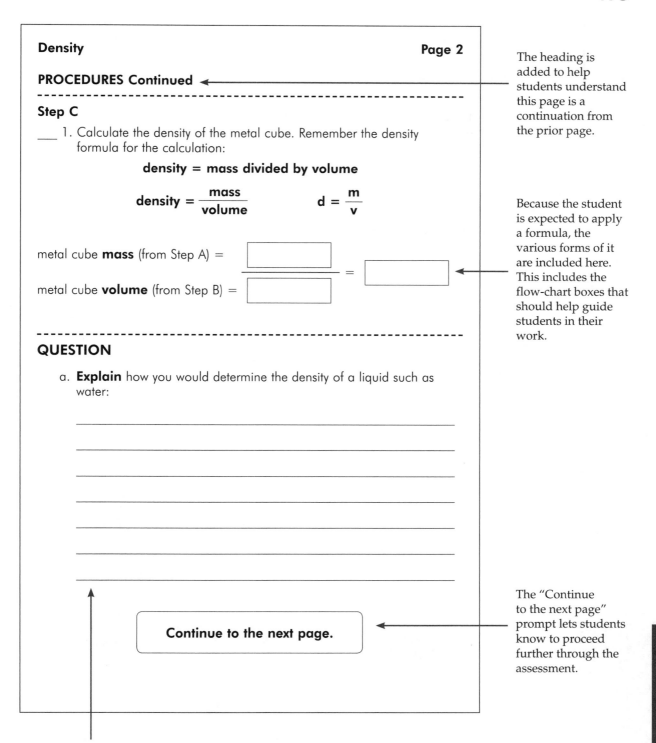

Density   **Page 2**

PROCEDURES Continued ◄————————————————————

The heading is added to help students understand this page is a continuation from the prior page.

- -

Step C

___ 1. Calculate the density of the metal cube. Remember the density formula for the calculation:

density = mass divided by volume

$$\text{density} = \frac{\text{mass}}{\text{volume}} \qquad d = \frac{m}{v}$$

metal cube **mass** (from Step A) = ☐

metal cube **volume** (from Step B) = ☐

= ☐ ◄—

Because the student is expected to apply a formula, the various forms of it are included here. This includes the flow-chart boxes that should help guide students in their work.

- -

QUESTION

a. **Explain** how you would determine the density of a liquid such as water:

_____

_____

_____

_____

_____

_____

_____

_____

| **Continue to the next page.** | ◄—

The "Continue to the next page" prompt lets students know to proceed further through the assessment.

Each procedural step is separate from the others and clearly labeled (e.g., Step A, Step B, Step C), and the subparts of each step are clearly labeled.

Middle-School Level Performance-Based Science Assessment
Annotated Revised Assessment: Density

Density   **Page 3**

- -

Step D

___ 1. Determine the actual density of water. Follow the procedure you explained in the question on page 2. Be sure to show your work in the space below.

Mass of water = _____

Volume of water = _____

density = mass divided by volume

$$\text{density} = \frac{\text{mass}}{\text{volume}} \qquad d = \frac{m}{v}$$

metal cube **mass** = [_____]

_____ = [_____]

metal cube **volume** = [_____]

Density of water = _____   ← Write your answer from the box to this blank space.

The flow-chart format for using the formula is repeated, and a directional arrow shows students where to insert their answer.

- -

QUESTION

b. **Explain** why the metal cube would probably sink in water while a wooden cube would probably float in water:

_____

_____

_____

Key action verbs are highlighted in boldface to draw students' attention to what they are being asked to do.

- -

YOU ARE NOW FINISHED. PLEASE BE SURE THE WORK STATION AREA IS *CLEAN* AND DRY, AND THAT EVERYTHING IS PUT BACK IN ITS PLACE BEFORE YOU LEAVE.

Students are clearly informed when they are at the end of the assessment.

Although not apparent on this reduced-size copy, the font changed to one that lacks serifs. In addition, it increased in size to 14 point.

CONCLUSION

Throughout this chapter, examples of science assessments were provided in different forms: the original version, a revised version that follows the guidelines and suggestions from Chapter 3, and then a revised version with annotations added to specifically indicate what revisions were made and rationales for why they were done. As with the activities in Chapter 4, assessment samples in this chapter included the range of science disciplines, from biological to earth to physical sciences; and a range of grade levels, from primary through middle school. Although more examples could be provided, the ones included in this chapter should be sufficient models to help teachers in their attempts to take the guidelines and apply them to both traditional and performance-based assessments from their own classrooms. To reiterate part of the concluding comments from Chapter 4, teachers may wish to keep their first efforts more manageable by revising smaller or shorter assessments until they are practiced in the process, or they may prefer to revise certain portions of larger assessments rather than the entire assessments. Whatever course of action taken, the teacher must remember that these revising protocols are to help with the delivery of inquiry-based instruction, not to replace it.

6

Developing and Using Rubrics to Evaluate Student Performance

INTRODUCTION

Sometimes it is difficult to understand the difference between assessment and evaluation. Even though a teacher might understand the definitions, it can be difficult to apply that information. This chapter is designed to assist teachers in their efforts to better understand what is involved with assessment and what is involved with evaluation, particularly with respect to students with special learning needs through differentiated science instruction. As a starting point, the chapter begins with some brief information about assessment and evaluation, and then also briefly discusses rubrics. Much more detailed information on these topics can be found in other books available to teachers through various outlets. The latter half of this chapter applies this information to two student work samples.

VIGNETTE WITH MS. JANIS

Ms. Janis is a new second-grade teacher. While in college, she really enjoyed her science classes, and actively sought out experiences where she could engage in science activities and investigations. She feels she learned much from those experiences, and believes her own students will also benefit from good quality, hands-on/minds-on science activities. What students wouldn't like to dig into investigating mealworms, for example? Hands-on/minds-on activities are also a great way to get her students with special learning needs more involved in doing science.

So, this is exactly what Ms. Janis plans and implements in her instruction. When observing in her classroom, Mrs. Mekam, the principal, asks her how she assesses the learning the students are getting from doing activities like the mealworms. After all, teachers must be accountable to the school, state, and parents for student outcomes. This includes how Ms. Janis will derive grades and justify them to both students and parents. Ms. Janis thus needs have some understanding of assessment and evaluation, and have specific criteria to follow to support her classroom instructional decisions. How, then, can Ms. Janis do this? One way is for her to find or create appropriate science assessments, and to complement them by locating or developing, and then using, rubrics in her teaching.

DIFFERENTIATING BETWEEN ASSESSMENT AND EVALUATION

Ms. Janis and other educators often use the terms *assessment* and *evaluation* interchangeably. Although the two terms are related to one another, they are not synonymous. Similarly, the terms *test* and *assessment* are often used as if they are one and the same. In order to better understand the development, design, and use of assessments appropriate for specific populations of learners, Ms. Janis should be aware of the difference between these terms.

Assessment Defined

Assessment is more than simply testing. When teachers test, they use a relatively specific and narrow set of questions or tasks in a way that is typically highly structured and can be completed in a limited amount of time. Assessment, by its nature, includes gathering or collecting information from multiple sources. Usually, *assessment is seen as an organized effort to obtain information about what a learner knows and can do*, and employs various means by which that information is obtained. A test may or may not be part of an assessment. Teachers like Ms. Janis can assess students' learning with other tools including portfolios, checklists, observations of learner performance on a task, one-on-one interviews, and so forth. Teachers should understand that one often assesses a situation but does not necessarily make any judgment as to whether it is good or bad (the value of the information gathered), which is the evaluative aspect of the picture.

Evaluation Defined

By its nature, evaluation necessarily follows assessment. Even without thinking about it, when teachers evaluate something or someone, they have previously made some assessment (albeit very short and limited ones at times). When teachers evaluate, they apply the assessment outcomes to some criteria, such as specified levels of skill, grade ranges, or eligibility for admittance to a particular group. In other words, teachers make a judgment about the value of assessment information available. During evaluation, teachers interpret the assessment data to arrive at a judgment, or conclusion. Hopefully, when teachers evaluate, they take into account such things as the context in which the assessment occurred, the climate or circumstances during assessment, and the nature and characteristics of the learner.

TYPES OF ASSESSMENT

Teachers have at their disposal many types of assessments, and a book such as this cannot do justice to all of them (e.g., authentic assessments, portfolios, etc.). For the purpose of helping teachers like Ms. Janis, subsequent attention focuses briefly on two types of assessment: forced-choice (or objective) and performance-based (or complex-generated response) assessment. There are both high-quality and poor-quality forced-choice assessments, and the same applies to performance-based assessments. Simply because a teacher has one type of assessment does not necessarily imply it is of poor quality. Further, both types of assessment have their place in education, and both must be designed carefully and with clear intention in mind (Abell & Volkmann, 2006; Stiggins, 1987). A growing number of educators promote assessing learners with a combination of the two. There are various sources from which teachers can obtain forced-choice and performance-based assessment items. These range from published commercial assessments to locally developed assessments (including teacher developed). Whatever the source or type, there are pros and cons for teachers to consider, summarized as follows (Stiggins, 1987).

Forced-choice assessments are characterized as providing learners a stem or stimuli that they must respond to, along with a set of responses from which they must select an answer. Examples include, but are not limited to, multiple-choice and matching questions. Formerly, most standardized tests were largely comprised of forced-choice items. Many standardized tests today include performance-based items as well. Advantages of using forced-choice items for standardized assessment include the ease and efficiency with which it can be completed and scored. There is one "correct" response for an item and performance results are likely to be the same regardless of who scores the assessment. Forced-choice assessments are effective for assessing knowledge and understanding. They are efficient and can be very reliable. They are usually constructed from clearly defined content. However, they cannot easily assess most performance skills very well, and they tend to assess lower levels of thinking (as per Bloom's taxonomy). Common drawbacks to these assessments include items that are poorly written, administration of the assessments in poor conditions, and a tendency for students to guess on responses. Since virtually every state now has standardized testing as part of their accountability criteria, teachers need to know how to effectively use these assessments to support their instructional decisions.

Performance-based types of assessment (product, portfolio, performances, etc.) are alternatives to traditional paper and pencil testing for knowledge. Performance-based assessments require learners to construct their responses to questions, using prior knowledge and pertinent skills to solve realistic problems (Office of Education Research, 1993). Performance-based assessment attempts to apply skills in a manner similar to the method the student uses during the learning process. It is an active, hands-on form of assessment and allows learners to demonstrate their understanding of concepts and apply acquired knowledge and skills. In order to assess specific knowledge, critical thinking, and problem-solving skills, the teacher must carefully construct performance-assessment tasks. They can be short tasks (requiring just a few minutes for students to do), or more extended or enriched activities (requiring days to complete) (Baron, 1990). Scoring criteria (i.e., rubrics) must also be carefully developed and shared with students. If constructed properly, performance-based assessments can be very reliable and fair. Among the drawbacks are that they can be very time consuming to construct and administer, and can be expensive in terms of energy and resources. One consequence of this is that some performance-based assessments tend to cover too few topics or concepts. As with forced-choice assessments, performance-based assessments can be poorly written, administered under poor conditions, or simply not sufficiently designed to cover necessary content.

Performance-based assessments lend themselves well to science. Hein (1991) and Hein and Price (1994) identified six categories of performance assessments that are easily used by science teachers: (1) using graphical and symbolic representations from graphs, tables, charts, and other visuals; (2) using apparatus such as measuring instruments or microscopes; (3) making, interpreting, and using observations and predictions; (4) interpreting and applying data and information; (5) planning investigations, including formulating hypotheses and ways to test them; and (6) performing investigations. The national standards (see the Resource section at the back of the book) place much emphasis on having students learn science by doing it, as well as teachers assessing science by having students do it. (See also Atkin, Black, & Coffey, 2001.)

It is congruent and consistent to have hands-on/minds-on science instruction coupled with performance-based assessment. In addition, performance-based instruction can lead teachers to include more and better quality hands-on/minds-on science instruction, and to integrate more content threads together. Once a decision is made with respect to the particular assessments and evaluation criteria, the next step is to design or select appropriate rubrics to go along with those assessments.

THE BUSINESS OF RUBRICS

Today, teachers often hear the term *rubric*, particularly when they work with assessments. What, then, is a rubric? What purpose does a rubric serve? How important is a rubric? Such questions are common among teachers. Here, a brief summary of relevant information helps answer these questions.

Rubrics Defined

A rubric is a guide to follow when scoring assessments. Some prefer the term *scoring criteria* to rubrics. The original definition of *rubric* comes from "marks in red," a phrase used in former days, likely as a result of grading student papers. Today, the term refers to the guidelines, sometimes in a document, describing how to score all of or parts of an assessment. Such guidelines can come in a variety of forms, but two are generally recognized: *analytic* and *holistic*. The type of rubric designed or selected for any particular assessment varies depending upon a number of factors, including but not limited to (1) the focus or intent of the assessment, (2) the type of instruction preceding assessment, and (3) personal preferences of the person doing the assessing.

Role and Importance of Rubrics

When teachers write assessments, they likely have some idea of what they expect as "correct" answers. For forced-choice assessments, teachers are apt to make a scoring key to accompany the assessment. For essay questions, this may include the salient points a student must communicate in order to receive a certain number of points. These are essentially rubrics. However, a rubric is somewhat more formalized than simple scoring keys. Rubrics often provide some preliminary information on the context in which, and conditions under which, the assessment is administered. They provide detailed breakdowns of points to be awarded for student responses, and how those points are to be awarded. In short, rubrics are designed to measure student progress by awarding points for specific responses to each component of an assigned academic task.

The criteria teachers employ in the rubric should be established prior to giving the task to the student. This is to avoid problems the scorer (usually the teacher) may have with vacillating between awarding one set of points for a response and then awarding a different set of points for the same level of response on a different item or from another student. Establishing the criteria early also helps teachers be certain they are targeting the assessment on what they intend to focus. If the assessment and the rubric do not match, then an obvious problem occurs when scoring the assessment. Designing an appropriate rubric is just as important as designing the assessment, and sometimes requires about as much time and effort. As rubrics are written and implemented, they may require revision in order to best measure student performance. There are times, for example, when the specifically designed rubric fails to account for the range of possible responses that students provide.

Once the teacher establishes the rubric (scoring criteria), the assessment can be administered to students. For the assessment to be most effective, each student should be made aware of and come to understand the particular rubric prior to beginning the task to be assessed. The student then knows exactly what is required in order to demonstrate the targeted skills of the task. After the teacher administers the assessment, each student response needs to be matched with an acceptable response on the rubric. Then, a total or overall score for the assessment can be derived.

When used consistently, rubrics serve a dual purpose for both teachers and students—serving as assessment tools as well as vehicles for effective teaching. As an assessment tool, the rubric provides a standard against which student work can be compared and judged. The data derived from the rubric can be used to make performance comparisons across students as well to provide information about a particular student's mastery of targeted skills. To promote effective teaching, rubrics present a goal for student performance. That is, teachers can establish target goals for their students' performance. Rubrics can further be used to assess the efficacy of a particular curriculum. Data from a rubric allows teachers to determine if the curriculum is meeting the needs of the students, if topics need reteaching, or even if the instructional goals are inappropriate for the students. *Hence, it is very important at the outset to clearly establish the intent of the assessment and of the rubric. The intent for which the assessment is designed should match the design of the rubric.*

TYPES OF RUBRICS

Analytic Rubrics

Analytic rubrics assess student products based on elements of the assessment scale. That is, the teacher awards points for very specific responses on different portions of an assessment. All points from each part of the assessment are then added together to derive an overall score, and determine the performance of the student. Such scoring criteria are quite specific as to what can and cannot be awarded points. When teachers use analytic rubrics, they must analyze each response made by a student and score those responses according to the established criteria.

Analytic rubrics support a more objective and consistent assessment of student work. Data resulting from an analytic rubric gives the student specific, detailed feedback about the components of a task as well as an aggregate score. However, by their nature, analytic rubrics are more process than product oriented.

Analytic rubrics may be very restrictive or may allow for variability in student responses. For example, imagine a teacher plans to assess a student on her ability to accurately determine the mass of an object that the teacher knows to be 45 grams. An example of a restrictive rubric awards points is shown in Figure 6.1.

Figure 6.1   Restrictive Analytic Rubric Example

1 point	= Student determines mass of object at exactly 45 grams.
0 points	= Student determines mass of object to be other than 45 grams.

OR

Student does not attempt to fill the cylinder and/or fails to record an answer.

Now imagine that the teacher is concerned with the quality of the balance the student must use, or that the teacher believes time availability or student ability must be considered. In this case, the teacher may wish to use a rubric that has more variable scoring. This type of scoring uses error ranges that can be designated by percentage ranges or actual measurement values. Two examples of variable analytic rubrics are shown in Figure 6.2.

Figure 6.2   Variable Analytic Rubric Example

3 points	= Student masses object to within 0%–4% of 45 grams.
2 points	= Student masses object to within 4%–7% of 45 grams.
1 point	= Student masses object but mass is more than 7% from 45 grams.
0 points	= Student does not attempt to mass the object and/or fails to record an answer.

OR

3 points	= Student masses the object to 44–46 grams.
2 points	= Student masses the object to 42–44 grams or to 46–48 grams.
1 point	= Student masses object to mass less than 42 grams or greater than 48 grams.
0 points	= Student does not attempt to mass the object and/or fails to record an answer.

Each such measuring activity included within the assessment has specific scoring criteria. If there are three things the student must measure, then each has a range of possible answers analyzed and points assigned to each answer.

Holistic Rubrics

Teachers use holistic rubrics when they desire to assess the total, or overall, performance of a student or the overall quality of a student's response. Holistic rubrics are more product than process oriented. In other words, holistic rubrics are concerned primarily with the overall performance or product rather than with the individual steps made to arrive at the final product. Each individual step is not necessarily analyzed and scored as occurs with analytic scoring. However, criteria for holistic scoring should reflect specific and important elements of a solution to a problem or to other acceptable answers.

When developing holistic rubrics, teachers must first determine performance indicators, typically referring to superior, acceptable, inadequate, or unacceptable levels. In its purest form, a holistic rubric is not used to award points. Student products (or assessments) are simply rated according to the identified indicators. However, since most assessments used in schools lead to evaluation, points can be designated for each indicator. Doing this makes the rubric what is called quasi-holistic, since it is not purely holistic. Holistic rubrics should include details that describe each indicator (or level of performance). The rubric in Figure 6.3 could be used for assessing the work of students who have been asked to design and conduct an experiment.

Figure 6.3 Holistic Rubric Example

3 Points—*Superior Performance*
- The hypothesis is clearly stated and is limited to the variables involved.
- All variables are correctly identified and none are misidentified.
- All procedures are explicitly and clearly stated with no extraneous steps, but do include safety considerations, a complete materials list limited to only those items required, and clear and correct identification of any and all controls.
- The conclusion, including analysis and interpretation of data, is thorough and takes into account all data, is based on sound scientific principles that apply to the experiment, is not overgeneralized, and is clear.

2 Points—*Acceptable Performance*

- The hypothesis is somewhat clear but may include some extraneous variables or may omit needed phrasing about one variable.
- All but one variable are correctly identified.
- Most necessary procedures are clearly described, but they may include one or two minor extraneous steps, or have unclear safety considerations; materials list is incomplete or has needless items; or the control includes a minor omission or addition.
- The conclusion takes into account most data and tends to be based on scientific principles that apply to the experiment, and is basically clear, but may overgeneralize to a slight extent.

1 Point—*Poor Performance*

- Hypothesis is somewhat unclear, fails to include most variables involved, and may even include some extraneous variables.
- Two or more variables are not correctly identified and/or other variables are misidentified.
- Few procedures are stated or procedures are stated unclearly; the steps include too many unnecessary steps or fail to include those needed to complete the experiment; the materials list is incomplete or includes many unnecessary items; and the control is not clearly described and may or may not include omissions or additions.
- The conclusion fails to take into account major portions of data or attempts to include data not obtained directly from the experiment, and/or tends to overgeneralize, misapply scientific principles, or include other significant errors.

0 Points—*Not Applicable or No Attempt*

- Hypothesis has little or nothing to do with the experiment or no attempt is made to make a hypothesis.
- Variables are identified but they either have little or nothing to do with the experiment, they are completely misidentified, or no attempt is made to identify and deal with variables.
- Procedures given are vague or unclear and do not address the experiment; materials listed are inappropriate, too few, or include too many unnecessary items; control is absent or not appropriate for the experiment; or no attempt is made to describe procedures.
- The conclusion does not take into account most or all data collected, ignores data and/or focuses on data external to the experiment, and/or misapplies scientific principles; or no attempt is made to analyze and interpret data and draw conclusions.

Teachers may find preparing a grid, or matrix, to represent the holistic rubric helpful. The indicators are usually arranged across the top while specific performances are arranged in a column along the left. Descriptions are provided in each cell (box) of the grid. Such grids allow the advantage of creating a rather comprehensive holistic rubric which encompasses several performances, and which alleviates the need for multiple pages of the rubric. An example of the holistic grid rubric can is shown in Figure 6.4.

Figure 6.4   Experimental Design Rubric (Holistic Grid or Matrix)

Experimental Element	Superior	Acceptable	Poor	Not Applicable or No Attempt
1. Hypothesis	Hypothesis is clearly stated, limited to variables involved, and made in general terms.	Hypothesis is somewhat clear, may include extraneous variable(s), or omit needed phrasing about one variable.	Hypothesis is somewhat unclear, fails to include most variables involved, or may include many extraneous variables.	Hypothesis has little or nothing to do with experiment at hand, or no attempt made to provide a hypothesis.
2. Variables	All variables are correctly identified and none are misidentified (e.g., dependent variables identified as independent, etc.).	All but one variable are correctly identified.	Two or more variables are not correctly identified and/or other variables are misidentified (e.g., dependent ones identified as independent).	Variables are identified but they either have little or nothing to do with the experiment; they are completely misidentified; or no attempt is made.
3. Procedures and materials	All procedures are explicitly and clearly stated with no extraneous steps; safety considerations are present; all materials needed are clearly identified and do not include unnecessary items; and all controls are clearly and correctly identified.	Most necessary procedures are stated clearly, and may include one or two minor extraneous step(s); safety considerations are not clear; the materials list is either incomplete or includes one or two unnecessary items; and the control includes a minor omission or addition.	Few procedures are stated and/or are stated unclearly and without detail; steps include too many unnecessary procedures or fail to include those which are needed; materials list is incomplete or includes more than two unnecessary items; and control is only partly included and may or may not include inappropriate omissions or additions.	Procedures are vague and/or unclear, and/or do not address the experiment at hand; materials listed are inappropriate, too few, or include too many unnecessary items; control is absent, or not appropriate for experiment; or no attempt is made.
4. Conclusion, analysis, and interpretation	Conclusion is thorough, takes into account all data, is based on sound scientific principles that apply to the experiment, does not overgeneralize, and is clear.	Conclusion takes into account most data, tends to be based on scientific principles that apply to the experiment, may overgeneralize to a slight extent, and is basically clear.	Conclusion fails to take into account major portions of data or attempts to include data not obtained directly from the experiment, and/or tends to overgeneralize, misapplies scientific principles, etc.	Conclusion fails to take into account most or all data collected, ignores data and/or focuses on data external to experiment, and/or misapplies scientific principles; or no attempt is made.

USE OF RUBRICS IN INCLUSIVE SETTINGS

An analytic rubric may be most appropriate for teachers to use with students who have exceptional learning needs. With these rubrics, such students (as any student) can receive credit for the process skills required to complete the task rather than simply being restricted to the product itself. In comparison, a holistic rubric is more product oriented and is used to measure the overall quality of the learner's response.

Because they measure different aspects of a task, it is possible for analytic and holistic rubrics to be used together. A science experiment might be scored holistically for all students as a screening procedure to determine overall quality of the product. As a follow-up, an analytic rubric can help assess the work of the students who did not produce an experiment with satisfactory results. In some instances, a quasi-holistic rubric may be most appropriate, because it has qualities of both analytic and holistic scoring.

While many of the benefits of rubrics are clear, establishing rubric criteria can be problematic. At first, teachers may feel compelled to fit any and all scoring into a certain scheme. For example, they might try to have all questions worth 10 points, and thus try to fit a rubric into a 10-point scale. This may or may not work. If only 5 points are justified by the rubric, then imposing them onto a 10-point scale is inappropriate. Typically, and particularly for analytic rubrics, three to six categories or levels of response are common. Lower grade-level students may require rubrics having fewer response levels. This may be useful for adapting rubrics for use with students with special needs as well. That is, the teacher can adjust the rubric to more appropriately assess the performance of students with exceptionalities.

Teachers working with students with special educational needs may find a 3-point rubric useful for the following reasons. First, the 3-point rubric is relatively easy to write because responses are based on the scale of above average, average, and below average. Second, the distinction between the three response levels is easily defined and recognized. When creating a 3-point rubric, the top score is for students who demonstrate an exceptional understanding of the component of the task being analyzed. The middle score is for students who show a satisfactory understanding, and the lowest score is for students who demonstrate an incomplete understanding or unsatisfactory performance.

Teachers may want to use a 4-point rubric because the 4 points translate easily into the traditional A, B, C, and D grade categories. It is not necessary to limit the criteria in each category of the task to the same number of response levels. In other words, one task may have three response levels while another has five. As an example, in an assessment on measuring, the teacher may choose to have only two response levels for the measuring of the mass of an object, but then have five response levels for the measuring and calculation of the density of the object. This is justifiable because the second one requires more of the student.

The total number of points that a rubric provides should emerge as the rubric is developed, rather than be forced. If a rubric ends up with a total of 40 points, the teacher should use that value rather than attempting to impose 50 points onto the rubric value. If teachers then wish to convert the rubric total scores into something more preferable, such as a value on a 100-point scale, they can do so. For the 40-point example, if a student earns 36 points, this equates to 90 percent. The teacher can record either 36 out of 40 points or 90 out of 100 points in the grade book.

Teachers may want to solicit student input on creation of rubrics. This process can make students more aware of task expectations and also help them to achieve at higher levels. As a teaching tool, a rubric provides a target example for students. To demonstrate the range of teacher expectations for specific tasks, sample rubrics as well as completed papers can be organized into a three-ring binder and made available to both students and parents. For students, these samples provide document responses at each level of the rubric. Similarly, for parents, the collection of rubrics shows examples of the teacher's expectations, and how capable a learner is in meeting those expectations, as compared to the rest of the students in the class.

When used consistently, rubrics can serve a dual purpose for students and teachers. First, the rubric serves as a standard against which student work can be judged. To promote effective teaching, rubrics establish a goal for student achievement and progress. Second, students, when informed early of levels of performance expectations, are much more likely to complete the tasks successfully.

Finally, if a teacher like Ms. Janis still doesn't feel she is informed enough to begin making her own rubrics from scratch, she can access rubrics through many of the teacher guide materials that accompany her text, or she can access samples via the Internet that she can modify to fit the particular needs of her situation. Rubistar, for example, is a well-known Internet rubric site that may be a starting place for her (see http://rubistar.4teachers.org/).

THE PRACTICE MATERIALS

This section contains an assessment activity, an analytic rubric to be used to score that activity, and some background information about the class in which the assessment is given. The assessment activity, titled Rubber Band Stretch, would be administered to students after instruction on measuring, hypothesizing, graphing, predicting, identifying and controlling variables, and understanding the elasticity of various materials.

To note, this assessment is not a revised version. This is intentional so its use helps illustrate some potential difficulties a student might have when doing the assessment. The first artifact in the chapter is an unmarked copy of the assessment activity. Immediately following the activity is the second artifact: an analytic rubric for the assessment activity. The third and fourth artifacts are Rubber Band Stretch papers completed by two students, Michelle and Heath. The fifth artifact is background information that includes data the teacher gathered using the same materials given to students, and class scores (individual students' scores) on the activity.

The reader's task is twofold. Each step is described as follows. Complete Step 1 before you continue on to Step 2. Consider writing down answers to questions posed in each step and reflect more on them later.

Step 1

Examine the Rubber Band Stretch activity, and then the analytic rubric that follows it. Become familiar with the rubric's content. Then, use the rubric to score both Michelle's and Heath's papers. Use the score form provided after the rubric, or something similar, to record the two students' work. (Do not be concerned at this time with other students' scores on the same activity. However, the information the teacher gathered may prove useful later.)

Discussion

By examining the two student papers and applying the criteria in the rubric, the teacher is *assessing* the work—determining what an individual knows and can do. From this assessment, a teacher gleans a general idea as to the level of understanding each student possesses about the process skills and concepts taught prior to assessment. The teacher thus determines whether or not each student knows how to correctly construct a data table, graph data from a data table, and interpret that graph. In addition, the teacher determines whether or not each student understands how to formulate a good hypothesis, and identify specific types of variables. Further, the teacher determines whether or not each student can expand upon what they learned from the activity and project thinking to future possibilities (such as what could be tested for later; see Question 12).

Consider the following sampling of possible questions, and contemplate to arrive at some conclusions before going on to Step 2:

- Overall, how would you summarize Michelle's grasp of the process skills and concepts?
- How would you summarize Heath's?
- Overall, were either or both students successful?
- What do the results suggest: is it time to move on to the next unit, or is it time to provide remediation?
- Would such results cause the teacher to reconsider the way in which the lessons leading up to the assessment were taught or presented?

(Original Activity)

STATION: *Rubber Band Stretch*

Name: _____

1. Compare your workstation with the diagram to the right. Be sure each thing is present in its location as shown on the diagram. When you complete this station's activities, be sure each thing is placed back where it belongs at this workstation.

What You Should Have & Where It Should Be

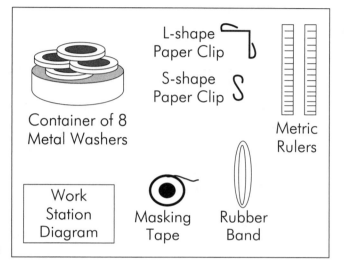

2. Tape the L-shape paper clip to one metric ruler. Part of the "L" should hang over the edge of the ruler (see diagram below).

3. Hook the rubber band on the L-shape paper clip. The rubber band should hang freely. Then hook the S-shape paper clip on the lowest end of the rubber band. You should now be able to set the metric ruler on the table, with the paper clip end hanging over the table edge (see diagram below). The rubber band and S-shape paper clip should hang freely and not touch or bang into the table. Tape the metric ruler to the tabletop so it does not move.

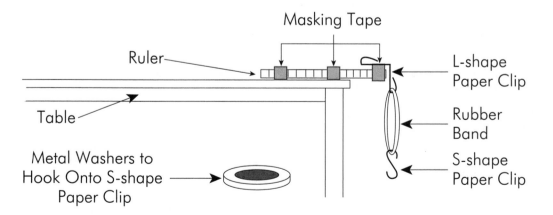

4. Make a data table. Let one column be for "rubber band length," and let the other column be for "number of washers." Use the data table at the top of the next page.

5. Use the second metric ruler to measure the length of the rubber band. Be sure to measure only the length BETWEEN paper clips! Record the measurement in your data table for zero (0) washers.

Rubber Band Stretch   Page 2

Data Table

6. Add two (2) washers to the hook of the S-shape paper clip. Measure the rubber band length, and record it in the data table. Then add two more washers to the S-shape paper clip. Measure and record the rubber band length. Continue adding washers by twos, measuring the rubber band length and recording in your data table, until all the washers are used.

7. Graph the data you have recorded in the data table. Use the graph paper on the next page to do this.

8. Write a hypothesis describing the results of this experiment: _____

_____

_____

_____

9. What would be the rubber band length if you used five (5) washers? _____

10. How many washers would be needed to stretch the rubber band to a total length of ten (10) centimeters? _____

11. For this experiment, name the following:
    a) independent variable: _____
    b) dependent variable: _____

12. Name at least TWO other variables that you could test for in this experiment:
    a) _____
    b) _____

WHEN FINISHED, REMOVE TAPE FROM ALL OBJECTS, CLEAN UP YOUR WORK STATION, AND REPLACE MATERIALS AS SHOWN ON THE FIRST DIAGRAM.

Rubber Band Stretch

Page 3

ANALYTIC SCORING RUBRIC FOR RUBBER BAND STRETCH

Grade Level(s): 6–8

Concept(s): elasticity, cause-effect relationships

Objective(s): Students will be able to make an accurate prediction based upon data collected and patterns observed in the stretching of a rubber band, and will be able to generate a hypothesis useful for further testing.

State Goal(s): I, III, IV

Process Skill(s): observing, measuring, using numbers, interpreting data, identifying variables, controlling variables, predicting, formulating hypotheses

Learning Outcome(s): Students will be able to recognize cause-effect relationships in the natural world, and be able to make predictions based on those relationships.

SCORING

Question #		Points
4–6	Data Table	
	Student correctly constructs data table, complete with proper column headings and units of measurement, and has all data for one variable recorded in either ascending or descending order and all data for other variable arranged so as to correlate with the first variable's data.	4
	Student correctly constructs data table, complete with proper column headings and units of measurement, but the recording of data is not in complete ascending or descending order for either variable.	3
	Student correctly constructs data table, complete with proper column headings and units of measurement, but has serious errors in recording of data.	2

OR

	Student has correct data but fails to include proper column headings and/or units of measurement.	2
	Student has significant errors in construction of data table and in recording of data.	1
	Student does not attempt.	0

Rubber Band Stretch   **Page 2**

Question #		Points
7	Graph	
	Student constructs graph correctly with all axes correctly divided, increments on axes proportional, increments reflecting total range of data, axes labeled correctly with values and measuring units, and all data points correctly plotted and connected with a line.	4
	Student constructs graph as above but with one or two minor errors, such as axis increments not proportional throughout axis, omission of measuring units, misplotting of data, omission of graph line connecting points, etc.	3
	Student constructs graph but has three or more minor errors as described above.	2
	Student constructs graph that contains significant errors.	1
	Student constructs inappropriate graph, graphs irrelevant data, or does not attempt.	0
8	Student generates hypothesis that is general in its wording and takes into account the interrelationship of the variables involved. For example, the amount of stretch of a rubber band will increase with unequal but larger lengths as equal amounts of weight are added to it.	3
	Student generates hypothesis that is not general in its wording, but takes into account the interrelationship of the variables involved. For example, this rubber band stretched in increasing amounts as more weights were hung on it.	2
	OR	
	Student generates hypothesis that is general in its wording, but fails to take into account the interrelationship of the variables involved. For example, the amount of stretching of a rubber band gets longer when weight is on it.	2
	Student generates hypothesis that is not general in its wording, and fails to account for the interrelationship of the variables involved. For example, my rubber band got longer.	1
	Student generates a hypothesis that is not related to the activity.	0
	OR	
	Student does not attempt.	0

Rubber Band Stretch   Page 3

Question #		Points
9	Student correctly determines rubber band length with 0% error.	3
	Student determines rubber band length with 1%–5% error.	2
	Student determines rubber band length with 6%–10% error.	1
	Student error is greater than 10% **or** student does not attempt.	0
10	Student correctly determines number of washers with 0% error.	3
	Student determines number of washers with 1%–5% error.	2
	Student determines number of washers with 6%–10% error.	1
	Student error is greater than 10% **or** student does not attempt.	0
11	Student correctly identifies weight (or number of washers) as the independent variable and rubber band stretch as the dependent variable.	2
	Student correctly identifies one of the two variables, but fails to correctly identify the second.	1
	Student fails to correctly identify either variable **or** does not attempt.	0
12	Student correctly names two variables. For example, rubber band age, rubber band thickness, type of rubber in rubber band, number of times rubber band has been used, rubber band width, etc.	2
	Student correctly names only one variable.	1
	Student fails to correctly name either variable **or** does not attempt.	0

End of Rubric

Rubber Band Stretch

Page 4

RUBBER BAND STRETCH—SCORE FORM		
Student Name:		
Item	**Comments or Rationales for Scoring**	**Score**
Questions 4–6: Data Table		
Question 7: Graph		
Question 8: Hypothesis		
Question 9: Rubber Band Length Determination		
Question 10: Number of Washers Determination		
Question 11: Identifying Dependent and Independent Variables		
Question 12: Naming of Two Other Variables		
	TOTAL SCORE =	

(Original Activity)

STATION: *Rubber Band Stretch*

Name: *Michelle*

1. Compare your workstation with the diagram to the right. Be sure each thing is present in its location as shown on the diagram. When you complete this station's activities, be sure each thing is placed back where it belongs at this workstation.

What You Should Have & Where It Should Be

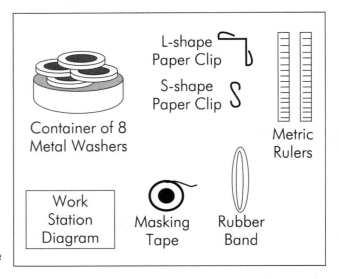

2. Tape the L-shape paper clip to one metric ruler. Part of the "L" should hang over the edge of the ruler (see diagram below).

3. Hook the rubber band on the L-shape paper clip. The rubber band should hang freely. Then hook the S-shape paper clip on the lowest end of the rubber band. You should now be able to set the metric ruler on the table, with the paper clip end hanging over the table edge (see diagram below). The rubber band and S-shape paper clip should hang freely and not touch or bang into the table. Tape the metric ruler to the tabletop so it does not move.

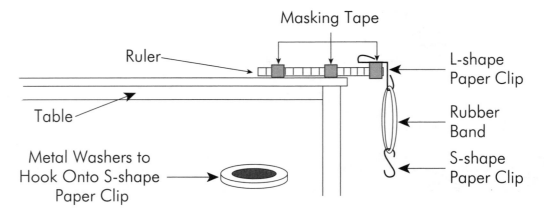

4. Make a data table. Let one column be for "rubber band length," and let the other column be for "number of washers." Use the data table at the top of the next page.

5. Use the second metric ruler to measure the length of the rubber band. Be sure to measure only the length BETWEEN paper clips! Record the measurement in your data table for 0 (zero) washers.

Rubber Band Stretch   **Page 2**

Data Table

Number Washers	Rubber Band Length
0	6.5 cm
2	10 cm
4	16 cm
6	22 cm
8	27 cm

6. Add two (2) washers to the hook of the S-shape paper clip. Measure the rubber band length, and record it in the data table. Then add two more washers to the S-shape paper clip. Measure and record the rubber band length. Continue adding washers by twos, measuring the rubber band length and recording in your data table, until all the washers are used.

7. Graph the data you have recorded in the data table. Use the graph paper on the next page to do this.

8. Write a hypothesis describing the results of this experiment: *If more washers are added then the length of a rubber band will increase.*

9. What would be the rubber band length if you used five (5) washers? *19 cm*

10. How many washers would be needed to stretch the rubber band to a total length of ten (10) centimeters? *2*

11. For this experiment, name the following:

    a) independent variable: *# of washers*

    b) dependent variable: *length of rubber band*

12. Name at least TWO other variables that you could test for in this experiment:

    a) *different types of rubber band*

    b) *different ways the "S" hook is made*

WHEN FINISHED, REMOVE TAPE FROM ALL OBJECTS, CLEAN UP YOUR WORK STATION, AND REPLACE MATERIALS AS SHOWN ON THE FIRST DIAGRAM.

Rubber Band Stretch   **Page 3**

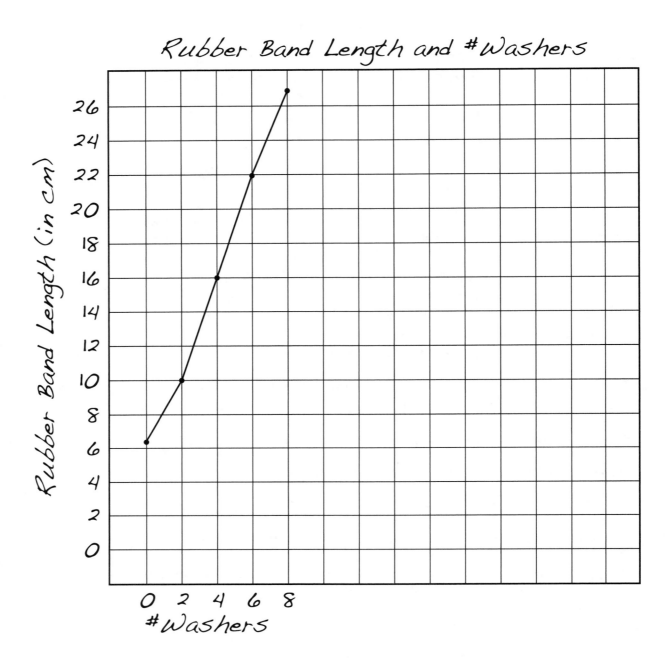

(Original Activity)

STATION: *Rubber Band Stretch*

Name: *Heath*

1. Compare your workstation with the diagram to the right. Be sure each thing is present in its location as shown on the diagram. When you complete this station's activities, be sure each thing is placed back where it belongs at this workstation.

2. Tape the L-shape paper clip to one metric ruler. Part of the "L" should hang over the edge of the ruler (see diagram below).

3. Hook the rubber band on the L-shape paper clip. The rubber band should hang

What You Should Have & Where It Should Be

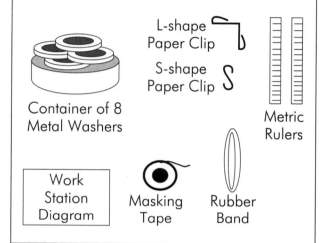

freely. Then hook the S-shape paper clip on the lowest end of the rubber band. You should now be able to set the metric ruler on the table, with the paper clip end hanging over the table edge (see diagram below). The rubber band and S-shape paper clip should hang freely and not touch or bang into the table. Tape the metric ruler to the tabletop so it does not move.

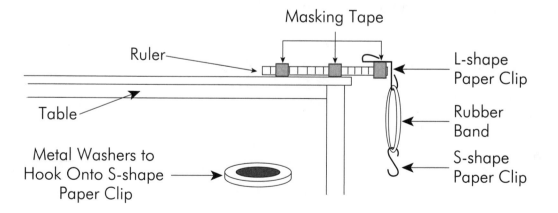

4. Make a data table. Let one column be for "rubber band length," and let the other column be for "number of washers." Use the data table at the top of the next page.

5. Use the second metric ruler to measure the length of the rubber band. Be sure to measure only the length BETWEEN paper clips! Record the measurement in your data table for zero (0) washers.

Rubber Band Stretch   Page 2

Data Table

Washers	Length
2 4 6 8	11 15 22 26

6. Add two (2) washers to the hook of the S-shape paper clip. Measure the rubber band length, and record it in the data table. Then add two more washers to the S-shape paper clip. Measure and record the rubber band length. Continue adding washers by twos, measuring the rubber band length and recording in your data table, until all the washers are used.

7. Graph the data you have recorded in the data table. Use the graph paper on the next page to do this.

8. Write a hypothesis describing the results of this experiment: _____ *I believe that when washers are added to this they will weigh it down more and more.*

9. What would be the rubber band length if you used five (5) washers? _____ *1*

10. How many washers would be needed to stretch the rubber band to a total length of ten (10) centimeters? _____ *almost 2*

11. For this experiment, name the following:

    a) independent variable: _____ *washers*

    b) dependent variable: _____ *weight*

12. Name at least TWO other variables that you could test for in this experiment:

    a) _____ *size of paper clip*

    b) _____ *strength of rubber band*

WHEN FINISHED, REMOVE TAPE FROM ALL OBJECTS, CLEAN UP YOUR WORK STATION, AND REPLACE MATERIALS AS SHOWN ON THE FIRST DIAGRAM.

Rubber Band Stretch

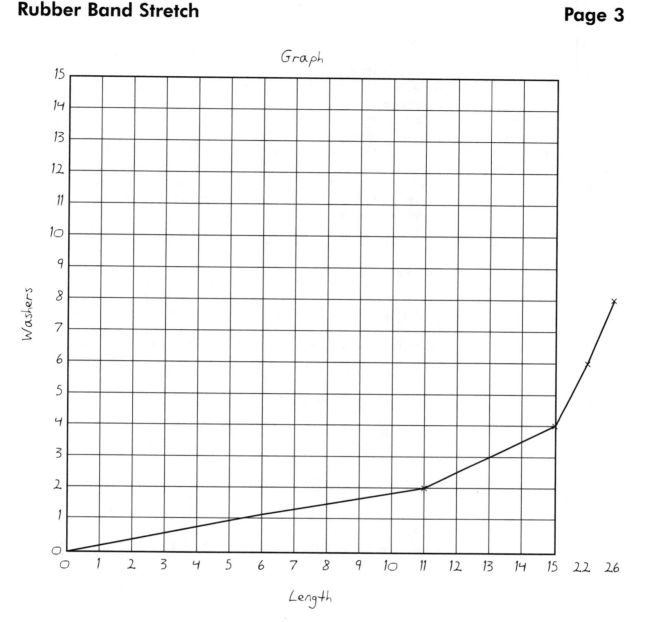

Determining Rubric-Based Scores

A scoring form has been completed for both Michelle and Heath. Compare these scored forms with the scores and rationales you derived for each of the two students. Based on the rubric provided, there is a total 21 possible points for the best performance.

The way Michelle's work was scored indicates she earned a total score of 17 points. Heath's work was scored at a total of 7 points. These point totals were determined through a relatively strict interpretation of the criteria described in the rubric, however some teachers prefer to be more flexible in their interpretations of the criteria. Reasons for more flexibility include factors such as how much class time has been devoted to teaching the topic and student practice with the topic, the extent of depth into which the topic was explored, and so forth.

For this activity, to provide more context for the students' work, Michelle's and Heath's teacher performed the assessment before administering it to students, and recorded the expected results if students performed at the best level. Before going further, examine the teacher's results for the assessment in the following section.

Teacher-Generated Results for Rubber Band Stretch

- For this activity, the students were to use the same rubber band.
- The teacher pretested the rubber band's elasticity as described in the instructions.

The teacher's pretest results are shown as follows, along with the teacher's graph for Questions 8 and 9:

Rubber Band

# Washers	Length (cm)
0	8
2	10
4	15
6	22
8	27

Rubber Band Length vs. Weight

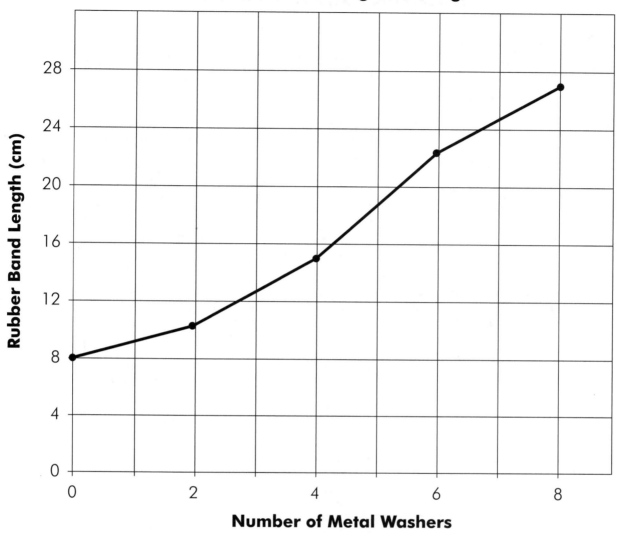

If more than teacher uses the Rubber Band Stretch assessment and its accompanying rubric, the teachers need to agree on the way to interpret the rubric criteria before scoring the students' work. Although this does not necessarily ensure they will each score any single student's work identically, it should help their end results to be within 1 or 2 points of each other. (This is one way to check inter-rater reliability for the rubric.)

RUBBER BAND STRETCH—SCORE FORM

Student Name: Michelle

Item	Comments or Rationales for Scoring	Score
Questions 4–6: Data Table	Each column of the table has clearly identified headings; the column with measurements includes the units of measurement; all data have been recorded, with values in descending order in one column and with correlating values in second column.	4
Question 7: Graph	Graph is titled. Each axis is correctly divided in equivalent sized units, and each axis is correctly labeled with the name of the variable and units of measurement where needed, and independent variable is on proper axis; horizontal axis does not make use of majority of space available on grid; the data point for 0 washers is not plotted and the graph line does not include the 0 value.	3
Question 8: Hypothesis	The hypothesis includes wording that addresses the relationship between the two variables, and is basically general in its phrasing. However, the relationship described does not include the idea that the rubber band stretching may increase with unequal but larger lengths as equal amounts of weight (or number of washers) are added.	2
Question 9: Rubber Band Length Determination	Based on the student's graph, the student has correctly interpolated the correct value with no error.	3
Question 10: Number of Washers Determination	Based on the student's graph, the student has correctly interpolated the correct value with no error.	3
Question 11: Identifying Dependent and Independent Variables	The student identified the variables as number of washers and length of rubber band. Although the number of washers determines the weight applied to the rubber band, this was not expressed sufficiently.	1
Question 12: Naming of Two Other Variables	The student correctly identified one possible variable as being the type of rubber band. The other variable identified would have no effect on the results.	1
	TOTAL SCORE =	17

RUBBER BAND STRETCH—SCORE FORM

Student Name: Heath

Item	Comments or Rationales for Scoring	Score
Questions 4–6: Data Table	Table has columns labeled, but the labels are incomplete (lack specifics such as "number" for washers or what the "length" is of), and lack units of measurement. The data are arranged in one column in descending order with correlating data in the second column, but missing data for 0 washers.	2
Question 7: Graph	Graph is titled but the title does not describe what the plot is about. The axes are labeled, but the labels are incomplete (e.g., needs # of washers); vertical axis values have equal increments, but horizontal axis does not, and student did not fit axis values within bounds of available grid (extra values were added to right of grid); the independent variable is shown on the wrong axis; all data points have been plotted and graphed on the line provided.	1
Question 8: Hypothesis	The hypothesis only mentions a single variable; it is not stated in general terms.	1
Question 9: Rubber Band Length Determination	Using the student's graph, the correct answer is between 15 and 22 centimeters (likely 18 cm). The answer provided is incorrect by more than 10%.	0
Question 10: Number of Washers Determination	Using the student's graph, the answer is about 1.8 washers. The answer provided is "almost 2." The student's answer is at 10% error.	1
Question 11: Identifying Dependent and Independent Variables	Student identifies "washers" as independent variable but does not state what property of the washers is relevant. Student fails to identify a valid dependent variable.	1
Question 12: Naming of Two Other Variables	The student names two other variables. The size of paper clip is not a relevant choice. The strength of the rubber band may be considered appropriate.	1
	TOTAL SCORE =	7

Step 2

Now that the rubric has been used to assess the work of Michelle and Heath, their work needs to be evaluated. Refer to the Background Information for Rubber Band Stretch section, showing how other students in the class performed on the assessment. The teacher's task now is to determine the following two things:

(1) Where do Michelle and Heath fall within the student rankings?

(2) What letter grades should be awarded to Michelle and to Heath?

Teachers may opt to use the grading scale specified by their own school or district, or may use some other grading criteria. For example, a teacher may use a straight grading scale such as the following, or choose to grade on the curve.

Scale		
Grade	Points	Percentage
A	19–21	90–100
B	17–18	80–89
C	15–16	70–79
D	13–14	60–69
F	0–12	0–59

Whatever choice for grading is selected, the teacher writes down the information concerning the grading applied so that it can be easily explained to others. Using the grading scale here, if Michelle's performance is scored as 17 points, the grade assigned her is a B. Similarly, Heath's grade is an F. Looking at the grading from a slightly different perspective, Michelle's performance is in the top five of the class (or the upper 25%), while Heath's in the bottom three (lowest 25%).

Background Information for Rubber Band Stretch

CLASS SCORES ON RUBBER BAND STRETCH
(BY DECREASING ORDER WITH 21 POSSIBLE POINTS)

	Student	Score	% of Total
1.	Shannon	20	95
2.	Mark	20	95
3.	Deanna	19	90
4.	Jill	17	81
5.	John	16	76
6.	Matt	16	76
7.	Jason	15	71
8.	Meg	15	71
9.	Carrie	15	71
10.	Chris	14	67
11.	Nancy	14	67
12.	Ben	13	62
13.	Thomas	12	57
14.	Marcie	12	57
15.	Donnie	11	52
16.	James	9	43
17.	Elizabeth	9	43
18.	Danielle	8	38
19.	Steven	6	29
20.	Randy	5	24

Extending the Discussion on the Determination of Grades

The process of ranking Michelle and Heath amongst other students and assigning grades is *evaluation*. In this process, the teacher compares students' assessment scores with a particular standard. That standard may be a grading curve derived from all students' scores, it may be a grading scale imposed by the school district, or it may be some criteria the teacher has established. Whatever the standard selected for comparison, when teachers engage in the process of evaluating, they are placing Michelle and Heath somewhere in the continuum between the highest-performing student and the lowest-performing student. Based on the evaluation, the teacher then makes some decisions.

Although there are a number of questions that could be posed at this point, consider the following:

- Do Michelle and Heath qualify to proceed on to the next unit?
- What grades will be recorded in their report cards?

- Or, more high stakes, do they qualify to graduate to the next grade level?
- Does either student require remediation, and if so, what should it entail?

Answering these questions certainly requires some further analysis and additional information.

Michelle is an exceptionally bright student who seems to effortlessly learn material. She does quite well on objective tests in particular. Her performance on the Rubber Band Stretch assessment is probably not what the teacher expected from her. There may be any number of reasons why this occurred. For example, consider the following possibilities (the list is not all-inclusive):

- Michelle may have been absent during one or more days when the lesson upon which the assessment is based was taught.
- The particular concepts and skills involved may be difficult for her (many students experience occasional aberrations such as this in their schooling).
- She may have been extra tired or not feeling well the day of the assessment.
- There may have been other distractions during the assessment that contributed to breaking her concentration (e.g., something happening outside the classroom).
- Something may have occurred in her life the night before or morning of the assessment.

The teacher may not know the reason, and is simply left with the bare results. A grade of a B is probably justifiable. There is no indication that Michelle is in need of remediation. This qualifies Michelle to move on to the next unit (or to be promoted to the next grade level).

Next to be examined is Heath's performance, which could be considered in two possible ways, depending upon the circumstances affecting him. These circumstances are illustrated in the following two scenarios.

Scenario 1

Heath is intelligent and potentially a very capable learner. His performance on the assessment could be indicative of some of the same possible reasons Michelle did not perform as well as expected, or it could also be that he simply didn't pay much attention to either the instruction or to the assessment task. Knowing his potential, the teacher likely expected much better performance from him. Provided the teacher finds he was just being inattentive or careless, the grade of an F is probably defensible. This does not mean Heath should receive no remediation. The teacher should attempt to ascertain the reasons behind Heath's performance. If it turns out to be that he discounted the assessment, then some discussion about the importance of trying one's best each time would be warranted. Unless this type of performance is an obvious and ongoing pattern, it probably doesn't disqualify Heath from moving on to the next unit or grade level.

Scenario 2

In this scenario, Heath came into the class at the beginning of the year and struggled with proper handling of laboratory equipment. Further, he consistently demonstrated difficulties in making measurements of sufficient accuracy for science activities at this grade level. Heath may have a learning disability that thus far isn't severe enough to warrant special education services, so the teacher does not have an IEP or 504 plan for him. Given these circumstances, the teacher may determine that Heath has demonstrated some significant strides in learning. Compared to most other students, his performance is subpar, but it is good for him. With respect to a grade for the assessment, the teacher is faced with a dilemma and may see one of three possible actions to take: (1) award Heath a grade that shows his level of performance in context with the other students who took the assessment, (2) award Heath a grade that shows his level of performance in relation to his growth and learning since the previous assessment, or (3) award a grade somewhere in between the two extremes.

Both the pros and cons must be weighed. For the first choice, the grade could be disheartening to Heath and potentially contribute to his withdrawing or reducing his efforts in science. This choice would also not truly reflect the improvement he has made from prior assessments and learning tasks. If the second choice is selected, the grade might reflect Heath's improvement, but could give a false impression about his ability to effectively deal with the science and his readiness to proceed further. The third choice may be one the teacher selects since it seems the most fair. However, it fails to adequately show where Heath is with respect to other students or with his own improvement. Some school districts have developed grading policies that could help a teacher in such a situation. For example, the school may allow for a grade of C/F which shows Heath's self-improvement (the C) but also his performance relative to other students (the F). This could provide him some incentive to continue working to improve and learn, but does not yield false impressions. The teacher would probably decide Heath can move on to the next unit, but whether he moves to the next grade level depends upon which grading option the school allows the teacher to select.

Differentiation of Instruction for Heath

Aside from making the decisions about Heath's grade on the assessment and his readiness to move on, the teacher needs to take a closer look at Heath's strengths and weaknesses and consider some differentiation that could help him. One avenue the teacher should pursue is to apply the school district's RTI protocols. This helps the teacher document Heath's abilities to perform on a variety of learning tasks, and brings to the fore additional strategies to facilitate and measure Heath's learning. These include some remediation and revising written materials for Heath, particularly in the instructional phase when students engage in activities and construct their learning.

An examination of Heath's assessment results reveal his difficulties likely lay with a good understanding of how to clearly identify variables, how to formulate a workable hypothesis, and how to present data in a graphic form. Such deficiencies warrant the teacher providing Heath some remedial instruction in these processes, and the teacher could select several process-based activities to help Heath. An example includes working with simple pendulums, in which he could identify variables, change variables, test the results, and so forth. Another example is to build and test paper airplanes. The teacher may also provide Heath some additional work with graphing data from simple data tables. To facilitate these process-based remediation efforts, the teacher can revise the written materials to make things clearer to Heath. The teacher may also consult colleagues (such as a special educator or someone who specializes in mathematics) to see what kinds of strategies can help Heath.

CONCLUSION

People familiar with assessment are apt to encourage teachers to use multiple assessments, and use multiple forms of these assessments. For example, a performance-based assessment might be used along with an objective test (and perhaps even with a series of laboratory activities) to assess a student's understanding and learning. Such an approach provides the teacher a much clearer idea of what the student knows and can do than using any single assessment by itself. Basically, as a teacher gleans more, and more varied, information about a student, the more accurately the teacher can assess the student. This, in turn, leads to more appropriate evaluation of the student. This should then facilitate the teacher's further analysis of a student's performance, and provide guidance with respect to the kinds of remediation and materials' revision that are necessary and appropriate for the circumstance.

Resource

Scientific Literacy, Standards, and State Goals

VIGNETTE WITH THOMAZ

Thomaz is an elementary teacher who has recently been assigned the task of teaching science to all the fifth-grade classes in his school building. He knows that he needs to select science activities from the current adopted curriculum. Consequently, Thomaz also knows he must have some protocol to follow in selecting curriculum materials. In addition, those curriculum materials need to be suitable for use with students who have been mainstreamed into the classroom. So, Thomaz wonders, where does he begin? What guidelines can he use to select the best curriculum materials, and be sure those materials are appropriate for use with all his students?

INTRODUCTION

As teachers like Thomaz may realize, the enterprise of science education is vast. Over the past four decades, numerous publications have been produced intended to serve as guides for teachers and teacher educators in their efforts to teach science. Understanding what these publications say is a foundational starting point for teachers. To establish a foundation upon which to build the retooling of science activities and assessments, this book focuses on five of these (four national level and one state level).

NATIONAL STANDARDS

National Science Teachers Association and Scientific Literacy

The oldest of these publications deals with what constitutes scientific literacy, and was produced during the early 1970s through the auspices of the National Science Teachers Association (NSTA) by Showalter, Cox, Holobinko, Thomson, and Orledo (1974). Despite its age, *Program Objectives and Scientific Literacy* does an excellent job of thoroughly dealing with the topic. The subsequent science education literature certainly is filled with numerous articles that contribute different definitions of scientific literacy. Indeed, some of those definitions are much shorter than the one provided in *Program Objectives and Scientific Literacy*. Sutman (1996), for example, has proffered the definition that

... an individual is (totally) science literate when that person's background and experiences develop his/her ability and willingness to continue to learn science content on his/her own, to continue to develop and use science processes on his/her own and be willing and able to communicate effectively with others and/or involve others in these experiences and understandings. (pp. 459–460)

Program Objectives and Scientific Literacy begins by stressing that the principal overall objective of science teaching is the *development of satisfactory levels of scientific literacy among all learners*. Essentially, the document defines scientific literacy as, "that which every person should understand, know, and feel at least to some extent about the realm of science" (p. 1). This has been a goal of science education since the late 1950s, and continues through today. As defined in this document, scientific literacy is divided into seven dimensions, each of which is composed of various elements or factors, as derived from research. Included in these dimensions are:

- **Nature of science** refers to the characteristics of scientific knowledge as well as how one comes to learn and understand it.
- **Concepts in science** include the "big" or "unifying" ideas that thread through each of the science disciplines.
- **Processes of science** are the process skills used to actually do science.
- **Values in science** are the qualities of science considered worthwhile or desirable, such as honesty.
- **Science and society and technology** refers to the interrelationships between each of these components and how one influences the other.
- **Interest** involves one having an interest in science and a positive or favorable attitude toward it.
- **Skills** include the knowledge and ability to use a variety of instruments, equipment, devices, machines, and other hardware in the pursuit of doing science.

Along with Showalter and colleagues' groundbreaking publication, three additional national-level publications will be of help to teachers. The *National Science Education Standards* (*NSES*) published by the National Research Council (NRC) in 1996 as well as the American Association for the Advancement of Science's (AAAS) *Benchmarks for Science Literacy: Project 2061*, published in 1993, both operationally define science literacy throughout their entire texts. A complementary document, crafted by the NSTA and released in 1993, *Scope, Sequence and Coordination* (*SSC*) (Pearsall, 1993), provides additional teacher guidance. These three publications help clarify and delineate what quality science education looks like. However, translating that into pragmatic classroom practice is difficult for many teachers. To help, NSTA produced the *Pathways* publications; in particular, the *NSTA Pathways to the Science Standards: Elementary School Edition* (Texley & Wild, 1997) and *NSTA Pathways to the Science Standards: Middle School Edition* (Rakow, 2000) are useful translational tools.

Even with the *Pathways* text in hand, teachers should understand that the "scientifically literate" person described in any of these publications does not emerge during a single school year, or even within just elementary schooling—becoming scientifically literate is a growth process that continues throughout life. The work teachers do with their students is but one part in a long sequence of teaching and learning that occurs in each student's lifetime.

If there is a single theme embedded throughout the *National Science Education Standards* (*NSES*) (NRC, 1996) and the AAAS (1993) *Benchmarks*, it is that inquiry, investigations, and problem solving are critical elements of any science program. The *NSES* makes explicit points that the ability to do inquiry should be something students develop at each grade range (K–4, 5–8, and 9–12), as well as come to understand the process. Students should be engaged beginning in their early years with investigating and actively constructing ideas and explanations. In the middle grades, students should begin to recognize relationships between explanations and evidence and progress from partial inquiry toward more full inquiry. The AAAS *Benchmarks* note that scientific inquiry is complex and demanding, is far more flexible than often given credit in textbooks, and is more than just doing experiments (see AAAS, Chapter 1, Section 1B, p. 9).

Another common theme teachers will recognize throughout each of these standards documents is the *science is for all students* to learn and do, not just for those in special groups such as accelerated classes. To that end, the standards information presented in these publications should be viewed with the perspective that science can and should be done with both students in the general education population as well as in the special education population. To help teachers get started, the following pages of summarize what these national-level standards publications contain. Teachers are encouraged to go beyond these summaries and locate and become familiar with the original standards documents.

NRC *National Science Education Standards (NSES)*

NSES *Learning and Teaching Standards*

The *National Science Education Standards (NSES)* (NRC, 1996) details what all students must know and be able to do with respect to science learning experiences. These standards provide specific criteria to make judgments about teaching and learning. However, the standards go beyond teaching and learning and examine assessment, programs, and systems (e.g., the system at a national level). In total, *NSES* emphasizes the clear alignment of learning opportunities to the standards. The phrase *all students* means there is the expectation that the standards are to apply not to just certain groups of students, but to every student, regardless of background, ambition, or circumstances.

Some basic principles guide the *NSES*, including the following:

- All students should be afforded the opportunity to attain high levels of scientific literacy, and that opportunity should occur regardless of gender, cultural or ethnic background, physical or learning disabilities, future aspirations, or interest and motivation in science.
- The attainment of science knowledge and understanding is something that all students can accomplish. Students must be given sufficient time to develop the deep understandings of essential scientific ideas rather than more superficial knowledge with many isolated facts.
- Students must engage in science as an active process if it is to be learned appropriately. They must ask questions, construct explanations of natural phenomena, test those explanations in various ways, and communicate ideas to others.
- The modes of inquiry that characterize the practice of contemporary science, including rules of evidence and ways of formulating questions, must be reflected in the science done in schools.

NSES *Content Standards*

The *NSES* content standards are not intended to represent a science curriculum, but are intended to convey the breadth and depth of science knowledge and understanding necessary for a learner to be scientifically literate. The content described in these standards includes structure, organization, balance, and presentation of content, and clearly defines what should be included within specific grade-level ranges. Within each grade-level range, the content standards are split into eight categories: (1) science as inquiry, (2) physical science, (3) life science, (4) earth and space science, (5) science and technology, (6) science in personal and social perspectives, (7) history and nature of science, and (8) unifying concepts and processes. The fundamental understandings reflected in the standards emphasize the need for the following:

- Representation of central scientific ideas and organizing principles
- Guidance for fruitful investigations
- Application to everyday situations and common contexts
- Linkages to meaningful learning experiences
- Developmental appropriateness for students at specified grade levels

Therefore, although not specifying a science curriculum, the *NSES* content standards certainly clarify what science curriculum should be like and include. This information should help teachers as they select their curriculum.

NSES *Assessment Standards*

The assessment standards focus on the quality of assessment practices designed to measure student attainment and the quality of science learning opportunities. The standards identify the essential attributes of exemplary assessment practices. Those best practices include:

- Deliberately designing assessments with clear purpose and coordinating them with those purposes while insuring they have internal consistency
- Measuring student attainment and science learning opportunities with a focus on the science content that is most important for students to learn while reflecting the complexity of the various dimensions described in all the *NSES* standards
- Making use of quality assessment processes (e.g., inclusion of authentic assessment tasks, appropriate time periods between assessment measurements, etc.) and the data derived from them so that informed decisions can be made with respect to actions to be taken in improving science education
- Being aware of and sensitive to biases (gender, racial, ethnic, physical disabilities, language, student experiences, etc.) and avoiding them
- Making inferences that are sound and refer to the assumptions upon which they are based

AAAS *Benchmarks for Scientific Literacy*

The American Association for the Advancement of Science (AAAS) *Benchmarks for Scientific Literacy* is divided into key chapters that cover the nature of science, the nature of mathematics, the nature of technology, the physical setting, the living environment, the human organism, human society, the designed world, the mathematical world, historical perspectives, common themes, and habits of mind. Each of the chapters in *Benchmarks* provides specifics about what learners should know. These are broken down into what is appropriate at specified grade-level ranges: kindergarten through Grade 2, Grade 3 through Grade 5, Grade 6 through Grade 8, and Grade 9 through Grade 12.

In the *nature of science, Benchmarks* covers scientific inquiry and the scientific enterprise (the "doing" of science). Patterns and relationships and mathematical inquiry are covered within the *nature of mathematics;* and the relationship between technology and science, design and systems, and issues in technology are covered under the *nature of technology.* The *physical setting* deals with the universe, the earth, processes that shape the earth, the structure of matter, energy transformations, motion, and forces of motion. The *living environment* deals with the diversity of life, heredity, cells, the interdependence of life, flow of matter and energy, and evolution of life. Human identity, group behavior, social change, social trade-offs, political and economic systems, social conflict, and global interdependence are covered within *human society.* Agriculture, materials and manufacturing, energy sources and their use, communication, and health technology are addressed in the *designed world.* The *mathematical world* looks at numbers, symbolic relationships, shapes, uncertainty, and reasoning. *Historical perspectives* provides an examination of science throughout human history and how it has led us to where we are now. *Common themes* examines some of the "big conceptual ideas" of science, including systems, models, constancy and change, and scale. Finally, *habits of mind* delves into values and attitudes, computation and estimation, manipulation and observation, communication skills, and critical-response skills. As the teacher might discern, many of the terms and broad topic titles are present in the NSTA scientific literacy document and *NSES* standards described earlier in this chapter.

NSTA *Scope, Sequence, and Coordination;* and *Pathways*

The National Science Teachers Association (NSTA, 1996) *Scope, Sequence, and Coordination (SSC)* differs somewhat from the other publications already described in that it places primary emphasis on curriculum reform rather than systemic reform in K–12 science education. However, similar to the other documents, the foundational context of *SSC* is the development of science literacy. *SSC* seeks to guide science educators in appropriate directions with respect to the scope of science education programs, sequencing of content and processes in those programs, and coordination amongst and between components of those programs. The document promotes concrete to abstract sequencing of content through a spiraling curriculum approach (i.e., the spacing of and repetition of topics over a time period that is typically seven years). *SSC* recognizes the interdependence of the various science disciplines, and promotes the integration of them at the middle-school level.

STATE GOALS FOR LEARNING IN SCIENCE

A final publication for teachers designing learning in science is their state's goals and standards for science. There are inherent similarities in the core content of each state's definitions of scientific literacy, and teachers are encouraged to familiarize themselves with their own state science education standards. The state goals to apply in science teaching parallel many of those articulated in the national standards documents. They emphasize students will have a working knowledge of the following:

- Concepts and basic vocabulary in the life and physical sciences and how they apply to life and work
- Implications and limitations of technological development and its interactions with society
- Principles of scientific research and their application in simple projects
- Processes, techniques, methods, equipment, and available technology of science

Again, although the specific wording varies from state to state, many have language that parallels that from other states, as well as that in the national standards.

CONCLUSION

Teachers will find that these aforementioned publications consistently overlap in many areas, yet each is also unique in its focus and in the manner in which the science education enterprise is detailed. As teachers explore these resources, they will also find that different levels of learner performance and acquisition of particular aspects of science literacy are grouped by grade ranges (e.g., K–4, 5–8, and 9–12) rather than being specific to individual grade levels. Most are also divided into different science domains, such as earth science, life science, physical science, society, and so forth. If teachers have a sense of what each of these standards-related documents convey, then they will, at the very least, begin on the road to appropriate science teaching, and, at best, refine their efforts beyond what they presently practice. By following the standards, teachers will embark on the path to selecting the necessary and appropriate science curriculum materials—activities and assessments that will have utility for all their students.

References

Abell, S. K., & Volkmann, M. J. (2006). *Seamless assessment in science: A guide for elementary and middle school teachers.* Alexandria, VA: National Science Teachers Association.

Access Center. (2004, September 26). *Computer-assisted instruction and writing.* Retrieved from http://www.k8accesscenter.org/training_resources/computeraided_writing.asp

American Association for the Advancement of Science. (1961). *Science: A process approach.* New York: Oxford University Press.

American Association for the Advancement of Science. (1993). *Benchmarks for science literacy: Project 2061.* New York: Oxford University Press.

Atkin, J. M., Black, P., & Coffey, J. (2001). *Classroom assessment and the National Science Education Standards.* Washington, DC: National Academies Press.

Baron, J. B. (1990). Performance assessment: Blurring the edges among assessment, curriculum, and instruction. In A. B. Champagne, B. E. Lovitts, & B. J. Calinger (Eds.), *Assessment in the service of instruction* (pp. 127–148). Washington, DC: American Association for the Advancement of Science.

Cell. (n.d.). *Wikipedia.* Retrieved from http://en.wikipedia.org/wiki/Cell

Chapman, M. (2003). *The effect of motivation on learning extrinsic versus intrinsic.* Retrieved January 24, 2005, from http://www.siue.edu/~micchap/Research.html

Cotton, K. (n.d.). *Instructional reinforcement.* Retrieved January 20, 2006, from http://www.nwrel.org/scpd/sirs/2/cu3.html

Education Development Center. (1960). *Elementary science study.* Cambridge, MA: Author.

Friend, M. (2005). *Special education: Contemporary perspectives for school professionals.* Boston: Pearson Education.

Friend, M., & Cook, L. (2007). *Interactions; Collaboration skills for school professionals* (5th ed.). Boston: Allyn & Bacon.

Goldstein, A. P., & McGinnis, E. (1997). *Skillstreaming the preschool child or the elementary child—or the adolescent.* Champaign, IL: Research Press.

Gunther, N. (Executive Producer), Bieber, J. (Producer), & Lavoie, R. D. (Writer and Presenter). (1997) *When the Chips are Down* [Educational Video]. United States: PBS Video. (Available from www.ricklavoie.com/videos and www.shoppbs.org)

Hein, G. E. (1991). Active assessment for active science. In V. Perrone (Ed.), *Expanding student assessment* (pp. 106–131). Washington, DC: Association for Supervision and Curriculum Development.

Hein, G. E., & Price, S. (1994). *Active assessment for active science: A guide for elementary school teachers.* Portsmouth, NH: Heinemann.

Institute of Education Sciences, U.S. Department of Education. (2007a). *Contexts of elementary and secondary education: Special programs indicator 31.* Retrieved from http://nces.ed.gov/programs/coe/2007/section4/indicator31.asp

Institute of Education Sciences, U.S. Department of Education. (2007b). *Fast facts.* Retrieved from http://nces.ed.gov/fastfacts/display.asp?id=59

Jensen, M. M. (2005). *Introduction to emotional and behavioral disorders.* Upper Saddle River, NJ: Pearson Education.

Jordan, D. R. (2006). *Attention deficit disorders* (4th ed.). Austin, TX: Pro-ed.

Kirk, S., Gallagher, J. J., Coleman, M. R., & Anastasiow, N. (2009). *Educating exceptional children* (12th ed.). Boston: Houghton Mifflin.

Levine, M. (2003). *A mind at a time.* New York: Simon & Schuster.

Lipson, M. Y., & Wixson, K. K. (2003). *Instructional resources.* In A. M. Ramos (Ed.), *Assessment and instruction of reading and writing difficulty* (pp. 189–190). Boston: Pearson Education.

Medina, J. (2008). *Brain rules.* Seattle, WA: Pear Press.

National Research Council. (1996). *National science education standards.* Washington, DC: National Academies Press.

National Science Teachers Association. (1996). *Scope, sequence, and coordination: A framework for high school science education.* Alexandria, VA: Author.

Office of Education Research. (1993). *Consumer guide, Number 2.* Retrieved from http://ww2.ed.gov/pubs/OR/ConsumerGuides/perfasse.html

Pearsall, M. K. (Ed.). (1993). *Scope, sequence, and coordination of secondary school science: Volume I—The content core.* Alexandria, VA: National Science Teachers Association.

Rakow, S. J. (Ed.). (2000). *NSTA Pathways to the science standards: Middle school edition.* Alexandria, VA: National Science Teachers Association.

Rhode, G., Jenson, W. R., & Reavis, H. K. (1992). *The tough kid book.* Longmont, CO: Sopris West.

Rosenberg, M. S., Westling, D. L., & McLeskey, J. (2008). *Special education for today's teachers.* Upper Saddle River, NJ: Pearson Education.

Showalter, V., Cox, D., Holobinko, P., Thomson, B., & Orledo, M. (1974). *What is unified science education? (Part 5) Program objectives and scientific literacy, Prism II.* Alexandria, VA: National Science Teachers Association.

Stiggins, R. J. (1987). Design and development of performance assessments. *Educational Measurement: Issues and Practices, 6*(3), 33–42.

Sutman, F. X. (1996). Science literacy: A functional definition. *Journal of Research in Science Teaching, 33*(5), 459–460.

Texley, J., & Wild, A. (Eds.). (1997). *NSTA Pathways to the science standards: Elementary school edition.* Alexandria, VA: National Science Teachers Association.

Index

NOTE: Illustrative material is identified by (figure), (table), (activity), and (assessment).

DATE DUE

APR 0 1 20

GAYLORD

The Corwin logo—   open book—represents the union of courage
and learning. Corw   improving education for all learners by publishing
books and other p   velopment resources for those serving the field of
PreK–12 education. By providing practical, hands-on materials, Corwin continues to
carry out the promise of its motto: **"Helping Educators Do Their Work Better."**